Other Books by Reuben Fine

THE PERSONALITY OF THE ASTHMATIC CHILD
FREUD: A CRITICAL EVALUATION OF HIS THEORIES
THE PSYCHOLOGY OF THE CHESS PLAYER
THE HEALING OF THE MIND (2 editions)
PSYCHOTHERAPY AND THE SOCIAL ORDER (editor)
PSYCHOANALYTIC PSYCHOLOGY
PSYCHOANALYSIS AS A PHILOSOPHICAL SYSTEM
A HISTORY OF PSYCHOANALYSIS
THE INTIMATE HOUR
THE LOGIC OF PSYCHOLOGY
THE MEANING OF LOVE IN HUMAN EXPERIENCE
PSYCHOANALYSIS AROUND THE WORLD (editor)
NARCISSISM, THE SELF, AND SOCIETY
THE FORGOTTEN MAN

TROUBLED MEN

Reuben Fine

TROUBLED MEN

The Psychology, Emotional Conflicts, and Therapy of Men

 Jossey-Bass Publishers

San Francisco • London • 1988

TROUBLED MEN
The Psychology, Emotional Conflicts, and Therapy of Men
by Reuben Fine

Copyright © 1988 by: Jossey-Bass Inc., Publishers
350 Sansome Street
San Francisco, California 94104
&
Jossey-Bass Limited
28 Banner Street
London EC1Y 8QE

Library of Congress Cataloging-in-Publication Data

Fine, Reuben, date.
  Troubled men.

  ✓ (The Jossey-Bass social and behavioral science series)
  Bibliography: p.
  Includes indexes.
    1. Men—Mental health. 2. Men—Psychology.
3. Psychotherapy. I. Title. II. Series. [DNLM:
1. Men—psychology. 2. Psychotherapy. WM 420 F495t]
RC451.4.M45F56 1988   155.6'32   88-42788
ISBN 1-55542-105-9 (alk. paper)

Manufactured in the United States of America

The paper in this book meets the guidelines for
permanence and durability of the Committee on
Production Guidelines for Book Longevity of the
Council on Library Resources.

JACKET DESIGN BY WILLI BAUM

FIRST EDITION

Code 8835

The Jossey-Bass
Social and Behavioral Science Series

CONTENTS

Preface   xi

The Author   xv

1.   Understanding Men's Emotional Problems   1

2.   Treating Men: Therapeutic Principles   25

3.   Problems of Loving   51

4.   Sexual Conflicts   96

5.   Pleasure and Pain   123

6.   Feeling and Reason   149

7.   Family Role   164

8.   Social Role   192

9.   Self-Image   218

10. Work: Curse or Blessing?   243

11. Inexpressive Man   262

ix

12. Creative Man   283

13. Epilogue   305

     References   309

     Patient Index   331

     Name Index   335

     Subject Index   341

PREFACE

THIS BOOK IS THE FIRST TO DEVOTE ITSELF EXCLUSIVELY TO the emotional problems of men. Until recently, the feeling—or even the firm conviction—has been that women have all the problems, while men have all the pleasures. That this is far from true is obvious to anyone who looks at the society in which we live, yet it seems to be an implicit assumption in many psychological writings. Thus, one key purpose of the present work is to explode the myth of the carefree and problem-free man. But equally critical goals are to explore in detail the kinds of problems from which men suffer and to offer a treatment approach that will help troubled men live happier and more fulfilled lives.

Because this book is about troubled men, it is appropriate for a broad audience—that is, virtually anyone interested in men's emotional problems. Primarily, however, it is addressed to all psychotherapists interested in the treatment of men. Although the point of view I take is psychodynamic, the material in this book will be useful for therapists of any and all persuasions, mainly because I stress the underlying philosophical roots of men's troubles, as well as specific therapeutic techniques I have adopted in practice.

Troubled Men is designed to serve three primary purposes: First, it will clarify the problems that men present in psychotherapy and the way in which these problems can be handled. Second, it will elaborate in detail on the concept of the ideally normal man—or what I have referred to in previous writings as the *analytic ideal*. Third, it will provide a detailed exami-

nation of the working-through process, the heart of all dynamically oriented therapy.

American society has always tended to emphasize wom-
en's problems and frailties and, correspondingly, to deny that
men have similar problems. The mere fact that far more women
than men go to therapists is seen as corroborating evidence.
However, an alternative explanation might be that men's denial
mechanisms are operating at full force. Most men in our culture
have a great need to pretend that they are macho, strong, reli-
ant, and successful; any break in this pretense is felt as extremely
humiliating, and hence is denied as much as possible. Willy Lo-
man, in Arthur Miller's great play *Death of a Salesman,* is a perfect example. To the very end he pretends that there is nothing
the matter, that a big kill is around the corner, and that he is a
successful, prosperous salesman, well liked by everybody. Then
the mask is removed, and he commits suicide. Naturally, most
men do not commit suicide (though actually more men do than
women, especially in the older age brackets), but the depression
that follows the loss of their fantasies is often severe.

Once a man is honest enough to admit that he needs help,
it often turns out that he has problems in many, if not all, areas
of his life. To approach these problems therapeutically, I center
on the analytic ideal, the component parts of which are the
topics of Chapters Three through Twelve. The ideally normal
man, who can reach the greatest degree of happiness, must be
able to love, to enjoy sex, and to experience pleasure. He must
feel—yet be guided by reason. He must have roles in a family
and in society and still have a strong sense of personal identity.
And he must have work he enjoys, an ability and willingness to
communicate, and an outlet for his creativity. If he has all these
things, it is likely that he will also be free from psychiatric
symptomatology.

Unfortunately, many men experience great difficulties in
all the above areas. And these difficulties eventually propel them
to do something about their distress. As the process of education continues to expand, more people understand how they
cause their own suffering, and as resistance to psychotherapy
eases, even more men will seek therapeutic assistance. It is now

estimated that one man in three will see a therapist at some time in his life.

Observers of the therapeutic scene point to the astronomical growth in the number of therapists in the last decade. Bellah and his colleagues (Bellah and others, 1985) state that we are in the midst of a therapeutic revolution. It is my hope that *Troubled Men* will serve to clarify some of the goals of the therapeutic revolution, as well as the procedures and processes that go into the art of psychotherapy.

While psychotherapists disagree considerably about philosophies and methods (as need scarcely be noted), most would agree that a great deal of effort is required to effect real change in the psyche of any human being. Freud referred to it as the *working-through process*. While different techniques are used and different goals are stated by the therapist at different times, in all cases, the working-through process is essential if some real change is to occur. There are no quick fixes, even though many such panaceas are offered to the gullible. Real psychotherapy requires a sincere commitment on the part of the client, as well as on the part of the psychotherapist, and a willingness to expend the effort needed to reach the goal.

Overview of the Contents

Chapter One is introductory. I review the literature on the psychology of men and discuss both the analytic ideal and the goals of therapy. Chapter Two delineates principles of the psychotherapy of men, focusing on the differences between the therapy of men and the therapy of women. The topic of Chapter Three is problems of loving. Contrary to popular opinion, men have at least as many difficulties in loving as do women. Chapter Four deals with the sexual problems of men. Primary among these are impotence, premature ejaculation, and a total retreat from sexuality. Men's need to suffer is discussed in Chapter Five. While all human beings seek pleasure in one form or another, men—as well as women—all too often unconsciously look for a way to suffer. In Chapter Six, I examine men's denial of feelings, along with the ideal of the macho, unemotional male. Chapter Seven addresses men's role in the family of origin. The emphasis here is on the life cycle before marriage. Chapter Eight considers the social role of men. Here conflicts surrounding love, marriage, and work are brought to the fore. Chapter Nine examines the importance of self-image for men, with emphasis on the pervasive feeling of failure produced when men cannot attain the impossible goals set for them by society. Work is the topic of Chapter Ten. For some men, work is a curse; for others, it is a blessing. Chapter Eleven investigates the inexpressive man and the forces that produce him. Chapter Twelve discusses the issue and importance of creativity for men.

In this volume I have included numerous clinical illustrations to show how change is effected in practice. Where necessary, the clinical material has been altered in some nonessential way to avoid identifying specific individuals. No direct reference to any particular person is intended or implied. Most of the patients discussed in this book finished treatment many years ago, so that the problems encountered in their therapy are no longer relevant to their lives.

Acknowledgments

I wish to express my thanks to A Steno Service for their usual excellent secretarial assistance, to my wife Marcia for her unfailing and unbelievable tolerance of my writing habits, and to William A. Kouw, Sanda Bragman Lewis, and Herbert S. Strean for their thoughtful critical comments.

New York, New York   Reuben Fine
August 1988

THE AUTHOR

REUBEN FINE IS A PSYCHOTHERAPIST IN PRIVATE PRACTICE IN New York City. He is also visiting professor at Adelphi University, director of the Center for Creative Living, and director of the New York Center for Psychoanalytic Training. He received his B.S. (1933) and M.S. (1939) degrees from the City University of New York, and his Ph.D. degree (1948) in clinical psychology from the University of Southern California.

Fine has long been active in the American Psychological Association (APA) and has been an APA fellow since 1955. He was president of the division of psychotherapy (1966–1967), a member of the council of representatives (1968–1970 and 1980–1983), and organizer and first president of the division of psychoanalysis (1979).

The author of numerous books, Fine also serves on a number of editorial boards and as consulting and honorary editor of such journals as *Psychotherapy, Book Forum, History of Childhood Quarterly, Journal of Psychoanalytic Psychology,* and *Current Issues in Psychoanalytic Practice.*

TROUBLED MEN

1 | Understanding Men's Emotional Problems

VIRTUALLY FROM TIME IMMEMORIAL THE MALE HAS BEEN RE-garded as the superior sex, and as such he can have no problems. Nor can he have a special psychology: psychoanalysis has a standard book on *The Psychology of Women* (Deutsch, 1944) but nothing on the psychology of men.

Not only has man been regarded as superior, but he has also been perceived as justified in being dominant. Women have been seen not only as weaker but also as subjects to be oppressed.

Thus in the Judeo-Christian tradition, Eve was formed from Adam's rib. The Orthodox Jew thanks God every day that he was born a male and not a female. When Christianity came along, women were seen as at best inferior creatures to be toler-ated. Worse yet: at the height of the witch craze of the Middle Ages, the Church officially declared that "a woman is beautiful to look upon, contaminating to the touch, and deadly to keep . . . a foe to friendship . . . a liar by nature. . . . There is no wrath above the wrath of a woman. . . . All witchcraft comes from car-nal lust, which is in women insatiable" (*Malleus Maleficarum*, [1484] 1928). At best, St. Paul declared, it is better to marry than to burn, recognizing at least that man's lustful desires were also hard to quench.

Nor were the enlightened Greek philosophers much bet-ter. Aristotle (1952) stated in *Politics* that "the relation of male to female is naturally that of the superior to the inferior—of the

1

ruling to the ruled" (p. 69). Aristotle was the leading intellectual authority for many centuries. His predecessors had had
even more contemptuous attitudes toward women. Thus the
Greek poet Palladas wrote, "Marriage brings a man only two
happy days: the day he takes his bride to bed, and the day he
lays her in her grave" (Hunt, 1959, p. 26). It was a common belief among everyday Greeks that the story of the Trojan War
represented a more profound truth: that women drove men to
war (Hunt, 1959).

Masculinity and Femininity:
A Review of the Literature

While these views naturally had no official role in the development of scientific psychology and biology in the nineteenth
century, it is noteworthy that they managed to infiltrate even
the greatest of thinkers. Darwin ([1859] 1958, p. 94) in *Origin
of Species*, his description of the evolutionary process, wrote of
sexual selection (which was then the major basis of his theory):
"This form of selection depends not on a struggle for existence
in relation to other organic beings or to external conditions, but
on a struggle between individuals of one sex, generally the males,
for the possession of the other sex. The result is not death to
the unsuccessful competitor, but few or no offspring." More
than 100 years later, the anthropologist Sarah Hrdy took exception to Darwin, dedicating *The Woman That Never Evolved*
(1981) to "the liberated woman who never evolved but who
with imagination, intelligence, an open mind, and perseverance
many of us may yet become."

The denigrating view of women was embodied in the
nineteenth century in the doctrine that a woman's whole personality was determined by the state of her sexual organs, which
were inherently weak. All kinds of disorders, physical and mental, were attributed to poor ovaries and their concomitant parts,
leading to what we would consider today overtly sadistic medical treatment of women, such as ovariotomy, or "female castration." In 1906 a leading gynecological surgeon estimated that
there were 150,000 women in the United States at that time

who had lost their ovaries under the knife (Ehrenreich and English, 1978, p. 111). Even worse, the removal of the clitoris had since the 1860s been urged as a cure for masturbation and other "sexual evils," and clitoridectomies were often performed—the last one, according to one researcher, as late as 1948 (p. 111).

In many parts of Africa today even more barbarous operations than the clitoridectomy are performed on girls and women to deprive them of the capacity for sexual pleasure (Hosken, 1979).

Freud's work, to be properly evaluated, must be considered in the light of this historical belief in the superiority of men, and the need to subjugate the woman and deprive her of sexual pleasure. As is well known, when Freud began in the 1880s, there was still the notion prevalent that hysteria, one of the most baffling disorders of that day, was caused by the uterus getting loose from its moorings and traveling around the body (Veith, 1965). Because hysteria (from the Greek word for *uterus*) was conceptualized in this way, men obviously could not suffer from it. Freud's early work (1886–1914; compare Fine, 1979b) established once and for all that hysteria is a psychological disturbance that can be effectively handled by psychoanalysis or psychotherapy and has nothing to do with the uterus as such.

In an era when many liberated men and women were arguing for better treatment for women (Ibsen, Shaw, John Stuart Mill, the sociologists, the suffragettes, and others), Freud was able to show that the sexual repressions forced on women led them to become physically ill. In this way he opened the door to the sexual emancipation of women. His observations, and those of other analysts, were largely confirmed by Kinsey and his associates (1948, 1953), in spite of Kinsey's pronounced antianalytic bias, and by the Masters and Johnson work from the 1960s on, again in spite of their lack of familiarity with psychoanalytic concepts. (The Masters and Johnson [1966] description of the female orgasm is virtually identical with the earlier work of Wilhelm Reich [1927] in *The Function of the Orgasm.*)

One consequence of Freud's study of the problems of women was that he came to investigate the problems of men as well. He discovered at an early age that men had just as many sexual problems as women. In 1898 he opined that it would take humanity 100 years to learn to come to terms with the claims of sexuality (SE III, p. 278).* In 1898 he wrote (SE IX, pp. 210–212), "To the uninitiated it is hardly credible how seldom normal potency is to be found in a husband and how often a wife is frigid among married couples who live under the dominance of our civilized sexual morality, what a degree of renunciation, often on both sides, is entailed by marriage, and to what narrow limits married life—the happiness that is so ardently desired—is narrowed down. I have already explained that in these circumstances the most obvious outcome is nervous illness."

It should be borne in mind that the whole Freudian system of psychology rests upon numerous bases. At first there was the unconscious, psychosexual development, and the transference-resistance phenomenon in therapy, later the ego and superego, then the role of the culture, more recently the self system and identity. Psychoanalysis has gradually expanded into a general psychology (Hartmann, 1964), although its tenets have yet to be formulated with sufficient clarity.

As psychology expanded its horizons, increasingly the problems of men came into focus. Initially they were limited to the sexual, which turned out to be serious enough.

Many types of neurotic and psychotic disturbances were then described in men: the men who wish to be God (Jones, 1951), the impostors (Abraham, [1925] 1955b), those wrecked by success (Freud, 1915: SE XIV), the exceptions (Freud, 1915: SE XIV), the phallic-narcissistic men (Reich, [1933] 1945), and a large number of others (see Fenichel, 1945).

Freud largely limited himself to the Oedipal situation, but he also ranged far and wide in his delineation of the human personality, both male and female. Thus in his paper on obsessional acts and religious practices (1907: SE VII), he saw the religious man (or woman) as an obsessional character; in his paper

---

*Unless otherwise noted, all Freud references are to *The Standard Edition*, for which full bibliographical information is provided in the References at the end of the book.

on the creative artist, he saw him as standing halfway between dreaming and reality (1948: SE IX). In *Totem and Tabu* (1913: SE XIII) he made the largest leap, laying the basis for extensive forays into cultural anthropology, and the analysis of cultures that was to begin in the 1920s.

For most of his life, Freud regarded the father as the chief determinant of character. Thus in *Moses and Monotheism* (1939: SE XXIII) he could still identify the authority of the parents with the autocratic father, threatening the child with his power to punish, and essentially disregard the danger from the mother. At the same time, from 1923 on he enlarged the concept of the Oedipus complex to what he called the "complete" Oedipus complex, in which the child has both sexual and aggressive wishes toward both parents and identifies to some extent with both, though the primary identification is with the parent of the same sex.

Before 1926 Freud had seen anxiety, at least in theory, as the result of repressed sexual desire—what he had earlier called the "actual neurosis." But even though he had in effect given up this theory, it was not until 1926 that he could formulate his second theory of anxiety: anxiety represents a fear of separation, originally from the mother, later from other persons who substitute for her. This laid the way for the investigation of the oral stage, which Freud himself had tended to neglect.

Once the investigation of the oral stage got under way, in the 1930s and 1940s, the significance of the mother in the development of psychopathology achieved increasing recognition. Melanie Klein (1947) may be credited with having been the first to examine mother-child pathology, though she paid little attention to what the mother actually did, seemingly placing virtually the entire burden on the child's projections and introjections. The first clear statement of the effects of bad mothering came in Margaret Ribble's book *The Rights of Infants* (1943). There after, numerous terms were coined to depict the bad mother: the castrating mother, the phallic woman, the overprotective mother, the schizophrenogenic mother, or simply the bad mother. Schizophrenia in particular was traced to very early frustrations with the mother—pathogenic experiences that took place well before the infant could verbalize anything. Schizophrenia was thus seen as an oral regression (Rosen, 1962; Frosch, 1983). In this way the pendulum made a sharp turn from seeing everything as due to the bad father to seeing everything as due to the bad mother. Sooner or later it was bound to swing to the middle.

The extreme emphasis on the mother was countered by an examination of the fathers of disturbed children and the role of the father in disturbed adults. It soon became clear that the father was as disturbed as the mother, if not more so (Lidz, Fleck, and Cornelison, 1965). Once again it was shown that men could be as afflicted as women. There was still lacking in analytic theory, however, the recognition that masculinity as such involves certain inevitable conflicts, in much the same way that (as Helene Deutsch demonstrated in her classic work on women [1944]) femininity as such has certain inevitable conflictual consequences. Thus in his final formulation on technique (1937: SE XXIII), Freud still stressed what he called the "biological bedrock"—passivity in men and penis envy in women—holding on to his earlier acceptance of the age-old notion that men are by nature active, women passive.

In the meantime significant developments occurred in other disciplines. Anthropologists began to go out into the field, studying other cultures. One of their first major findings was that the definitions of *male* and *female* varied from culture to culture. Margaret Mead (1935) made this most clear in her famous book on *Sex and Temperament in Three Primitive Societies.* She examined the gentle, mountain-dwelling Arapesh, the fierce, cannibalistic Mundugumor, and the graceful Tchambuli headhunters. Each culture had evolved a different conception of what is "naturally" feminine and what is "naturally" masculine. Her major conclusion was that the major determinants of masculinity and femininity in any culture are more cultural than biological. "The material suggests that many, if not all, of the personality traits which we have called masculine or feminine are as lightly linked to sex as are the clothing, the manners and the form of head-dress that a society at a given period assigns to either sex" (p. 206).

In a later work (*Male and Female,* 1949), Mead summarized the conclusions from her field work from 1925 to 1939 and made some pertinent comments about the American culture. "Human fatherhood is a social invention," she claimed. Further, she described the change in the ideals that had been set up for the average American. She wrote (p. 257) that "this discrepancy between the actuality and the ideal is experienced as a discrepancy between 'myself and the other,' a falling behind the standards of the block, the clique, the school class, the other men in the office, the rest of the faculty. . . . The old perfectly realizable Puritan imperative for the moment, 'Work, save, deny the flesh,' has shifted to a set of unrealizable imperatives for the future, 'Be happy, be fulfilled, be the ideal.' "

With regard to men specifically, she once more insisted that their role is culturally determined. Whole societies can build their male ceremonials on an envy of women's role and a desire to imitate it, in contrast to the denigration of women in our Western culture.

Mead was in the forefront of a whole group of what have been called "cultural relativists," who have almost no use for the biological foundations. Another cultural relativist, though still highly environmentalist, Kardiner in two influential books (1939, 1945) stressed the biopsychosocial determinants of personality. He coined the term "basic personality type" for that personality configuration in any society that is shared by the bulk of the society's members as a result of the early experiences they have in common. Because of the differences in early experience, personality norms for various societies will differ.

Mead was an anthropologist; Kardiner, an analyst (he himself had been analyzed by Freud). With Kardiner and his colleagues (Horney, Fromm, Sullivan, Thompson, and others), the role of cultural as contrasted with biological factors came to be stressed by one group of analysts, who have since come to be known as the "revisionist" or "culturalist" school. Their main contention is that while biology is relevant, culture plays the major role in the formation of personality.

While this view of culture-personality had a wide following, it also came to be attacked by many. It was argued first of all that when the modal or basic personality is investigated more closely, it is typical of only a limited section of the population. For example, Wallace (1970), studying the Tuscarora Indians, found that the modal personality, defined on twenty-one dimensions, was shared by only 37 percent of the sample tested. However, the commonsense observation that different cultural groups have different characteristics remains popular with many social scientists. The only question is how to define the similarities and the differences.

Sociobiologists, of whom E. O. Wilson is the most prominent, also questioned the various cultural hypotheses that had been set up. In his first book Wilson (1975) tried to show that the biological principles that now appear to be working reasonably well for animals in general can be extended profitably to the social sciences.

Wilson pointed to some basic similarities among all human societies with regard to the roles of the two sexes. In general, women are less assertive and physically aggressive. There has never been a single society in which women had absolute control. In about 75 percent of the societies studied by anthropologists, the bride is expected to move from the location of her own family to that of her husband, while only 10 percent required the reverse exchange. Lineage is reckoned exclusively through the male line at least five times more frequently than it is through the female line. Thus, he argues, the evidence for a genetic difference in behavior is varied and substantial. Society can respond in one of three ways: (1) condition its members so as to exaggerate sexual differences in behavior, (2) train its members so as to eliminate all sexual differences in behavior, or (3) provide equal opportunities and access to both sexes but take no further action.

However, the differences between the cultural and the biological points of view can be exaggerated as well. Fenichel (1945), when he reviewed the situation, wrote (p. 588), "The insight into the formative power of social forces upon individual minds does not require any change in Freud's concepts of instincts. . . . The instinctual needs are the raw material formed by social influence; and it is the task of a psychoanalytic sociology to study the details of this shaping. Different 'biological constitution' contains manifold possibilities; yet they are not realities but potentialities. It is experience, that is the cultural conditions, that transforms potentialities into realities, that shapes the real mental structure of man by forcing his instinctual demands into certain directions, by favoring some of them and blocking others, and even by turning parts of them against the rest."

In more recent years much attention has been focused on the self-image, a topic particularly pertinent to the present work. If the self-image varies with the culture, it stands to reason that it would be different in different cultures, especially those most unlike Western civilization. That this is indeed the case is demonstrated by the extensive field work carried out in the past 100 years, especially since the time of the Boasian revolution.

Geza Roheim (1932), reporting on his field work among the central Australian natives, wrote (p. 121), "Every society has a characteristic feature, something which strikes the eye of a human being who comes from another society. It seems probable that these peculiarities—the outsider's point of view—have their roots in tendencies which are universally human, yet particularly accentuated in the group in question. If we regard each type of society as a distinct neurosis, we might speak of the characteristic or governing symptoms of these social systems."

This distinct neurosis is best brought out by the culture's notion of the self or person. The anthropologist Clifford Geertz (1973, p. 48) asserts that "the Western conception of the person as a bounded, unique, more or less integrated motivational and cognitive universe, a dynamic center of awareness, emotion, judgment and action organized into a distinctive whole and set contrastively both against other such wholes and against a social and natural background is, however incorrigible it may seem to us, a rather peculiar idea within the context of the world's cultures."

It is especially through the definition and treatment of illness, both physical and mental, that anthropologists have approached the definition of the self for every culture. The most meticulous study of healing in the context of culture is the work of Arthur Kleinman (1980), a psychiatrist trained in anthropology who spent several years in Taiwan studying the dynamics of the healing process, both physical and psychological, in the native culture.

His work clearly confirms the general thesis that illness is a biased evaluation based on the superego and the cultural forces. Accordingly, all reports of dis-ease (discomfort) as well as claims of well-being must be regarded with a grain of salt. Thus in our own culture, the claim "I am normal," so frequently heard with regard to mental illness, is a defensive maneuver of the ego to protect the self from potentially damaging reproach and punishment.

As Shweder and Bourne (1984) emphasize, what makes Western culture special is the concept of the "autonomous distinctive individual living in society" (compare Marsella and White, 1982).

These considerations are especially applicable to the self-concept of "man" and the understanding of "emotional illness" in our culture. While the notion of the male role has certain biological roots, which are universal (his sexuality, development, and aggression), it also has significant cultural bases, which vary with the times. For example, even in our own century, the self-concept of the Japanese suicide pilots who deliberately destroyed themselves for the sake of the Emperor is incomprehensible to Western observers; the self-concept of the Nazis who deliberately murdered millions of people (not just Jews) in order to gratify their narcissistic ambitions may be incomprehensible even to the next generation of Germans. Similarly, the machismo of the American male, and his deep sense of failure if he does not reach sufficient financial success, are increasingly being questioned by many men on the current scene.

From physiological research come further data on the essential differences and similarities between men and women. It has been found that the hormonal differences between the sexes are not a matter of either-or but of proportion between estrogens (the feminizing hormones), androgens (the masculinizing hormones), and progestins or gestagens (the pregnancy hormones). All three of the sex hormones are closely related in chemical structure, although the level of testosterone in the younger male is ten times higher than in the female (Money and Ehrhardt, 1971, p. 207). Thus in the normal male the influence of the male sex hormone overrides that of the female sex hormone normally produced in the male body. Efforts to find hormonal differences in homosexual men have failed (Kinsey, Pomeroy, and Martin, 1948).

Money and Ehrhardt (1971), who have done the most extensive research on sexual anomalies, have also shown that whatever the biological deviation, the "gender identity" of the individual is established by the parental preferences. With their work and that of Stoller (1968), the concept of gender identity came to replace sexuality in theoretical discussion: sexuality is the physiological given; gender identity is the psychological preference. Thus here too, as in the anthropological research, biology proposes but culture disposes.

Animal psychology ("ethology") has also accumulated evidence for the relativity of the two sexes, rather than an absolute, unbridgeable difference (Wickler, 1972). In some cases some primitive organisms may play the part of the male at one time, the part of the female at another (p. 25). Even in as advanced a species as the bighorn sheep, both sexes play two roles —either that of the male or that of the female (p. 29). But this does not alter the fact that above a certain evolutionary level, the sexual characteristics are in general firmly differentiated.

Apart from sexuality per se, the most obvious difference between the two sexes is that of maternal and paternal role. Yet here too—even though the female is biologically equipped to be the mother, and functions as such—the male will adopt a caring paternal role with surprising frequency. Ridley (1978) has put together the evidence on this point for a variety of animal species.

Among monkeys and apes, Redican and Taub (1981) have summed up a variety of paternal behaviors among males. Males have been observed to assist during the births of neonates; to premasticate food for infants; to carry, sleep with, groom, and especially play with young; to defend young virtually without exception; to provide a refuge during periods of high emotional arousal; and to engage in many other behaviors that we associate with being a "good father" (p. 242). Males can also be destructive of the young infant, though the frequency of such destructive behavior has not yet been accurately determined (Hrdy and Hausfater, 1984).

Both psychologists and psychiatrists have also been busy attempting to see what differences can be found among men and women. In psychology, in the most careful and exhaustive investigation of sexual differences ever published (Maccoby and Jacklin, 1974), the authors explore a number of popular myths, such as that girls are more social than boys, that girls are more suggestible than boys, and that girls have lower self-esteem while boys are more analytical. The only fully established fact in this enormous literature is that boys tend to be more aggressive while girls tend to be more dependent, and even this is only a broad generalization, with many exceptions. The authors conclude their study with this sage comment (p. 374): "A variety of social institutions are viable within the framework set by biology. It is up to human beings to select those that foster the lifestyles they most value."

In psychiatry there have again been numerous attempts to establish sexual differences among the various disorders (Gomberg and Franks, 1979). Here too, while many loose statements are made, more careful research leaves us in the lurch. Gove (1979, p. 41) argues that "there are ample grounds for assuming that women find their position in society to be more frustrating and less rewarding than do men and that this may be a relatively recent development." Some studies do suggest that women present themselves for therapy more often than men, but first of all, this is probably a transient phenomenon, and not true of all kinds of therapy; and second, it does not show that women are sicker than men, merely that they are more willing to put themselves into a dependent position. Furthermore, the man's denial of his problems in our culture is all too obvious. With the cultural emphasis on machismo, the man more often than not will say, "I have no problems, and I need no help."

In the latest (1982) edition of their authoritative *Modern*

Clinical Psychiatry, Kolb and Brodie (1982, p. 159) sum up the situation as follows: "More men than women are admitted to hospitals for mental disorders, the ratio among first admissions being six men to five women; however, because of the greater longevity of women, there are more women than men in public hospitals. As indicated earlier, more women than men with psychiatric disability contact physicians in office and clinic practice. General paresis, alcoholic psychoses, psychoses with epilepsy, and psychoses with cerebral arteriosclerosis are more frequent in men. Manic-depressive psychoses, involutional melancholia, paranoia and psychoses with somatic disease are more frequent in women. Schizophrenia appears to be a little more frequent in women."

There is, of course, dispute about the value and validity of the various diagnostic categories used in psychiatry. What is clearest is, as Kolb and Brodie say (p. 179), that the parental relationship (they stress the mother, but the father comes in as well, of course) is the factor most determinative of the future mental health of the individual. When this relationship is disturbed, as is more often the case than not, the ego is weakened and the child reaches out in a variety of reparative and rehabilitative mechanisms, which later harden into a number of neurotic structures. Thus the sex of the individual is less important than how the child is treated by the parents.

The Myth of Male Superiority

One result of all these lines of investigation can be stated quite succinctly: male superiority is a myth. The man's presumed lack of problems rests on the mechanism of denial. There are conflicts inherent in being a man. In a culture changing as rapidly as ours, the traditional roles to which men were accustomed—husband, father, breadwinner, achiever, sexual conqueror—have all changed, or are in the process of changing. What many have called "gender-role strains" develop. Men need help.

Men's Health, a new journal, states that men are expected to have the mental clarity of a Zen master, the determination of Atlas, the stamina of a long-distance runner, the strength of a warrior, the resilience of Jim Brown, and the creativity of Baryshnikov. Because men cannot live up to this image, the journal argues that

> quite frankly, it hasn't looked too terrific for us men in recent years. Women continue to outlive us by eight to ten years, on average. We get more (by far!) heart attacks, ulcers, strokes and cancer than they do.
>
> The media maintain that we're not in touch with our feelings. Statistics say we still work too hard. Play too hard. Drink too much. Psychologists profess our stress is excessive. Doctors declare sperm counts are down and prostate problems are up. . . .
>
> What's a man to do? . . . Well, rouse yourself, my friend. Because the new answer is "Plenty!" . . . The good news, men, is that we can add many extra years to our lives. That most of the diseases that do us in are preventable. That there's an abundance of new ways we can shed our stress and keep our cool. Abandon macho yet maintain masculinity. All live, laugh and love longer than men have been able to since the beginning of mankind [1985, p. 1].

Once the recognition dawned that men have a physiological basis for their gender but that by and large what happens to them depends on the culture, a whole new literature on the problems of man, both popular and technical, began to emerge. Some of the more important works are mentioned below briefly:

• *The Grant Study:* George Vaillant (1977). The Grant study of successful male adults was conceived in 1937. The men were chosen while they were still college sophomores, on the assumption that there was a high likelihood of finding in that sample a large group of boys who would lead successful lives, regardless of the observer's bias. In all, 268 men were originally chosen. In his book Vaillant describes the steady follow-up interviews on 95 of the original sample.

What was different about the successful Grant study subjects was that they were happier. Their work was satisfying; their health, excellent; their mortality rate, 50 percent less than that of their classmates.

Yet in spite of their good health, there were none who survived the game of life without pain, effort, and anxiety. The psychiatrists who interviewed the subjects in college felt that over half the sample could have benefited from psychiatric consultation. By the time the subjects were thirty, 10 percent had seen psychiatrists, and by age forty-eight the number had increased to 40 percent.

Vaillant reaches five main conclusions: (1) while early childhood events have a role to play, they are not as powerful as psychoanalysts had supposed; (2) lives change, and the course of life is filled with discontinuities; (3) what he calls "adaptive mechanisms" are the key to making sense of mental illness and mental health; (4) human development is a lifelong process in which truth remains relative and can be discovered only longitudinally; and (5) positive mental health does exist and can be discussed operationally in terms that are at least in part free from moral and cultural biases.

• *The Seasons of a Man's Life:* Levinson and others (1978). Levinson and his colleagues planned their study of adult male development in 1966, at a time when the conceptualizations involved scarcely existed even in theory. They studied intensively forty men selected from four diverse occupational groups: hourly workers in industry, business executives, university biologists, and novelists. The men ranged in age from thirty-five to forty-five. Each man was interviewed for ten to twenty hours over a span of two to three months. Based on these interviews, detailed biographical sketches were built retrospectively for each man, portraying his individual life as it evolved over the years. From these forty biographies, the researchers derived generalizations about the life cycle in general.

Levinson and his colleagues found, as the title of the

book implies, that there are seasons in a man's life. These seasons, they claim, are relatively universal—essentially, the biological root. The major influences that come into play are the individual's (1) sociocultural world as it impinges on him; (2) self as it includes a complex patterning of wishes, conflicts, anxieties, and so on; and (3) participation in the world—his transactions between himself and the world.

While in Levinson's work *masculine* and *feminine* are conceptualized as polarities, they are somehow also complementary. This polarity continues to exist throughout a man's life, never to be fully resolved. In becoming a man, the boy selectively draws on and adopts the gender images of his culture. Through his relationship with mother, father, siblings, and others, he develops an internal cast of characters who represent the forms of masculinity of significance to him.

- *Beyond the Male Myth:* Pietropinto and Simenauer (1977). Pietropinto, a psychiatrist, and Simenauer, a psychiatric writer, published the results of a questionnaire that surveyed over 4,000 men—a random, national cross-section carefully controlled for age, education, income, occupation, race, and marital status.

  Some of their main findings: (1) it is passive not liberated women who cause impotence in men; (2) men want sincerity, affection, and companionship in women above all else; (3) men are made nervous by glamour, beauty, and brains; (4) men are devastated when they fail to bring their women to orgasm; (5) male homosexuality is not on the rise; and (6) men's sexual attitudes are now determined by age rather than class or status.

- *The Role of the Father in Child Development:* Lamb (1981). In this work Lamb revises his previously published work on the psychology of the father. A number of excellent papers are included, some of which will be referred to where appropriate. (Lamb has since also published a number of other significant works.)

- *Father and Child:* Cath, Gurwitt, and Ross (1982). This outstanding collection of papers is another sign of the growing interest in fathers. From a theoretical point of view, the two most significant papers are those by Greenspan and Herzog. Greenspan posits a dyadic-phallic phase of development based on the analysis of a five-and-a-half-year-old girl, in which there is a shift from dyadic to triadic relationships. Another way of putting this is to say that development proceeds from the mother to the father; thus object constancy (usually put at about three years of age) has to be evaluated in the light of this shift. James Herzog, in his chapter, introduces the notion of "father hunger" to describe the affective state and longing experienced by father-deprived children.

- *Men in Transition:* Solomon and Levy (1982). In this book, as the name implies, the authors consider the various roles that the man is called upon to play in a changing society; the male role is in transition. Among the problems encountered by men as a result of this transitional phase in the culture are male inexpressiveness, androgyny (that is, subscription to a self-definition that includes both masculine and feminine traits), problems faced by postparental fathers and by the older man, the lack of heroic stature, the male sex role, male homosexuality, and the abandoned husband.

- *American Couples:* Blumstein and Schwartz (1983). This study by two sociologists is based on a questionnaire study of 12,000 couples that centered on attitudes toward money, work, and sex. While much more egalitarianism was found by Blumstein and Schwartz (the man's home is no longer his castle), many of the traditional values and pulls remain; for example, the double standard in sexual infidelity, though breached, continues in the same direction. A surprising feature of this study is the inclusion of ninety lesbian couples and ninety gay male couples.

- *The Hearts of Men:* Ehrenreich (1983). The surprising thesis of this book is that it is men who have started the rebellion against their traditional role of breadwinner–success machine. Their demand that the old values must change is as great as that of women.

- *Feminist literature.* Mention may also be made of some of the feminist literature, because the women's movement has in its turn set off something of a men's movement, giving rise to, for example, men's consciousness-raising groups. A typical work is that by Colette Dowling: *The Cinderella Complex* (1981). Her thesis is that women fear that ambition, success, and the pursuit of money are not feminine traits. While she does not discuss men, it is obvious that when women change their roles, men will have to change theirs as well.

The above is merely a sample of what has been produced in the past ten years. Several major conclusions emerge from this entire discussion:

1. While there is a biological base to men's personality, the major determinants of male behavior are cultural.
2. Men's roles are changing, but many traditional reactions persist.
3. Just as the feminine role as such creates certain inherent strains, the masculine role in our culture does so as well.

The Analytic Ideal

One hundred years ago, when Freud began his research, only symptoms were recognized by the profession. The notion that these symptoms were embedded in a larger framework, which today we call the "character structure," was completely foreign to the professionals of that day. As time went on, even the character structure was recognized as a series of traits or forms of behavior that were intimately related to the culture in which the person lived. Further, the character structure of men was seen as being different in many significant respects from that of women.

As psychotherapy progressed, it was also seen that the incidence of emotional disturbance was far greater than had been previously supposed. The severe disorders, such as schizophrenia, manic-depressive psychosis, drug addiction, suicidal tendencies, and so on, had always been there. But the realization that anxiety, sexual disturbances, excesses of damaging feelings (such as rage outbursts), and similar manifestations were also widespread came more slowly. People with such problems have been given various labels: emotionally disturbed, normal-neurotic, and more recently, worried well.

Again this raises the question of normality. The assumption that people are normal if they work and "get along" somehow has not stood up to more careful scrutiny. Freud's formula for normality is the capacity to work and love. Simple as these requirements may seem, many people fail to live up to them.

Further, expanding on Freud's position, we can set up an analytic ideal that also brings out the differences between men and women. A certain image is set up for each sex by the culture and the family, and the man, willy-nilly, begins by conforming to this image; when he does not, he feels alienated, an outsider, plagued with a sense of the meaninglessness of life. Yet if he does conform, he feels other problems—boredom, inadequate social contacts, a fear that he has misused the best that life can offer him. If normality is defined as the analytic ideal, as it should be, then neurosis can best be defined as the distance from this ideal.

The analytic ideal could also be called the "humanistic" or "democratic" ideal. I prefer the term *analytic ideal*, because it embodies a point of view that I have reached after years of struggling to help people overcome their problems. The notion is by no means alien to the average man in our society.

The analytic ideal is the image that many men—as a result of intensive psychotherapeutic research as well as a more careful exploration of our culture—have built up as the closest that they can come to the good life. Briefly, the argument is that humans attain the greatest degree of happiness if they can love, enjoy sex, have pleasure, experience feelings yet be guided by reason, have a role in a family, have high self-esteem (good self-image), work, communicate, have some creative outlet, and be free from psychiatric symptomatology.

Veroff, Douvan, and Kulka (1981a, 1981b), in two books in which they compare surveys done in 1957 with surveys in 1976, stress the changes that have occurred in these twenty years in similar terms: more inner searching, better human relations, closer family ties, and the like.

While I am an analyst, this image of the good life can easily be absorbed by any competent therapist, regardless of orientation. The "rational living" that Albert Ellis preaches, Carl Rogers's notion of unconditional regard for the other person, the family therapist's stress on the family environment in which problems arise and therapy takes place, even the behavior therapist's attempt to recondition patients into more rational adult human beings—all these are compatible with the ideal, if not actually part of it.

There are naturally differences between the two sexes and the goals set by each. These differences will be highlighted throughout the book, which is organized around the various components of the analytic ideal. For the moment, however, the following observations are pertinent:

1. *Love.* While love is the central experience of every human being's life, its meaning varies for the two sexes. Traditionally, the woman has stressed being loved, while the man has emphasized the idealization of a woman. As a result, men are often caught up in a romantic love trap, which demands that they place the woman on a pedestal. Love is the answer, but it has to be pursued in a sensible way. The ideal is mutual love, yet as everyone knows, it is a goal that is hard to reach.

2. *Sex.* We are in the throes of a sexual revolution. The age of consent is constantly being lowered; the traditional battle in which men seek sex with no strings attached, while women seek a relationship of more permanent duration, still holds for many. There are men who have an enormous amount of sex with no gratification; others are caught up in the age-old taboos that teach them to avoid pleasure. One of the major myths about men is that they have no sexual conflicts; closer examination shows that often their sexual hang-ups are greater than those of women.

3. *Pleasure.* That life should offer a maximum of pleasure and a minimum of pain is a commonsense notion that is overlooked by many men, especially by those who are driven by relentless ambition. "Theirs not to reason why, Theirs but to do and die," Tennyson's motto for the Brit-

ish Light Brigade in the Crimean War in the middle of the last century, seems to be true of many men. "Teach your wife to be a widow" is more than an empty slogan. To relax and enjoy life is achieved more easily by women than by men.

4. *Feeling.* Men are notoriously reluctant to express their feelings openly—especially tender feelings. Women, on the other hand, are encouraged to do so. The "inexpressive man" who has to be brought out by a woman is depicted in one story after another.

5. *Reason.* Men are supposed to be more reasonable than women; this perceived strength goes together with a denial of feeling, which is reserved for the more "emotional" sex. Often enough, however, the man's rationality is little more than a defense against feeling. One consequence is that men are much more apt to deny their feelings, which leads them to stay away from therapy as "sissy stuff."

6. *Family role.* In the traditional culture men often feel the family as a burden, while women see it as the desired goal. In marriage emotional separation involving an overdevotion of the man to his work and of the woman to her children is all too common.

7. *Social role.* Men tend to judge themselves by their role in society much more than women. The result is often a feeling of tension because they fear that they are not living up to expectations.

8. *Self-image.* The self-image of the man depends most heavily on his achievements; for many men this becomes an oppressive idea, and again feelings of failure and inadequacy become strong.

9. *Work.* Men have to work to earn a living, so many men regard work as a curse rather than a blessing. In marriage many men do not realize that they have a legal obligation to support their wives and children. In the lower classes, especially, this leads to widespread abandonment of the family. While the man who runs away thus avoids immediate obligations, in the long run his isolation leads to a terrible sense of loneliness.

10. *Communication.* Traditionally, men are supposed to be

strong and silent, not communicative with their wives or fellow workers. This frequently makes it very difficult for them to express themselves. In contrast, women are encouraged to talk and try to get closer to people.

11. *Creativity.* The creative male artist suffers from many handicaps; boys, after all, are brought up to be military heroes, not creative people.

12. *Psychiatric symptomatology.* In terms of the traditional categories, women tend to be more hysterical; men tend to be more compulsive. The greater frequency with which women consult therapists has already been mentioned as indicating an excessive use of the denial mechanism by men.

Popular psychology books all disseminate the analytic ideal in one form or another. What they fail to take into account is that once a man is brought up in a certain way, it is extremely difficult for him to change. This is where therapy comes in. In a recent article in the *New York Times* magazine, Morton Hunt (1987) estimates that one person in three now seeks out a therapist at some time during any year. It is not surprising that some have called this a "therapeutic revolution" (Bellah and others, 1985).

The diagnostic categories that are more commonly used by professionals—schizophrenia, depression, and the like, as listed in the *Diagnostic and Statistical Manual of Mental Disorders* of the American Psychiatric Association—cut across the various components of the analytic ideal. Physiological factors play a role in some cases, and at times drugs are helpful. But while more is known about the mind-body problems nowadays, psychosocial factors still play the primary role in the great majority.

It is in the light of this background from anthropology, history, physiology, clinical psychology, and psychiatry that the problems of men in our culture and their therapy can be most fruitfully investigated.

Neurosis is a vague term. In one revision of the *Diagnostic and Statistical Manual,* the American Psychiatric Association (1980) considered the term so unclear that they omitted it.

Later it was included as *neurotic disorder;* the present manual (American Psychiatric Association, 1987) states the following (p. 9): "At the present time . . . there is no consensus in our field as to how to define 'neurosis.' Some clinicians limit the term to its descriptive meaning whereas others also include the concept of a specific etiological process."

As Laplanche and Pontalis (1973) have shown, the more precise definition of neurosis in psychoanalytic theory makes it virtually coterminous with that theory. As psychoanalytic theory has changed, and become steadily more comprehensive, the image of neurosis has likewise changed, culminating in such statements as Roheim's (1932), that every culture has its own distinctive neurosis.

Traditionally, the neurotic was regarded as a deviant. Older textbooks of psychiatry (those published before 1945) either did not include neurosis at all, or listed only the most severe neuroses, such as hysteria and obsessional neurosis. Today more sophisticated texts (for example, Freedman and Redlich, 1966) regard neuroses as psychosocial disorders and include in them virtually the entire gamut of human emotional disabilities.

I have tried to see the troubled man as suffering in some aspect of the analytic ideal—sex, love, ambition, and so on. In therapy the various diagnostic disorders are in fact handled in this way—for example, depression as loss, or sexual conflict as immaturity. When the individual is examined in this way, theory and practice come closer together, with mutually beneficial results.

The various aspects of the analytic ideal are under constant discussion. What is an ideal sex life? How much ambition is normal; or, put another way, at what point and at what cost does a man become a workaholic? Already some modern governments (for example, that of the Netherlands) have based some of their labor policies explicitly on the hypothesis that the work force of the near future will no longer adopt the conception of work as a moral obligation (Ellis, 1984). Is the family so essential to mental health? Can the family be altered so as to make it less constricting than it has been in the past? Every therapist knows that these questions come up continually in the therapy of every patient.

The procedure adopted in this book is to list each aspect of the analytic ideal and show how individual men display their conflicts in that area. Naturally men are often conflicted in many areas, but it is impossible to discuss them all at once. The connection between the area of conflict and the total personality will be made abundantly clear, together with the means for overcoming the discord.

Psychoanalysis embodies two visions: first, a vision of man as he is; and second, a vision of what he might become. Neurosis is the description of what he is at present; the analytic ideal is the image of what he might become in the future. How the therapeutic process leads the man from neurotic conflict to a happier life closer to the analytic ideal will be the main thrust throughout the work.

2 | Treating Men: Therapeutic Principles

TO A GREAT EXTENT THE PRINCIPLES OF THE PSYCHOTHERAPY of men are the same as or similar to the principles of the treatment of women. But in a number of important respects, there are significant differences. It is on these differences, as well as the basic question of technique, that this chapter will focus.

One preliminary comment is in order here. My point of view is psychoanalytic. This involves a certain attitude, or set of attitudes, toward the patient, the therapy, even the whole societal structure in which therapy takes place.

No apology is needed for adopting a psychoanalytic framework. In the first place, it is generally estimated that about one-third of the therapists in the country are either frankly psychoanalytic or strongly psychoanalytically oriented. Second, even those who are not psychoanalytic make extensive use of the principles and theories developed by Freud and his followers, as well as by the revisionist analysts who follow Freud in most respects but question some of his specific ideas, such as penis envy. Hence a discussion of the principles derived from psychoanalysis applies in greater or lesser measure to all forms of psychotherapy that make a serious effort to change the structure of the disturbed person who comes to the therapist for help. Because of the importance of the psychoanalytic framework—both for the approach of this book and for the larger society—I include a discussion of the personality and training of the psychotherapist.

The Personality and Training of the Psychotherapist

In a book describing the first ten years of the Berlin Psychoanalytic Institute, Hanns Sachs, the first training analyst, wrote (Maetze, 1970, p. 53),

> The church has always demanded of those of its followers who wished to devote their entire lives to it, that they undergo a novitiate. In this transitional period they must learn to view world events in a way that is different from the layman, they must learn to cast their eyes on the hidden rather than the obvious. . . . Analysis requires something which corresponds to the novitiate. With the accumulation of theoretical knowledge, no matter how thorough the book knowledge acquired, analysis is not satisfied. . . . The future analyst must learn to see things which other people easily, willingly and permanently overlook, and must be in a position to maintain this capacity to observe, even when it is in sharpest contradiction to his own wishes and feelings. . . . As one sees, analysis requires something which corresponds to the novitiate of the church. . . . The only way to acquire it is through the training analysis.

All therapists have two things in common: they must listen to talk of mental anguish all day long, tales that other people would rather avoid; and they must have empathy for human suffering, again something that the average person generally prefers to stay away from. Because of these two commonalities, it stands to reason that therapists would show many similarities, regardless of their theoretical orientations, and that their lives would run along parallel lines.

There are many studies devoted to the ideal personality and training of the therapist. Among the early ones are Holt and Luborsky (1958) on psychiatric residents, Kelly and Fiske (1951) on clinical psychologists, and Berengarten (1951) on social workers.

Undoubtedly the most important empirical work is the study done by Henry, Sims, and Spray, who investigated 4,000 therapists from the four main mental health fields: psychiatry, psychology, social work, and psychoanalysis. Their work is reported in two excellent and stimulating books (Henry, Sims, and Spray, 1971, 1973). They discovered that the entrants into any of these four health fields who finally do become psychotherapists are highly similar in social and cultural background. They come from a highly circumscribed sector of the social world, representing a social marginality in ethnic, religious, and political terms. As therapists choose among the offerings in their particular training systems, they do so in ways that appear to fit into the choices of these systems. In this process the members of these systems become again alike in emphasizing particular views and experiences, and each emerges at the end of training with a firm commitment to the psychotherapeutic stance. Members of each group triumph over the manifest goals of their particular training system and become, with time, increasingly like their colleague psychotherapists in other training systems. Because of these similarities, Henry calls psychotherapy the "fifth profession."

In a companion volume, Henry, Sims, and Spray (1973) found that the life ways of psychotherapists constitute an increasingly homogeneous and integrated system of belief and behavior that most often begins in early family-situated religio-cultural experiences and that progresses selectively toward a common concept of a psychodynamic paradigm for the explanation of all behaviors—a paradigm that guides their choices and behaviors as they emerge from the training years into the practice of psychotherapy.

Then they sum up: on the basis of previous training and experience, psychotherapists have learned not to rely on common, everyday criteria for categorizing individuals but instead view persons as concrete manifestations of a general theoretical framework. For most of the therapists practicing in Los Angeles, New York, and Chicago, this theoretical framework is composed of psychodynamic concepts—particularly psychoanalytic concepts derived from the Freudian and neo-Freudian schools of thought. Such concepts delimit the psychotherapist's world. The specialized world of the psychotherapist is one in which the

terminology of everyday conversation is avoided and psychodynamic language becomes the basic mode of communication.
To a certain extent, therefore, the psychodynamic paradigm
serves to redefine the social behavior of individuals so that they
come to be viewed as functions of specific personal dynamics.

The situational supports implicated in the development
of a psychotherapeutic relationship in practitioners' offices are
not, of course, found in their homes. Even though psychotherapists tend to use psychodynamic language to describe their
spouses and children, it is clear that the personal relationships
the therapists have with members of their families are qualitative-
ly different from the intimate relationships established with patients. The emotional gratification derived from therapeutic
relationships with patients can be used by psychotherapists to
offset the emotional deprivation incurred in lowering the degree
of intimacy in familial relationships.

The distinctive character of the therapeutic encounter
provides some basis for understanding aspects of the therapist's
personal life. Reliance on the psychodynamic paradigm requires
that psychotherapists be cognizant of their own inner life and
that they view their own personal dynamics as crucial equipment for understanding others.

In the everyday social world, "birds of a feather flock together," presumably in part because they talk the same language
and hence feel comfortable not only with the terminology used
but also with the trend and flow of the conversation and with
the cognitive and intellectual processes used in deriving conclusions. Because psychotherapists specialize in the performance of
verbal therapy, it is not surprising that they actively prefer patients who can speak their own language, or who learn their language quickly.

Given these considerations, it should be clear that the
heavy reliance on the psychodynamic paradigm by psychotherapists has implications not only for the quantity but also for the
quality of therapeutic relationships. Specifically, in terms of the
number of patients receiving treatment, the findings of Henry
and his colleagues clearly document the fact that private practice remains the primary context for the provision of intensive
psychotherapy.

Henry and his colleagues also note that, to a greater extent than is true of most other professionals, psychotherapists manifest a tendency to adopt a unidimensional view of both personal and professional relationships: the psychotherapist's therapeutic perspective becomes a world view, a way of viewing all personal relationships, and not only an orientation toward work. Henry and his group found psychotherapists detached from the everyday affairs of home and community.

Because psychotherapists rely on psychodynamic language to describe human motives and desires—their own as well as others'—we might expect therapists to feel closer to their colleagues than to others who do not speak their special language. To the extent that a sense of community derives from the utilization of a common shared vocabulary for accounting for one's actions, the findings of Henry's group clearly document the existence of a community of psychotherapists. Thus just as psychotherapists tend to describe family members in psychodynamic language, they also tend to describe fellow practitioners with the same language. The numerous arguments among psychotherapists may be related to the fact that psychodynamic language is itself heavily negative in tone.

Not only is membership in the psychotherapeutic community maintained by describing current relationships with a common language, but psychotherapists also share a tendency to describe their past biological experiences in a way that is consistent with the psychodynamic paradigm. Henry and his colleagues describe a remarkable homogeneity in the sociocultural origins of members of the four mental health professions. Specifically, there is a pronounced tendency for practitioners to claim a Jewish cultural affinity, to have Eastern European ethnic ties and foreign-born fathers, to have rejected, in adolescence, religious beliefs and political views of their parents, to have experienced, during their own lifetime, upward social mobility. These biographical characteristics have been found to be associated with those personal qualities that experts believe applicants to therapeutic training programs should have: an introspective orientation, an intellectual predisposition, and a relativistic perspective. Placed in the context of the patterns of professional selection and recruitment, the development of a

commitment to a psychodynamic paradigm can be viewed as
the product of the individual's total biography.

The most recent attempt to examine these and related
questions on a large scale is that by Wallerstein (1978), who surveyed the fifty-seven institutes then members of the International
Psychoanalytical Association, receiving replies from twenty-eight
(or half). Some of these replies were extremely brief; some,
lengthy and careful discussions of all the issues raised. In any
case, they offered a good cross-section of psychoanalytic thought
on the question of training that is no doubt still applicable. Wallerstein distinguished six major training issues on which a variety of opinions emerged from the institutes' responses. These
issues are:

1. The extent to which a real problem of training in compat-
    ibility is posed by our simultaneous intent to encompass
    two not necessarily congruent educational goals for our
    candidates in training—that is, educating for a science and
    training for a profession. About half of the responding in-
    stitutes saw no meaningful distinction between the two
    goals and therefore no problem; the other half saw a real
    and thorny problem.
2. Proper training prerequisites for psychoanalytic education,
    stated variously as the issue of medical versus nonmedical
    training or the issue of proper mixture of the potential stu-
    dent pool from which psychoanalysis should seek its re-
    newal. Here the debate has persisted unchecked during the
    more than fifty years since Freud's publication of his book
    on lay analysis, with extremes on both sides. (Here the law-
    suit brought by some American psychologists against the
    American Psychoanalytic Association and the International
    Psychoanalytical Association may ultimately create a more
    cohesive point of view.)
3. The kind of curriculum that is best suited to our training
    institutes. That which has been traditional in professional
    school education is the uniform or essentially lock-step cur-
    riculum, in which the total student body is held responsible
    for mastering a common body of professional knowledge,

skills, and attitudes. In graduate academic education in the university, however, that which has been more traditional is individualized or tailor-made sequences geared to the very specific, differentiated interests and career goals of each student.

4. The selection for training and the place of selection criteria, both positive and negative. Here we also had polar extremes: between the effort, on the one hand, at a total abolition of preselection, leaving anybody who was qualified free to go into analysis with any practitioner (in some instances, even with advanced students); and the effort, on the other hand, at the most rigorous screening and preselection before admission to training analysis under member institute auspices.

5. The expectable degree of personality alteration to be achieved in the personal analysis and in the overall training sequence. This issue is inextricably linked, of course, to the stance on the selection issue. Here there seemed to be a fairly reliable correlation with the position on the selection issue: the Kleinian-oriented institutes, which tend to have freer admission processes (based on a willingness to take gambles on candidates who might be deemed too "disturbed" by other institutes), tend concomitantly to engage in much longer analyses and to count on achieving more far-reaching personality changes.

6. Last in this listing, but probably first in heated and controversial attention in our current literature, is the role of the training analyst in the assessment of his or her candidates and in the monitoring of the candidates' progression through the institute. This is the distinction between reporting and nonreporting training analyses. Here again there was an equal division of voices into the two camps, with various positions in between.

In light of the wide range of differences found in the replies, Wallerstein concludes that "we have in full view now a range of experiments in training" (p. 503).

Overall, there is agreement on a number of points: therapists should be well educated, empathic, interested in people and themselves, eager to help, curious about the working of the mind, and so on. In this it is easy enough to recognize Freud as the ego-ideal that therapists take for themselves, whatever theoretical orientation they manage to end up with.

At the same time, practical considerations loom larger than theoretical views. The most effective psychotherapy is still private practice. Efforts to bring therapy under institutional control, such as those that resulted in the Community Centers envisaged by Kennedy in the early 1960s, have all failed. Psychiatric hospitals are still of generally poor quality, nowadays doing little more than keep the patients quiet with the use of drugs.

Psychotherapy is not taught in the universities, or if it is taught, it is not taught well. Some of the essential prerequisites for being a good therapist, such as the personal analysis or self-evaluation, are incompatible with university regulations.

Training for psychotherapy consists of a personal analysis (or personal therapeutic experience), theoretical courses, and practicing psychotherapy under close supervision. Because of the increasing prestige of psychodynamic thinking, the theoretical courses are now often taught in universities, but practice under supervision and personal therapy generally are not. This is why every group has elected to conduct its essential training outside the framework of the university. In time this may change, but it still remains the prevailing policy.

One consequence of the separation from the university is that politics of the training institute play a much greater role than is recognized in theory. Even a person ordinarily thought of as conservative, Otto Kernberg (1984), has recently written a paper calling the institutes paranoid—without even using quotes around the word *paranoid*. Mercano and colleagues (Mercano and others, 1987), in their review of the Latin American institutes, state that the students in general are exposed to many points of view, that they agree with the instructor because they have to to get through, but that once on their own they do whatever they want to do.

In a number of instances, persons high up in the mental health training system have broken off to form groups of their own. (This has happened so frequently that everybody comments on it.) Even Freud's own trusted secret circle of six, which was formed in 1913 to carry forward the cause, dissolved less than ten years later. The comment by Henry and his colleagues that psychotherapists tend to stick to their own groups is appropriate here. The difficulties inherent in doing therapy are handled by most through applying individualistic measures; by others, by adhering to a group where they can simply submit to the opinions of the leader.

There is no agreement on the preparatory experience for analysis or psychotherapy. I believe that the reason for this is that psychotherapy deals with human happiness, a subject that cannot be taught in any organized way. It embraces all the disciplines known to humankind. Thus the therapist should be seen as the secular philosopher of our times. This would eliminate the older philosophies, which were much too abstract, and create a new philosophy—more similar to that of groups such as the Stoics and the Epicureans.

Freud once wrote (in Freud and Pfister, [1928] 1963, p. 126), "I would like to hand psychoanalysis over to persons who need not be doctors but should not be priests." He opposed the psychiatric domination of psychoanalysis that has happened in the United States and hoped for a more liberal attitude—one that would stress the philosophical issues involved.

Another problem that has arisen in the field of psychotherapy is the payment for therapy through insurance. Insurance companies want to make money, so if they reimburse, they want some control. This problem is faced by medicine in general, and therapists must not fail to address it.

Nothing here has been said about drugs, which are so widespread in treatment. While some drugs are useful in some instances, the notion that a drug will be found for every illness—a notion propagated by some psychiatrists on the current scene—is merely another illusion. Aldous Huxley suggested it in his 1932 *Brave New World*, but the brave new world he caricatured there would not be very attractive to us today.

Therapy is intimately tied up with the social milieu. Different social milieus require different therapies, and some questions that are so heatedly discussed today are not really therapeutic problems at all (for example, the women's liberation movement, which has for all practical purposes nearly accomplished its goals). It is a simple fact that psychotherapy of the kind we practice is virtually unknown in the totalitarian countries; in the Soviet Union it is dangerous even to own a Bible. Perhaps this will change with *glasnost*, but it has not changed yet.

Because therapy is so closely connected with the social milieu, the therapist must have a working philosophy that deals with this social milieu as effectively as possible. The philosophy I suggest in this book and try to work out, at least in outline, is that of the analytic ideal.

Establishing the Analytic Situation

As I have noted, men come to therapy less often than women. The major reason for this male reluctance is that the man's self-image makes him more ashamed of his problems and therefore more reluctant to discuss them with another person. The strong macho image of the man admits no weaknesses. He is particularly afraid to admit to any fears, which make him feel humiliated and cowardly in front of his fellow men. And all psychotherapy involves the discussion of fear or anxiety; in theory, anxiety and the defenses against it lie at the root of all emotional disturbance.

As a rule men come to therapy with one specific symptom that they can no longer handle on their own. Knowledge of the analytic ideal enables the therapist to see that this symptom is part of a larger picture, the character structure. Many examples of this will be given throughout this book. The man is frequently only dimly aware of the defects in his character structure; often enough it takes him quite a while to see that his symptom—for example, drinking—masks a deeper disturbance.

If a problem is severe enough to bring the man to a therapist, commonsense advice and suggestions no longer can be of any great help; the man has had plenty of those already. What the therapist uses to get at the problem is one aspect of the analytic ideal that he or she can agree with the patient is of particular consequence. Hence in the beginning the analyst is limited to two activities: first of all, to listen carefully and find out as much as possible about the patient; second, to formulate as clearly as possible the characterological difficulties from which the man is suffering. Two relatively simple examples of that process follow.

John sought out an analyst because he had been sexually impotent with a woman he loved. At first he was very resistant to the idea of analysis; all that he wanted was to become more potent.

The course of the first sessions, however, revealed a rather meaningless life. At twenty-seven he spent most of his time at the track, trying to make money at horse racing. He had been to graduate school for a while, then had dropped out. The family background was bad: his mother was a suicidal depressive who eventually died a suicide.

When it was pointed out to him by the analyst that he was drifting through life, with no clear-cut goals and few real pleasures, and the suggestion was made that he should enter analysis, he saw the point and entered readily. Once the analyst had helped him see how much of the analytic ideal was missing from his life, he became deeply aware of how bad his situation really was.

In another case a peculiar resistance came out right away. Henry was a graduate student who could not complete his degree. In childhood he was the preferred darling of his mother, who made few demands on him and later seemed willing to support him forever. This did not bother him much until the analyst pointed out to him that he could not go through life expecting to find another indulgent mother.

Henry's most peculiar resistance came out in the early stages. He had gone to a number of analysts, all fairly well known, and asked them to reduce their fee for him. All had refused. When he came to his last therapist, the therapist suggested that they halve the usual fee for one month, then return to the regular amount. The therapist also pointed out that with the demand for a reduction in fee Henry was asking again for an indulgent mother who simply was no longer there. With the compromise on the fee and the interpretation of his wish to be dependent, he accepted analysis.

This latter example shows that in the early stages it is often necessary to maneuver the situation carefully to establish an analytic situation. Even with the most careful efforts, some patients will run away from therapy very quickly.

Transference. No matter how disturbed the patient's behavior may appear, as a rule rational explanations will effect little change. The reason for this is that the patient soon (sometimes even before analysis begins) establishes a relationship with the analyst that is in many ways a replica of relationships with early figures, especially the parents. This is known as "transference."

As a rule the patient will not recognize that he is producing transferences; to him, everything is reality. Wherever an opening presents itself, this reality must be challenged to help him see that he is dealing with a transference manifestation. But unless the resistance is exceedingly severe in the beginning, this kind of interpretation has to be postponed until the transference is more solidly established, which usually takes a little while (several months).

Some analysts jump the gun by pushing transference interpretations too soon. When that happens, the patient who is not ready for it will protest and often leave treatment. It is vital to understand that this early resistance, with the strong wish to terminate treatment, is frequent and powerful. It has been estimated that if the opening phase is not handled properly, between 30 and 60 percent of the patients will drop out after a few sessions (Stieper and Wiener, 1965).

Transference can be viewed phenomenologically, in terms of what the patient does; genetically, in terms of the roots of the various feelings; or both. Eventually it encompasses everything that goes on between therapist and patient, but for practical and theoretical reasons, sometimes one aspect is emphasized, sometimes another.

Usually transference is classified as positive, negative, or indifferent (Fine, 1982). The seemingly indifferent transference usually covers up a great deal of negativism, however; the indifference is a defensive pose.

It is sometimes thought, and taught, that it is a matter of indifference whether the patient's transference is positive or negative; whatever the transference, it has to be worked out. That is true, of course, but my experience indicates that the patient who is sharply negative, especially in the beginning, does not do as well as the one who at least starts with a positive transference.

Another way of looking at transference, tying it up with the analytic ideal, is this: the basic problem from which all patients suffer is a neurotic experience of love, which has left them shaken and frustrated. If they can start off on a positive note with the analyst, that at least betokens a positive attitude to love. This positive attitude can be used constructively, in the course of analysis, to work out a more mature love experience in the patient's private life. Of course, this does not alter the fact that many patients start off positively, then become negative, or the reverse. But such switches are less common than is usually thought. Excessive negative transference leads to premature termination, with little therapeutic effect. Positive transference is almost always therapeutically beneficial.

In the case of Irving, the patient revealed that when he was seventeen, his sister-in-law had seduced him; that was his first sexual experience. The analyst unwisely asked whether he thought that was "ethical," implying that it was not. Thereupon Irving decided that his financial circumstances could not permit him to enter this treatment, and he terminated immediately. He then went on to another therapist, who was not judgmental, and did beautifully.

In this case, the negative transference was in fact created by the therapist. Nothing is more detrimental to constructive therapy than a judgmental therapist who makes the patient feel guilty about his life.

Resistance. Allied to transference is the concept of resistance. Freud once stated that any procedure that takes transference and resistance as its starting points should be considered analysis, even if based on some theory other than his own. This view has been confirmed by several generations of therapists.

Why does the patient resist? For the same reason that people resist revealing their intimate secrets to others—shame, guilt, rage, competition with the other person, and the like. Resistance consists essentially of unacceptable feelings and the reluctance to express them.

Here, it is now recognized, gender differences come in. If the analyst is a man, the "fight" revolves around aggression (dominance) and homosexuality (submission). If the analyst is a woman, the "fight" revolves around sexuality: the male patient seeks to seduce the analyst, who is often seen in the unconscious as a prostitute.

Barney, a thirty-five-year-old store owner, approached his female therapist in terms of straight sex. He said to her, "Let's fuck." In reply to any interpretation, he said that that was all there was to do with a woman (even though he was married and had three children). She could not break through this resistance, and he left after three sessions. The analytic ideal of a loving relationship with a woman he could not grasp.

While the struggle with the female analyst usually takes a sexual form, with the male it is more often a constant fight with the analyst, which is based on a wish to replace him; originally this is the son-father complex. It matters little whether the patient has the ability to do what the analyst has done; he sees himself as a grown-up man who can do anything, just as the little boy puts on an aviator's cap and fancies himself a member of the air force. Use of the analytic ideal as a framework eventually helps the patient see himself as he is and adjust to what his real abilities are.

Abraham was a fifty-year-old man who had never finished high school. He came of a poverty-ridden family, and his father had committed suicide. He had never been able to relate to women, confining himself to occasional encounters with prostitutes, and now lived with his married sister and her husband.

In the analysis Abraham almost immediately developed the idea that he was going to be an analyst. He went back to high school, where for some reason the first subject that he took, and flunked, was trigonometry. So he dropped out again. The patient nevertheless kept on trying, insisting that he was going to be an analyst.

In reality he had a secure civil service job that was remunerative but somewhat boring. The conflict with the analytic ideal was that he had a grandiose self-image that interfered with his everyday functioning. As this was worked out, by consistent interpretations, he came to see himself as he was, gave up his wish to be an analyst, and contented himself with a more settled life.

This case brings out the fact that many patients in analysis wish to become analysts at some point in their therapy. Such a wish is perfectly understandable, since they wish to pass on their positive experience to others. But the wish must be accompanied by the determination and ability to pursue the necessary studies. (I may say that in my own life, this was the route that led me into analysis. I was more involved in chess, philosophy, and other topics until my personal analysis led me to become acutely interested in people and their problems.)

The Activity of the Patient

Unlike forms of therapy (such as drug therapy) in which the patient can play a passive role, in psychotherapy the activity of the patient is of prime importance. As a rule, the patient comes in with a specific problem, such as excessive fears, sexual difficulties, an unhappy marriage, headaches, and the like. These are the specific symptoms for which the patient demands immediate relief. Actually, most patients have already tried specific forms of relief, such as drugs, drink, divorce, shifting jobs, or the like, and these have not succeeded. Hence they come in in a state of great anxiety, sometimes panic.

The first job of both patient and analyst is to translate the immediate symptoms into a character problem, in accordance with the philosophy based on the analytic ideal. Identification of a character problem is a broader evaluation of the patient's whole life situation. It makes it intelligible to the patient that the problem is not merely one of a symptom, no matter how painful that may be, but of his entire approach to living. It is only when the symptom picture has been translated or transformed into a character disturbance that really effective psychotherapy can begin. This translation takes place only when a sufficient transference has been established to allow the patient to look at his entire life-style more objectively.

The patient's main task is to produce material that is relevant to his psychological problems. All other material, such as politics or general literary discussions, should be avoided, because it detracts from the necessary concentration on the relevant conflicts. Some patients talk easily and quickly become ideal patients. Others fight, hit, struggle, and resist all the way through. I have sometimes used the analogy that there are two main kinds of analyses: the dental and the obstetrical. In the dental, the analyst has to struggle in otherwise inaccessible areas, to scrape, push, manipulate in many ways. By contrast, in obstetrical analysis the therapist drops a seed and nature takes care of the rest. Unfortunately, the great majority of patients are dental, though occasionally an obstetrical case comes along.

Samuel was caught up in an unhappy marriage, which had led him to resume analysis after some years. He did not know what was wrong. Then he produced a dream: "I am about to give birth to a baby. But the insides of my body are rigidly laid out in squares and rectangles; there is no room for expansion, and hence no room for the baby to get out. I wake up in a panic." The dream clearly brought out his envy of his wife, who could stay home and take care of their baby, while he had to go out and work. With this dream and its interpretation by the therapist, he could see that at some level he wanted to be a woman. This dissatisfaction with his male role then became the character problem on which the analysis centered.

There are three requests that the analyst makes of the patient: to come at a certain time, to talk, and to pay an agreed-upon fee. Resistance may be revealed in the patient's response to any of these requests. Indeed, it is surprising how many variations are found in the way in which patients approach these three simple issues (Fine, 1982; Strean, 1985).

A typical example is that of Michael, who in the course of a long analysis went into a deep slump, the major manifestation of which was a refusal to comply with ordinary demands. He would not pay his rent, which led to his being evicted. He would not pay the small alimony ordered by the court, which led to a brief imprisonment. He would not pursue his regular profession, which led to terrible impoverishment. And finally, in the therapeutic situation, he refused to pay the fees. Because of his refusal to pay, the analysis had to be terminated. Clearly he wanted to be mama's little darling, and avoided the analytic ideal of maturity in relation to others. After a long hiatus, he straightened out his financial affairs, returned to analysis, and made an excellent adjustment.

The patient's primary instructions are to tell the therapist about himself. One phrasing that I have found helpful is, "Tell me all about yourself. The more I know about you the more I'll be able to help you." Some patients will talk endlessly about their childhood, with little reference to the present; still others will talk endlessly about the present, with little reference to childhood. There are virtually as many variations as there are people. The principle remains: the patient is to produce material, but each case is different.

As noted before, most patients take some time to get to the point where they can be fully open with the therapist. Until that time arrives, it is best for the therapist to wait until the true story comes forth—as true as it can be under the circumstances. The procedure in which the patient says everything that comes to mind, called "free association," is a useful technique for bringing that true story out.

In the way in which this request for free association is responded to, there are again innumerable variations (see Bellak, 1961). Some patients will repeatedly say, "Nothing comes to mind." Others will say, "I'd rather not talk about myself." Still others (the "obstetrical" patients) will associate freely and be fully cooperative. There are actually relatively few patients of this kind, which is why every textbook on psychoanalysis devotes a large part of its discussions to resistances.

The dream plays a special role in the therapeutic encounter. The reason for this is that even when the patient is completely cooperative, he is still dealing with powerful unconscious forces. These forces come out most effectively in the dream. Further, if the analyst offers an interpretation of the patient's comments, the patient may very well say, "That's *your* interpretation." But if the patient brings the material out in a dream, he finds it much harder to deny.

In our society people do not usually talk about dreams spontaneously. But they are there, right at the surface. To elicit dreams, all that the analyst has to do is inquire for them. Sooner or later most patients get into the habit of relating the dream they had the night before, or just recently. Some, however, will produce very few, no matter how strongly urged to do so. Each dream produced by such patients is all the more valuable, but at the same time the material remains scanty.

Still, no matter how much material is produced, the dream retains a special place. That most dreams are bizarre in one respect or another makes them all the more useful. Freud's dictum that the dream is the royal road to the unconscious is still true. Many instances will be given throughout the book.

The patient's capacity for production, including dreams, is an essential part of his character structure, which cannot be altered by artificial means (this is the reason why analysts in general have given up hypnosis). As a result of the analytic work, the patient's productions will alter in the long run. But to have that happen, the analyst must remain in an apparently passive stance. The stance is not really passive, however; if the therapist is there to listen, the difference from the childhood environment to the present will eventually impress itself upon the patient, who will then be able to change. For this reason I have suggested that such passivity be called "dynamic inactivity" (Fine, 1982).

The differences between men and women in divulging relevant information are those found in all similar situations in life. The woman will tend to be more seductive and sexual, the man (with a male analyst) more combative and resistant. Both reactions are material for analysis.

The Activity of the Therapist

The relative silence of the traditional analyst is a paradox to many and has to be clarified. It derives from the nature of the analytic ideal, as well as from the reality of interpersonal relations in our society.

First of all, it is a matter of empirical observation that the patient new to therapy either does not tell the truth, or does not tell the whole truth. In part this derives from seeing the therapist as a superego; in part it derives from the fact that unconscious distortions have become so ingrained in the person that he is no longer sure of what the truth is. Consequently, it takes time to uncover what really has taken place (see Spence, 1986, and commentary on his book). If the analyst talks too much, the patient will not be able to reveal his secrets.

Abe, a fifty-year-old man whose father had committed suicide, was very depressed. He often saw suicidal halos around the heads of other people. In therapy he sat in front of the desk; the analyst, behind the desk. The therapist was an extremely talkative person and bombarded the patient steadily with one interpretation after another. This prevented Abe from telling him about his great fear. After three months of this, Abe abruptly left treatment, frustrated by his inability to get his story out.

In this case it was a conscious revelation that the patient held back. In many other cases it is only after a long period of free association that new material comes to consciousness. Gradually, the superego of the therapist becomes milder and milder in the mind of the patient and material breaks through that he had consciously long since forgotten. A softening-up period seems necessary to allow shameful or guilt-laden memories to come to the fore. Here too any excessive activity on the part of the therapist would interfere with this process. So he or she keeps quiet until some data relevant to a clarification of the analytic ideal come to the fore.

Consider the case of Milton, who had begun to ejaculate at around age thirteen but had forgotten about it. After some time he revealed that for a while at that age he had noticed some white milky fluid coming out of his penis. Up to then he had denied masturbating before age nineteen. When the new memory came in, he realized that he had been masturbating all along, from age thirteen on, but had simply denied the significance of his action.

Choosing Diagnosis Versus Dynamic Assessment. Because the vast majority of analytic therapists come from one of three mental health professions, and have received part of their training in either mental hospitals or clinics for the seriously disabled, they have been trained to make diagnoses in accordance with the official criteria of the American Psychiatric Association (1987), as found in the *Diagnostic and Statistical Manual of Mental Disorders.* There is much that is faulty and even harmful in this diagnostic procedure.

Analysts have long been seriously critical of psychiatric nomenclature. Anna Freud (1965) wrote that "the descriptive nature of many current diagnostic categories runs counter to the essence of psychoanalytic thinking" (p. 110). Karl Menninger (1959) put it even more emphatically: "Diagnosis in the sense in which we doctors have used it for many years is not only relatively useless in many cases; it is an inaccurate, misleading, philosophically false prediction" (p. 672).

Menninger (1963) observed that the conventional psychiatric nomenclature has changed but little over the centuries, while Alexander and Selesnick (1966) showed how ideas once forgotten are revived over and over. Jung (1923), in his delineation of extraversion and introversion, devoted most of one book to a lengthy historical section in which he demonstrated how in one form or another the polarity of extravert-introvert has always characterized Western thought.

Because psychotherapy scarcely existed before Freud, the traditional, pre-Freudian systems took as their baseline the functioning of the individual in society. If someone could function, he or she was "sane"; if not, the person was "insane." The progress of psychological thought has completely demolished such an oversimplification. People can not only function with severe neurotic disabilities; they can even get along in many social situations with psychotic disturbances, such as hallucinations, delusions, and paranoid ideas. In fact, as Hartmann (1939) pointed out, many forms of psychopathology make for better social adjustment than what analysts would regard as mental health. Lasswell (1930) pointed out as early as 1930, on the basis of his empirical studies, that many of the leaders in our community have serious psychological problems. The dilemma even arises, and in some cases becomes acute, that paranoid indi-

viduals with no real convictions of their own are drawn to positions of power—and often reach them. Given that functioning in
society can certainly not be equated with mental health, the
conventional diagnostic system, based on such functioning, is
seriously flawed, in spite of all attempts to overhaul it.

Dynamic therapists have always emphasized the inner
psychological nature of mental and emotional disturbance. The
origin of mental disorder lies in the inadequacy of the early
family relationships, especially with the mother, who is the first
person to interact with the child. However, poor adjustment is
not all of one piece. Freud once put it this way (1937: SE
XXIII): every normal person is in fact normal only on the average. His ego approximates to that of the psychotic in some part
or other, and to a greater or lesser extent.

Since Freud's later work (after 1914), the emphasis has
been on ego structure, and on those aspects of the ego that are
growth-producing as contrasted with those that are growth-
inhibiting. It is from this background that I have developed the
conceptual framework of this book.

That normality involves love and work has long been
common currency. Add to these the other factors—sex, pleasure,
feeling, reason, family structure, self-image, communication,
creativity, and freedom from psychiatric symptomatology—and
you have the analytic ideal, a straightforward extension of
Freud's original thought.

It is through comparison of the individual man with the
analytic ideal that the nature of his inner disturbance is brought
to the fore. James Forrestal, while secretary of defense in the
Truman administration, became paranoid about the possibility
of an immediate Russian attack; in fact, he seems to have convinced himself that the Russians had actually attacked. He reacted by committing suicide. Later investigation showed that he
had strong paranoid tendencies all his life, which were concealed
by successful political activity. This is but one of many instances
of a seemingly highly successful man who is really sick underneath.

Maintaining an Attitude of Neutrality. As a rule, patients
feel guilty about many things in their lives. Fearful that the

therapist will censure them, they tend to withhold material. It is for this reason that the therapist must play a neutral role, in which patients feel no blame for past or present actions.

Victor, a forty-five-year-old homosexual, had developed a peculiar ritual. He would move up next to another man in the subway, spread a large newspaper, and gradually begin to masturbate the man sitting next to him. Once the man had developed an erection, Victor would immediately leave at the next stop. He must have developed a sixth sense of safety, because he was never caught. The first analyst whom he went to became alarmed and kept on saying, "You'll be caught and go to jail; stop it." This did not deter him. The second analyst said nothing, and as the roots of this odd behavior were uncovered, Victor eventually gave up the habit.

When the emphasis is placed on understanding the interpretation, advice and suggestion are necessarily relegated to a secondary role. Before, during, and throughout any therapeutic encounter, the patient is bombarded with the advice of friends, associates, and relatives. If the therapist does the same thing, he becomes no different than a friend or acquaintance. If instead he probes for the deeper meaning of the man's struggles, he takes on an entirely new and more fruitful role.

Modifying the Acting-Out Defense. Patients who act out their impulses rather than think about them engage in what has been called "acting out." Such acting out invariably interferes with the progress of therapy. This is why the treatment of alcoholics or drug addicts is hardest of all: as soon as these patients feel some anxiety, they resort to some acting-out defense. While it is not always possible to prevent this acting out, some modification is often feasible. Without such modification, the therapy often bogs down in an impasse.

In a case of drug addiction I treated (Fine, 1979a), the patient, a physician, was addicted to methadone (then referred to as Dolophine). His first therapist did not work out, so the patient went to a second analyst, who demanded that he give up the drug entirely. In retaliation, the patient would give himself a shot in the analyst's bathroom. When that analysis was likewise terminated, the patient came to me. I said nothing about the addiction, and eventually the deeper roots of his addiction were uncovered. He was particularly terrified of the anxiety attached to the third night of abstinence. It took more than a year of painstaking analysis of this fear to help him overcome it and give up the drug (see the more detailed handling of this case in Chapter Five).

Determining Frequency of Sessions. In classical analysis Freud originally saw the patient six times a week, though he did recognize that in milder cases three times per week was sufficient. Gradually these requirements have been whittled down, as experience has grown. In the study by Wallerstein (1986), even though only forty-two cases were covered, it became clear that classical analysis was by no means always the treatment of choice; many times patients in once-a-week therapy did better than those in five-times-a-week analysis.

Further, since Freud wrote, different modalities have come to the fore: group therapy, family therapy, brief therapy, and so on. All these modalities produce some change, and it has not yet been possible to differentiate which therapy is the most effective for any given case. At the present time it is best to let therapists use their judgment rather than prescribing some rigid rule.

Assigning Fees. The fee becomes an essential part of the therapeutic process. If it is too high, the patient cannot manage it; if it is too low, the patient loses respect for the therapist. In principle, it is best to set the fee at a level that the patient can manage for an indefinite period of time.

Here differences between men and women become apparent. Women often have their fees paid by their husbands. A problem is created if the husband rebels at the arrangement because of the resultant changes in his life. Lawsuits have been brought against psychiatrists and psychologists for interfering with the stability of a marriage. While such lawsuits have rarely been successful, the threat of one may impede the progress of the analysis. Wherever possible, it is best to have the patient pay for his or her own therapy.

There is no way that a child can manage the money, of course. Here arrangements have to be made with the parents (or guardians). When a positive transference to the analyst is established, the parents often become jealous and pull the child out of treatment. This is why in many clinics, a child will not be accepted for treatment unless the parents enter treatment as well.

Stages in the Treatment Process

The treatment process is by no means all of one piece; different strategies are applicable to each stage. In the beginning the therapist says relatively little, because he or she wants to find out more about the patient. In the middle phase the patient is used to the procedure and spends his time producing material, which the therapist then helps him make relevant by tying it up with the various components of the analytic ideal. In the final stage termination is the prime consideration; in spite of all efforts to reach a "pure" ending that would last the rest of the patient's life, such an outcome is rarely feasible. Some practical compromise is reached, so that the termination of analysis is a practical affair.

The Analytic Honeymoon. When things go well, there is often an analytic honeymoon, in which the patient, with little help from the analyst, experiences a great deal of relief. Factors that go into this analytic honeymoon are a lack of superego criticism, production of new or hitherto unnoticed material, establishment of a new kind of relationship, absence of a time limit, and reestablishment of hope. But after a while the superego reasserts itself and the old problems come back, though they can then be worked out more effectively. There is rarely any analytic process that works with complete smoothness.

The First Treatment Crisis. After the analytic honeymoon there is almost always a negative reaction; the course of true analysis, like that of true love (with which it may be compared in more than one respect), never runs smoothly. Dynamically, the superego reasserts itself; it will not let the patient off the hook so easily. Because the unconscious command of the parents was, "Don't be so damn happy," the patient unconsciously has to obey. Thus starts a tug of war between the punitive parents on the one hand and the encouraging analyst on the other.

In the case of Richard (presented in Chapter Nine), the fear of speaking at first seemed incomprehensible: he did not have to give speeches, so the fear seemed out of place in his life. Yet the fear persisted, to become an integral part of his psychol- ogy. Here lies the paradox of pathotherapy: in spite of their seeming irrelevance, fears come to the fore, and persist for a long time.

At this stage in the process, it is essential that the ther- apist should persist with an interpretive stance; in fact, the ther- apist can do little at this point but interpret. Suggestions, persua- sion, commands all prove either to be useless or to even backfire.

Nathan, a schizophrenic young man, used to get his sex- ual kicks by going to prostitutes in the massage parlors, usually picking some woman with extremely large breasts. Naturally these experiences with hostile women in the long run proved frustrating. He was encouraged to visit a halfway house, where there were many young women his age who were also interested in sexual contact. Finally he picked one up and went to her room, where they had intercourse of a sort. Shortly thereafter, he cracked up again and had to return to the hospital.

This example again shows the power of the superego. Even though consciously Nathan enjoyed the sexual experience, unconsciously he punished himself for it, which led to another breakdown. Incidentally, earlier in his life this man's mother had told him not to go with girls until he had plastic surgery on his nose, which she considered too large. He obeyed literally, but the feeling of sexual inadequacy that this taboo left with him lasted a long time. It was, in fact, responsible for some of his recurrent breakdowns. (Nathan is also discussed in Chapter Six.)

The Working-Through Process. There are no more kings or royal roads to success in psychotherapy than anywhere else. Incidentally, this is one reason why analysts are skeptical about the quick results allegedly achieved by other methods. Every analyst has had in his practice numerous cases where the patient felt miraculously better for a short while and then relapsed. Freud must have gone through this many, many times, until in 1914 he formulated the principle of *working through* as the heart of analysis. The major themes have to be repeated, the major explanations have to be analyzed and reanalyzed, until the patient has reached a level where he can really handle things on his own. This process of working through (from the German *durcharbeiten*) is an indispensable part of every serious therapeutic undertaking.

Regression and Social Problems. There are, of course, many special problems that come up, especially in the early stages of analysis: suicide, psychosis, deep regressions, senseless drifting, excessive substance abuse, and the like. No hard and fast rules can be given about any of these. I would stress here my own experience that regression during the analytic process never goes beyond the deepest regression previously experienced in life. This means that if a patient has never attempted suicide before analysis, he will not do so during analysis; similarly, if he has never been psychotic before, analysis will not produce a psychosis. Beyond that, emergencies have to be handled by whatever means seem suitable in the situation.

Termination. Any kind of serious psychotherapy is a long-term affair. It may last for many years. In the beginning the patient does not want to stay; after a while he does not want to leave.

The problem of adequate termination is a difficult one and will be discussed more fully from time to time in the body of this work. Here it will suffice to say that the goal of analysis is to help the patient come as close as possible to the analytic ideal. The judgment of when that has happened is a subjective one; it also depends very heavily on what the patient wants out of life. Because no two people are fully alike, no unbending procedures can be set up. In addition, events may depend to some extent on external circumstances beyond the control of either patient or analyst. Thus, while theoretically the process of analysis may go on all through life in some informal way, the termination of an actual analytic experience is a practical affair. For example, therapy may stop when the patient marries or moves to a new city for a better job. But such temporary changes should not be seen as a total reform of the character structure.

3 | Problems of Loving

"DOUBT THOU THE STARS ARE FIRE; DOUBT THAT THE EARTH doth move; Doubt truth to be a liar; But never doubt I love." Thus spoke Hamlet (Act II, scene ii) 300 years ago. It became one of Freud's favorite quotations, just as Shakespeare was one of his favorite authors. A man who does not love, said Freud, is bound to fall ill.

Love is the central experience of every human being's life. This is just as true for men as for women, although many people underestimate the man's need for a woman's love. Every therapist learns the truth in Freud's remark—that a man who does not love is bound to fall ill—even if entirely extraneous symptoms dominate the man's psyche (1914: SE XIV).

The values that have dominated my life are those derived from the main tradition of Western European humanism: truth, love, achievement, reliance on reason in place of authority, and a search for happiness on earth rather than in heaven. No one can practice as intimate a discipline as psychoanalysis without conveying his values to his patients, nor do I see any particular value in concealing them. What must be avoided is the seductive opportunity to become the almighty authority who forces his life on others.

The unifying thread in my own life, both personal and intellectual, has been love. Through my own analysis I was able to find love, and through practicing analysis I have been able to teach others how to love. The proper elucidation of the nature of love is, to my mind, *the* problem to be faced by all the sciences concerned with humanity. Insofar as they deal with love,

51

they further human knowledge; when they do not, they are trivial or simply talk gibberish. I need not conceal the fact that love has been so important to me that this chapter may justifiably be considered a piece of an autobiography (compare Fine, 1972).

The literature on love is enormous and endlessly fascinating. Rohner (1975), the anthropologist, was able to show that in societies where the children are loved by their parents, they grow up happy, with a reasonable degree of contentment; where they are not loved, they grow up depressed, unhappy, violent, always resentful.

The search for love is universal, even if it is not reached too often. Love poetry, which gives expression to the longing for other people who will love, is found everywhere. Zablocki (1980), in his study of isolated communities in the United States who retreat from the world to their own private paradise, found that residents of such communities invariably state that what they are looking for is love, away from a cruel, heartless world that gives them so little of it.

While love enters into every component of the analytic ideal, in this chapter I shall confine myself to those situations in which love per se is the center of discussion. For the great majority of male adults, it is the love for the adult woman that forms the pivot of existence. Among the most common problems encountered are the rejected lover, boredom and infidelity in marriage, homosexual love, and lack of love.

Development of the Male Love Impulse

Love develops; it does not come into existence overnight. The image of the perfect woman who walks through the door unexpectedly, the feeling of "falling in love" without knowing anything about the woman, almost endless searching for the ideal woman (Dante went through hell and purgatory to find his beloved Beatrice, only to find himself spurned by her): all these are illusions—shared by many men, yet illusions all the same. Love has to grow and be nurtured; it cannot appear as if by magic.

A review of the development of the love impulse in men

is useful at this point (for a fuller discussion, see Fine, 1985). Every man begins with mother, of course, and the quality of the interaction between the mother and her son is determinative for the remainder of his life. Almost all studies indicate that mothers are closer to their daughters than to their sons, which means that the man starts life with a certain amount of rejection from the mother. The amount of rejection and acceptance naturally varies. Mother love is by no means universal in the animal kingdom (Hrdy, 1977; Reite and Caine, 1983; Hrdy and Hausfater, 1984), so it need cause no surprise that it is far from universal among human mothers. De Mause (1974) has shown how long infanticide persisted in human societies; in fact, it is still going on. The vicissitudes of the mother-son relationship now are summed up in a voluminous literature (see, for example, Bowlby, 1969, 1973, 1980).

The man's development can be viewed as moving from one relationship to another throughout life, and here we concentrate on the relationships with women. The bond with mother, of course, depends heavily on the bond that exists between mother and father. The triangle of boy-mother-father reaches a climax somewhere between the ages of three and five, which is known as the "Oedipal period." During this Oedipal period the boy finds himself attracted to mother, feels threatened by father (who, after all, has all the rights over mother), and is *rejected by mother.* This latter point has received insufficient emphasis. The incestuous wish of the boy for mother is universally present and universally forbidden; this rejection carries with it for the boy the feeling that he is unworthy or inadequate for the idealized mother, a feeling that carries over into adult life.

For the child (as for the adult, though to a lesser extent), love is expressed physically; hence love and sex go together. What no one realized before modern psychology is that the sexual wish of the boy for his mother, and the love connected with it, create terrible torments in his little soul. Usually people laugh at the little boy, but his feelings have to be taken seriously.

A seven-year-old boy came home from school to find his mother lying down on the couch. He got up on top of her, fully clothed, and said to her, "Is this how you do it?" She assured him that he was correct but suggested that he wait till he was grown up and could try it with another girl. A better solution at that age cannot be found. But at the same time, without any wish on the mother's part to convey rejection, the mere facts that he is in reality sexually inadequate for her and that mother is a taboo object create feelings of inadequacy. (These feelings of inadequacy linger: David Reuben opens his best-selling book on *Everything You Always Wanted to Know About Sex* with the observation that every man is afraid that his penis is too small—small in comparison with father's, and for what he imagines mother to be like.)

Before or after the Oedipal period, the boy begins to interact with girls of his own age. As Galenson and Roiphe (1981) have shown, this interaction from about fifteen months on leads to sexual desires, which again are taboo. Thus the boy's sexual-love frustrations begin early.

Right after the Oedipal period, the boy usually gets involved in a love affair of varying intensity with a girl of his own age. This may be something simple, such as carrying her books to school, or more complex, such as attempting sex play. But for the boy it is a highly meaningful experience, again carrying with it for the majority of boys a stigma of failure, because they cannot perform as they wish.

During the school years (what psychoanalysts call the "latency period"), feelings for females are generally confined to mother, though there are many exceptions. For example, many boys are sincerely affectionate toward their younger or older sisters. But as a rule, boys at this age avoid girls, and continue to avoid them until puberty.

It is with such a background that the boy approaches his love objects in puberty. On the one hand, he has to overcome the infantile attachments to the parents; on the other, he has to move to new girls. One common sequence is that the new girls, now also for the most part taboo objects, are idealized in much the same way that mother was idealized in the Oedipal period. But then the boy discovers that while the "good" girl does not have sex, there are many "bad" girls who do. Thus the split emerges between the virgin and the whore—a split that may remain part of the boy's perception into adulthood. While many changes have occurred as a consequence of the sexual revolution of the past twenty years, these changes affect only a relatively small percentage of the population, and even with these the traditional psychology (the virgin-whore split) often remains firmly entrenched.

A fifteen-year-old boy in therapy was fully informed of the sexual activities of his classmates. One girl, whom he idealized but could not bring himself to take out, was attracted to older boys. She would tell him of her sexual exploits, particularly of how good she was at performing fellatio on a number of the boys. In spite of that, she complained, the boys would drop her very quickly. The stage was set for the classical split even before this boy had fully reached puberty. He had no use for her.

The above vignette describes a boy from a fairly sophisticated modern family. In spite of such sophistication, the familiar problems emerge. In less "modern" families, the customary problems are as prominent as they were in previous generations. Even when the man finally marries, the split will remain and burden him for many years, if not for the rest of his life.

Once the boy grows up, the sex-love problem remains acute. If he "goes steady" too early, he misses out on the excitement that has always been such a hallmark of adolescence. But if he does not go steady, the fortunes of adolescent turmoil may overtake him. Twenty-three hundred years ago Aristotle wrote in *Rhetoric,* "If the young commit a fault, it is always on the side of excess and exaggeration . . . for they carry everything too far, whether it be their love or hatred or anything else" (1952, pp. 164–166). A similar observation would be equally pertinent today.

In adolescence or early adulthood, the man makes up his mind to get married or not. "Marriage," wrote Samuel Johnson several hundred years ago, "has many pains, but celibacy has no pleasures." Many a young (and older) man has experienced the same torments as Johnson without finding an adequate solution, although most men do marry.

The therapist approaches the marriage dilemma with two ideas in mind. First of all, love is frequently a transference reaction—that is, it is a carry-over from the earliest longings for mother. In the course of therapy, this transference is shifted to other people. Eventually the man is freed from his compulsive transference to one woman and can make a choice on a reasonable basis. Second, even if the love object *is* a transference, she can have such realistically desirable qualities that married life becomes preferable to single life.

Love and Transference

When the love is a transference, the man finds himself in a masochistic position, in which he pursues a woman who is constantly rejecting him. Sometimes the more she rejects him, the greater does his "love" become. Here therapy becomes particularly effective, because the idealization of the woman comes to the fore and the painful rejections become all the more undesirable.

Harvey was twenty-six when he came to analysis. He was on the rebound from an unhappy love affair; the woman whom he idealized had simply kicked him out. Yet he was still in love with her.

About a year before coming to analysis, he had met Mimi, with whom he fell violently in love. Angered by her "establishment" parents in another city, she had moved to New York, where she more or less lived by her wits. She was a gay, carefree girl with no thought for the morrow. Naturally she had a whole string of men in her life, of whom Harvey was probably the least important. But he was dependable, especially when she was in financial trouble, which was quite frequently.

Mimi and Harvey lived together for about six months. In that time he was deliriously happy, even though she treated him very shabbily. Then one day she literally threw him out, telling him bluntly that he was too dull for her and that she had found a more exciting man.

This rejection led him to an analyst. Some six months later, Mimi called him up, asking to see him. He was in seventh heaven until he learned why she was calling: she was pregnant by another man and wanted Harvey to pay for the abortion (this was in the days before abortion was legal). At this request he was crushed, yet it helped him to see the nature of his "love" for her.

After this incident a long analysis ensued, in which the need for such a masochistic love was fully explored. Harvey was the youngest of six children, most of whom had experienced much turmoil in their lives. The relationship between mother and father was so bad that once, when father was out of work, she had him jailed for nonsupport. Occasionally mother worked as a practical nurse. But she was hypertensive, demanding, quarrelsome, depressed, and overly possessive. Harvey, the youngest, was the particular object of her venom.

As far back as he could remember, Harvey had been a timid, frightened little boy. Mother kept on bawling him out: he was a no-good bum, just like his father (who had died early). In analysis it did not take long for him to see that Mimi was in many ways a repetition (transference) of his mother—bawling him out, having no use for him. The major difference was that on the surface Mimi was a carefree girl who could enjoy life, but this image evaporated when he realized that her enjoyment of life derived from the exploitation of men.

Once the transference to Mimi was worked out sufficiently, Harvey could allow himself to experiment with other women. He was also able to finish the last eight credits of college. After college he found a job in a field that he enjoyed and began to experiment with various women. Eventually he found one who was healthy and who pleased him; this was a different kind of love, with joy and mutual gratification. His analysis ended with his marriage to this young woman.

In Harvey's case the analytic ideal helped him to concentrate on the neurotic character of his love for Mimi. His attachment to the analyst allowed him to grow, both in his profession and in his love life.

It is of more than passing interest that this kind of love, with its idealization of the woman, has been an essential aspect of male psychology since the twelfth century, when romantic love became the ruling passion at the court of Eleanor of Aquitaine in southern France (Fine, 1985). John Donne, one of the greatest love poets (sixteenth century), expressed it thus: "Twice or thrice had I loved thee, Before I knew thy face or name; So in a voice, so in a shapeless flame, Angels affect us oft, and worship'd be."

Thus the beloved woman becomes an angel. In Victorian times the poet Coventry Patmore wrote a best seller entitled *Angel in the House* (Hunt, 1959). In that age the woman was to be revered as an angel; this is the thesis of his book. It goes without saying that an angel is a disembodied fantasy, so when the man gets too close to her he is sure to be disappointed. And of course it also goes without saying that many women are not angels, in any sense of the term.

Reactions to the Unattainability of a Love Object

The classic novel depicting the psychology of the rejected lover is Somerset Maugham's *Of Human Bondage*. The plot can be briefly described.

Philip Carey, the hero, falls in love with Mildred, a waitress in a restaurant he frequents. Philip is a medical student who had wanted to be a painter (as was Maugham, who actually completed medical school but then did not practice, becoming instead a writer). Later Maugham was to write, "It is not an autobiographical novel; fact and fiction are inextricably mingled; the emotions are my own but not all the incidents are related as they happened and some of them are transferred not from my own life but from that of persons with whom I was intimate."

Philip selected Mildred because unconsciously he sensed her as someone who would be cruel to him. Maugham himself had had a most unhappy childhood, in which both parents died young; he was brought up by a cold, cruel uncle.

Philip sought the humiliation of being in bondage to a woman whom he despised. "He hated himself for loving her. She seemed to be constantly humiliating him, and for each snub that he endured he owed her a grudge." Mildred is shallow, callous, greedy, unintelligent, and utterly conventional. She goes to church one day a week because it "looks well." When Philip kisses her, she says, "Mind my hat, silly."

Finally Mildred goes off with Philip's friend Griffiths. Masochistically, Philip, who is rich, offers them the money for the trip, becoming their accomplice. (Compare the way in which Mimi, in the previous case, tried to extract money from Harvey in order to rid herself of the baby of another man.) Maugham admitted that at one time, seized by a devil of self-torture, he actually gave a rival five pounds to finance a trip with another person whom he loved.

Maugham's novelistic description grew out of his marriage to a woman who humiliated and tortured him and who revealed his homosexuality to the world, an act that made him furious. He rejected his wife and wanted nothing more to do with his daughter. It is not surprising that with this long series of painful experiences with women he gave them up altogether and turned to homosexuality, which had intrigued him since childhood.

Homosexuality. The question of homosexuality, which served as Somerset Maugham's lifelong resolution of his problems, has become very controversial. Some maintain that it is a perfectly normal variation of the sexual impulse. The majority of professionals, however, agree with the commonsense notion that if there is an exclusive attachment to a person of the same sex, something is wrong.

Psychoanalytic theory explains homosexuality in the man as an excessive Oedipal desire for the mother, coupled with a cold, rejecting father (Bieber and others, 1962). The man feels two barriers to the woman: first, she reminds him too much of mother; and second, father forbids it. Many men go through periods of heterosexual experimentation, then give up on women and turn exclusively to men. There are many variations possible. Maugham is an excellent example of this theoretical paradigm. It is not surprising that in his will he stipulated that no biography of him should be written; obviously he wanted to be known by posterity as a great writer, and there were many aspects of his life that he wished to conceal. (See Chapter Four for a fuller discussion of homosexuality.)

Depression. The loss of the love object is one core of the depressive reaction, according to contemporary theory. In infancy the loss of the mother may be such a blow that the infant will die (Spitz, 1965). Hence it comes as no surprise that later in life, when the man finds that the woman he adores does not respond, he becomes depressed.

A good example is seen in Donald, a twenty-three-year-old man who married young. His love for his wife was passionate, at times wild, and she loved him too. The first six months were a honeymoon for both.

Unfortunately, Donald's wife suffered from juvenile diabetes, which she had told him about, but he had not grasped its significance. The diabetes, which is often referred to as the "psychosomatic psychosis," in turn made her depressed, affecting her view of her body and all its function. In this state of depression, she turned away from further sexual relationships with him. (Actually, as he later learned, she started an affair with her physician, a man old enough to be her father and whom she later married.) Eventually they were divorced.

Donald was severely hurt by his wife's rejection, which he rationalized but could not understand. For the two years before he came to analysis, he did not have sex with any women except prostitutes, from whom any rejection was meaningless. Within a few months of beginning analysis, however, he had gone back to dating women in his social class. He went into an analytic honeymoon about his analysis in much the same way that he had experienced his marriage as a honeymoon. Eventually he was able to get over the rejection by his wife and move on to other women.

What did the analysis do to bring about this transformation? In the beginning the therapist simply listened to Donald's story. Donald was the son of divorced parents. Early in childhood he had loved his mother passionately, only to suffer severe disappointments in his feelings about her as he grew up. She was an embittered woman whose desertion by her husband had turned her away from all men, so she focused for many years almost exclusively on Donald. He was to make up to her what her husband (whom she could never refer to by name) had not given her. In addition, she was a quarrelsome woman with few friends, few interests in life, and a chronic resentment about much that had happened to her.

Donald's first dream in analysis was a simple one: "My

wife has a baby; I leave her." The dream represented the wish to become a father and to leave both his mother and his ex-wife. (Later he did remarry, have a baby, and leave his second wife.)

After a while the analyst began to give some unadorned interpretations. Donald's wife was a mother-substitute. He had married her after a lonely adolescence, in which there had been hardly any sexual experience. He was so attached to his mother in that period that he rarely even dated. Thus the love that he felt for his wife was a combination of many feelings. First, there was the memory of the mother of childhood, whom he had loved so much. Second, the marriage was a way out of the attempted domination of his mother, who demanded his financial support, among other things. And finally, in his eagerness to get close to a woman, he had misjudged the reality of his first wife; in reality, she was a sick woman who longed for her father and the serenity of her early childhood more than anything else. With these explanations, and with the attachment to the analyst in firm position (providing what Winnicott [1986] calls the "holding environment"), Donald was able to overcome his transference love and move on to other women.

It is important to note here that Donald's love for his wife was actually replaced by another love, that for his analyst. There was no doubt that this was a transference love; in fact, it was pure transference. So it was easy for Donald to see that his first love was also a transference, and one that did not have to hold him in its clutches all his life.

Revenge. Another common consequence of the loss of a love object for a man is feelings of rageful revenge. This can take many different forms; even outright murder occurs occasionally. The situation is again a transference from early childhood; if mother leaves the little boy alone, he flies into a fury. Then his fury is understandable, because he has no control over where she is going or when she is coming back. This is one reason separation anxiety has become such a key concept in modern theory.

But as an adult, the man need not be tied to the woman who rejects him. If he is, her rejection becomes a crushing transference. Many men do live out their lives this way, staying away from other women and brooding about the wrongs that the lost love object has done to him. If children are involved and she takes the children away from him, which is so often the case, an additional deprivation is piled on to his other woes. Thus he lives out his life in a state of bitter anger.

Roger, a thirty-five-year-old mathematician, was married for eight years. His background was a bad one: father had committed suicide; mother clung to Roger in compensation and was always ill. He knew little about sex, as did his wife, so that their sex life was a shambles. Actually, she left him for another woman.

When he came to analysis, he brooded constantly about what had happened to him. In this brooding he had one repetitive fantasy: his ex-wife would come back to him in a state of destitution and ask him for money. He would refuse her, driving her into a fury. This fantasy was repeated over and over in his mind; it was a real obsession. It took years of analysis to help him to see that he had made her a mother-figure on whom he could take revenge for all the wrongs of his childhood.

The healing process required years of analysis for Roger because of the working-through process (discussed in Chapter Two). The persistence of infantile attachments is so great that it is not sufficient to give only one interpretation, at which the infantile despair will miraculously dissolve. The circumstances of this man's life had to be recapitulated over and over; the anger at the analyst had to be overcome; the fear of other women had to be surmounted. All of this took many years.

Don Juanism. One of the most common ways that men react to the unattainability of a love object, both in fantasy and in reality, is "Don Juanism," more recently referred to simply as "womanizing." Here the man seduces a number of different women, whom he then drops as revenge against the woman he cannot obtain. In the most common literary version, the Spanish, Don Juan seduces the daughter of the commander of Seville and then kills her father in a duel. When he mockingly invites a statue of her father to a feast, it comes to life and drags Don Juan to hell. Don Juanism is a device used by women as well; in fact, it is actually somewhat more painful in women, because the man can, as a rule, replace the rejecting woman more easily than the woman can replace the rejecting man, especially if there are children involved.

Although ours has been a monogamous society for centuries, in this respect behaviorally it is in the minority. Polygyny (marriage to several wives) is by far the most widely preferred kind of marriage. Frayser (1985) found polygyny in 82 percent of a sixty-two-society sample; only 16 percent of the sample insisted on monogamy; while polyandry (marriage of a woman to many husbands) was found in only 2 percent (p. 252).

Many men use facts such as these to justify their attraction to many women. In addition, they say, "Animals do it"— which is a gross oversimplification, because animals mate only at certain times of the year and are indiscriminate rather than polygamous. In any case, whatever the anthropological and biological facts, in our own society the socially accepted arrangement is monogamy, and polygamy induces enormous psychological conflicts as well as legal problems of all kinds.

According to the latest data from the U.S. Census Bureau, 13.8 percent of thirty- to forty-four-year-old men have never married, a significant increase from the 9 percent of never-married men a decade ago (Gabriel, 1987). Not since the Great Depression (when the economic cause was obviously significant) has there been such a high proportion of bachelors in this age bracket. Barbara Ehrenreich (1983) argues that there has been a rebellion against marriage on the part of men. Most unmarried men have sex lives of one kind or another; hence they adhere to the common male image of plural wives—the Don Juan syndrome. However, when this pattern is scrutinized more carefully, it turns out to be a retreat from disappointment in love rather than an alternative, exuberant life-style, as its adherents so often claim.

Many variations of the Don Juan psychology are found. A typical one is that of Ronald, a twenty-seven-year-old man who had had sex with hundreds of women. He was the son of a wealthy businessman, who supplied him with a car, credit cards, and a nice apartment. Unaware of any problem in his way of life, Ronald went on with casual relationships for several years, often with two or even three different girls a night. Then one day, as he was standing in a bar looking around, a man eyed him, came up to him, and said, "You're one of us [referring to homosexuals]. Why are you fooling around with so many women?" Ronald was driven into a panic by the idea of homosexuality, which led him into psychoanalysis.

In analysis what came out first of all was the up-and-down nature of the fortunes of his family. Grandfather had been a millionaire, then had lost it all in the crash of 1929. The family had had to move to more modest quarters, but Ronald never forgot the lavish houses and apartments that grandfather had provided. Father recovered somewhat but lost his money too. By the time Ronald came into analysis seriously, he was on his own.

In his womanizing, the analytic ideal of love was missing. For years all he had wanted to do was have sex. An attempt at college had ended in failure. Sex was all that counted in life. Most of the women he had sex with were pick-ups, girls he met at bars. For a period he frequented prostitutes.

The purpose of his almost insatiable drive for sex was conquest—specifically, conquest of the fortune grandfather had lost in the Depression and the money father had later squandered. One of his fantasies was that he was sitting on top of Manhattan and defecating on the city (a fantasy similar to that of Rabelais's character Pantagruel, who thought of urinating on Paris).

The emptiness of his ceaseless search for a new girl had already hit home when he met the homosexual in the bar. He had also realized that he had to find some way of making a living.

One day he met a woman, Frances, wealthy and somewhat older than he. Dutifully he started an affair with her, and for the first time he felt fondness for a woman. It was this fondness that the analyst had to nurture along and prevent him from destroying.

Dreams were helpful. In one he was in an apartment with Frances; the walls were gone, except for the two-by-four framing. A black man was standing there watching them. Ronald went over and beat him up.

In this dream he brings his wishes for Frances out into the open (the bare room) but also shows Frances how powerful a man he is by beating up the black man.

In another dream: "Jean [a Frenchman who lived in the building] and Frances are together. I'm on the bed in what used to be Jean's room. Suddenly the door opens; a man comes in—a monster with a claw, with bleeding, matted hair on his chest, bloody, crying."

One association to this dream was the bleeding: he once had had minor surgery on his head. Afterwards the doctor said he had been very brave. The dream crying represented a release of the emotions he ordinarily held in check (the image of the strong, silent man). The monster was the man he would like to be—sadistic, powerful, vastly wealthy.

Eventually he was able to give up his wish to conquer every woman, as well as his wish to recapture the millionaire's paradise of his childhood. He settled down with Frances in a happy marriage, in which both worked and shared expenses.

In this case what the analyst did was to help Ronald pull his life together. The period of almost continuous sexuality was one in which he was showing off how great he was to women (ultimately, mother). This bravado covered up his fear of weakness—that he might really be a homosexual. When the man in the bar claimed that Ronald was a homosexual, this brought out his latent fear and he was driven to seek out a therapist. The vicissitudes of the therapy need not be traced here: he alternated between being a great rich man and a weak poor one. Eventually, with the help of the analyst, he gave up his childhood fantasies and settled down to a more sensible life.

One variation of the Don Juan syndrome occurs when a man sees a beloved woman in the distance, one who is unattainable to him, and then compensates by getting even on a variety of different women. The woman in the distance represents mother, whom he can never have; the other women are the vehicles on whom he takes revenge. Because he is basically tied to mother, he can never allow himself to love any other woman. And because of the tie to mother, a sharp split develops between the forbidden woman (mother) and the permissible woman (all others). Usually this split is accompanied by boasting, a wish to conquer, fear of homosexuality, and fear of the father.

A case of this kind was seen in Arnold, a refugee from Nazi Germany. As a university student in his native Germany, he tutored the children of a beautiful young woman with whom he soon started an affair. Because of the war, both left for America —she for California, he for New York. She was married, and stayed with her husband. He too married, but he remained unhappy with his wife all his life and eventually divorced her.

In New York Arnold entered a profession allied to medicine, and he treated many women. Because he was tall and handsome, many of them asked him to have sex with them, and he obliged. But none meant anything to him. His heart was with his beloved in California.

For two weeks during the year, he would travel to California, where he could see his beloved. She, still married, was uncertain of his love; besides, she was considerably older. While still in her fifties, she developed cancer of the spine and died. He was heartbroken. Although he continued his extramarital adventures for a long time with a long series of women, he could never get over the one woman he had loved from adolescence on.

The historical model for such a personality is Casanova (1725–1798), who recounted the story of his amours in six volumes. In childhood he was abandoned by his parents, who turned him over to a disinterested grandmother. At fifteen he was expelled from the University of Padua for excessive gambling debts; and at sixteen, from a Venetian seminary for immoral and scandalous conduct. For the rest of his life, he alternated between gambling and sex.

In his memoirs, Casanova ([1788] 1932) described 116 mistresses by name and claimed that he had been with hundreds of women. His first completed sex act consisted of coitus with two young sisters in one bed, all three of them enjoying the performance both as participant and spectator.

Naturally he contracted venereal disease many times, eleven of them described in his memoirs. Much of his work recounts his scrapes and fights, in a number of which his life was endangered. As though in anticipation of Freud, the wish to marry entered his mind only once when, as an older man, he met a beautiful young girl at the opera. He was so smitten with her that he proposed at once. Then he recognized her mother as an old mistress, which brought the realization that the girl he had proposed to was his daughter. He then made love to the mother with the daughter watching (again two women, and this time violating the incest taboo). Several years later he again met his daughter, who was then married to an impotent nobleman. Casanova had sex with her and got her pregnant.

As the years wore on, he became increasingly miserable. In his forties he started collecting pornographic pictures, was inflamed by caressing a nine-year-old girl, and as part of a swindle had sex with a seventy-year-old woman as a participant in a magical ritual.

Clearly, what was lacking in Casanova's life was the capacity to love a woman. Today we know that the loss of the mother in early life is one of the most severe traumas that a man can experience. Bowlby (1980) describes the sequence of protest, despair, and detachment that the child goes through when the mother is absent or lost. In Casanova's case, as in that of many others who often appear as patients on the therapeutic scene, the detachment was at the basis of his life of card playing, orgies, constant sex, and physical violence. Errol Flynn, in his autobiography, describes a similar existence. His remark that "behind every girdle there's a lawyer" (in those days women still wore girdles) epitomizes the constant scrapes that he got into with his seduction of married women or women who were linked with other men.

In many men there is a cycle of love and hate—love for one woman being replaced by hatred of many. The love is accompanied by idealization; the hatred, by extreme promiscuity (Don Juanism). Again here the love is the yearning for mother; the hatred, the anger that results when the man's wishes are frustrated.

Total Retreat from Love. Finally, there is the reaction that is in some ways the most pathological of all: a total retreat from any effort to love a woman. If she (any woman) rejects me, the man argues, nobody will accept me. At bottom it is obvious that in such cases the woman is mother; if she rejects the boy, no woman will ever go near him. This often becomes the genesis of some form of schizophrenia or borderline schizophrenic personality.

In our clinic, the Center for Creative Living, which treats persons with moderately severe disturbances, we often have as patients young men who are unable to relate to women, dropped out of school at an early age, and are overattached to their mothers. Frequently they are in treatment with young, pretty social workers. Feelings of love for the therapist often emerge. Typically, a triangular battle occurs: the young male patient forms an alliance with his therapist against the mother, who is trying to keep him infantilized. Usually the mother becomes a serious problem to the therapist in such cases. In one, the mother made every effort to break the treatment, and when she could not do so, moved off to Florida. Her son had to go along, because he did not work and did not have the means to sustain himself without her. Here, as in so many cases of this type, the father stayed out of the battle, allowing the mother to handle everything.

Every man at some time in his development has to free himself from mother. When the mother is particularly adamant about keeping him infantilized, it creates a difficult situation with which many men are unable to cope. Yet liberation from the parents is part of the analytic ideal. If a man cannot handle the liberation, he can easily break down.

Sometimes, as in the case of Tom, men are able to get past a seriously disturbed childhood in spite of the efforts of the parents (especially the mother) to keep them ill. At the time that Tom came to analysis, he was thirty years old and only partially employed, living on a combination of unemployment relief and odd jobs; most of his time he would spend alone. He had been rejected by the army during World War II because of his social isolation (suspected schizophrenia), which prompted him to see a psychiatrist. This resulted in some benefit but had to be discontinued when he took a job to which the psychiatrist could not accommodate his hours. After a brief hiatus he undertook some analytic therapy with another analyst.

The patient resolved to carry through his analysis on the basis of a rather unusual inner battle. He had been brought up a Catholic. In reading Dante, and feeling rather sorry for people in the Inferno, he came across the old problem of free will and the foreknowledge of God. He finally concluded, after much thought with his first analyst, that he did have free will (in contrast to the teachings of the Church). He no longer feared that he would go to hell for disobeying the Catholic dogma.

It was this determination that carried him through the second analysis. When the analyst pointed out how he stayed away from girls and sex (he was afraid even to masturbate with his hands) because of the early indoctrination, he was able to begin to relate to women and feel freer within himself. This persistence carried him through to better jobs, and eventually to one as a reporter on a small-town newspaper, which had always been his goal.

Although his capacity to relate to women remained at a primitive level, at least he had taken the beginning steps and was aware that many of his problems were tied up with his fear of the opposite sex. He grasped enough of the analytic ideal to realize that he had to have women in his life, and went about changing things in his typical, methodical way. As a result, his life moved forward in spite of the negative pressures put on him by his family.

This case is a good example of the basic therapeutic principle that the therapist should never give up on a patient. In the beginning Tom's case looked pretty grim, but with his persistent desire to improve, he was able to achieve considerable progress.

Marital Conflicts

Although the storybooks say that love and marriage go together like a horse and carriage, unfortunately that is all too often untrue. It is common knowledge that we are in the midst of a revolution in marriage customs and attitudes. Figures vary, but it is often stated that one marriage out of two ends in divorce. Because marriage is held out as the place where the ideal of love is to be realized, this major breakdown of the marriage contract strongly affects the man's ability to find love in his life.

There are many ways of classifying marriages, but most of them stress external arrangements rather than internal feelings. The novelist John O'Hara once wrote, "A married couple always presents an absurdly untruthful picture to the world, but it is a picture that the world finds convenient and a comfort."

The classification of marriages that I have found most useful is one proposed by sociologists John Cuber and Peggy Harroff in *The Significant Americans* (1965). Their work is based on in-depth interviews with 437 distinguished Americans, all in the upper reaches of society in Ohio. They offer a gross sorting of marriages into *utilitarian* and *intrinsic* marriages. The utilitarian is more often seen as a marriage of convenience; the intrinsic is the true love match. Cuber and Harroff break down the utilitarian category further into *conflict-habituated, passive-congenial,* and *devitalized* marriages. Intrinsic marriages are described as either *vital* or *total.* Vital marriages are those where each partner has a vital interest not shared with the other person. The total marriage is one where everything is shared and enjoyed by both. By far the largest number of marriages studied by Cuber and Harroff fell into the utilitarian category. The role that the man plays in these various types of marriages is illustrated in various case studies throughout the book.

Although each of these categories is useful, it is the conflict-habituated marriage I will focus on here. The name is sufficiently indicative: these are marriages in which the partners are always fighting—and are used to it. In more formal language, these are often referred to as sado-masochistic marriages, in which one partner is sadistic toward the other, while the other plays the masochistic role. (For a fuller discussion of masochism, see Chapter Five.) What keeps these marriages together is the hatred. In a recent paper, Galdston (1987) calls hatred "the longest pleasure." He divides people into three categories with regard to hatred: those who cannot stop hating, those who are unable to hate, and those who have learned both to hate and to get over hating. All three abound in varying degrees in the conflict-habituated marriage.

An extreme instance was seen in the case of Charles and Myra. When they decided to marry, Myra was pregnant by another man. Charles agreed to marry her on condition that she give up the child to adoption after it was born, to which she agreed. They then married and had four children together.

For the first ten years of the marriage, Charles was cruel in the extreme. He beat Myra, called her names, and on a number of occasions even tried to strangle her. His ostensible reason was that she deserved all the punishment: she had had a child out of wedlock. In this period he could not stop hating; yet she could not fight back, because of her guilt about the illegitimate child.

Finally she rebelled, and he had a change of heart. Instead of being so sadistic, he became excessively submissive and self-punitive. He took on three jobs, working all the time. He left the house to live in a furnished room. Work was his only activity; all pleasure was denied.

Thus the conflict went on for some twenty years—the first ten with sadism on his side, masochism on hers; the second ten with the reverse. Finally they decided to reach some compromise and to bring resolution through divorce. She sued him for support, but the judge was merciful to him and actually reduced support below the amount that he had been voluntarily paying her. Myra found another man; Charles lived an isolated existence. Many such arrangements, often never coming to the surface, are found in our society.

A somewhat different pattern was observed in the marriage of Ira and Ruth. Before marriage she had been very promiscuous, picking up men on the street, sometimes having sex with them right then and there. He was the opposite, staying away from women, fearful of people around him, at times coming close to the suicidal impulses that had ended the life of his father.

When they met, she saw a chance to give up the promiscuous life that she had led by finding some stability in marriage; while he in turn was motivated by a chance to have a sex life and—less consciously—by the wish to rescue her from her life of shame. (The wish to rescue the prostitute from her miserable life is one that is found in many men and has often been the subject of novels and stories. In these men the hostility of the women who discards one man after another is denied by the man.)

The marriage yielded one child, a boy. At an early age he developed a problem that called for psychiatric intervention, which brought the whole family into therapy. When the therapy started, Ira and Ruth were constantly bickering; time and again they would agree to a divorce, draw up papers in front of a lawyer, then call it off at the last minute.

Both had sexual problems: he suffered from premature ejaculation, while she found her greatest delight in anal play. He acquiesced, willing to do anything to keep her in the marriage.

She was also terribly afraid to be alone, no doubt fearful that the sexual impulses that had driven her to such promiscuity earlier in life would recur. For the seventeen years prior to analysis, he had never gone out alone because of her fears. She felt great contempt for him, because he was so subservient to her. He in his turn liked to play the role of the warm, nurturing parent he had never had in his unhappy childhood. He had been one of twelve children in a poverty-stricken environment, and his father had committed suicide, unable to tolerate the suffering any longer.

Ruth's family background included a brutal alcoholic father who would often get drunk and sit around throwing knives on the table. Ruth suspected that he had had sex with one of his other three daughters. A second had become a prostitute; a third had become a kept woman, eventually committing suicide; and Ruth herself had been promiscuous. Only one of the four girls had led a reasonably normal existence.

In this family the therapy led to very positive results. The analyst helped them to see that in the fights they were taking out their childhood frustrations, each blaming the other. Her wild sexual youth was treated by the analyst with compassion and understanding, which helped her to overcome the guilt that she felt for what she had done. His premature ejaculation was traced to his fear of his sexual aggression.

Unlike Myra and Charles in the previous case, this couple stayed together until the end. After a while the analysis helped them to see that their anger was directed not at the spouse but at some figure from their childhood. The son helped to cement their marriage, because they both loved him and were willing to forgo some of their own desires for his sake.

As a rule, in the sado-masochistic marriage the husband is more brutal, because he is stronger and because that brutality fits in with a certain image of the he-man that prevails in our society. But there are innumerable cases, such as the one above, where the wife is the sadistic one. Regardless of who is the aggressor, research has shown that people are more likely to be killed, physically assaulted, beaten up, slapped, or spanked in their own homes by other family members than anywhere else. Some observers (Gelles, 1972) have proposed that violence in the family is more common than love.

Conflict-Prone Husbands

In many marriages, conflict is so close to the surface that any triviality may bring it out. The "reasons" are just excuses; the two people are just looking for a fight.

The Violent Husband. Although the topic of battered women has assumed considerable prominence in American society, the violent husband rarely comes to therapy. As a rule, if he mistreats his wife or children, he feels justified in the mistreatment and blames them. It is well known as well that violence is far more common in the lower socioeconomic classes than in the middle or upper classes, and psychotherapy is rarely resorted to in the lower classes. Further, much of the violence is directed to the children, who can put up less of a defense; thus the violence can remain concealed.

Violence is understood primarily as a response to frustration. Consider David, who was a thirty-year-old actor trying to break into the movies. In spite of looks and training, he had no success. He came from a wealthy family who had wanted him to go into their business, which he considered mundane and beneath him. He moved to Los Angeles, married a woman with money, and devoted his time to seeking out work at the studios. At one point his wife objected, and he beat her up so badly that she had to be hospitalized. (She did not know that he also had sex with numerous women he met in his job search.) When he continued to fail at his efforts in the theater, he beat her up a second time. This was too much, and she left him.

The story has a curious dénouement. David moved to a foreign country. Because he had no gift for languages, he spoke the new language terribly, like a "typical American." This inability got him parts in the movies as a boorish American who could not adapt to the country. In the foreign country he married again, repeating the sado-masochistic pattern of his first marriage but at least avoiding the violence.

The Henpecked Husband. More common in therapeutic practice is the henpecked husband, who is kept in check by a domineering woman. To the outsider such a woman looks very masculine, while the henpecked husband looks very effeminate. Such an arrangement is, of course, far from the analytic ideal. Sooner or later many of these marriages end up in the analyst's office.

After years of fighting, Eric and his wife, Sally, came for therapeutic help. Though he was a highly successful school administrator, Eric was completely submissive at home. In the early years he had on a number of occasions beaten the two children badly, but now that they were grown up he could find no outlet for his anger.

Theirs could be seen as an example of Cuber and Harroff's (1965) devitalized marriage, discussed earlier. Outside his work Eric seemed totally stripped of any capacity to organize his life. Dutifully he did whatever his wife told him. Once he came to therapy with a large scratch on his face. He said to the therapist, "Look what I did. I forced my wife to scratch me because of the way I was behaving."

Clearly this situation is a repetition of the mother-child conflict. After releasing his aggression in the early years of the marriage, Eric was lost in his own home. The question of love between him and his wife had long since flown out of the window. All he wanted to do was survive. Therapy did help, but it did little more than soften the worst aspects of the conflicts.

The Drifter. Although love and marriage are the conscious

goals of the vast majority of women, many men are so obsessed with other desires that they disparage love and do not appreciate the gratifications and emotional stability that can be derived from marriage. When such men do not give up on marriage completely, grinding ambition is probably the chief source of their unhappiness. If they do marry, they gradually drift away from their wives, or their wives drift away from them.

Marshall was typical of men who are obsessed with money. Although a lawyer by profession, he had not succeeded at law in any noticeable way. For this he blamed his wife and her "nagging."

In reality, he was deeply troubled by an unhappy childhood. At the age of five, he had smelled his mother's panties, which left him feeling very guilty. At fifteen he had had his first sexual experience, with a prostitute (without using a condom). Even though he never had any symptoms, he became convinced that he had acquired syphilis from her, a conviction that could not be shaken by medical evidence. In his first attempt at marriage, he had walked away from the altar right before the ceremony started. This too he had never forgotten.

When he finally did get married, he could not remain faithful for long. There were no children, and the marriage soon drifted apart. Instead, he took up with another woman, one who had been his secretary at one time. Twice she became pregnant by him, and each time he denied that he was the man, accusing her of affairs with other men. Then he turned to gambling, where he would occasionally win large sums, then lose them again.

In therapy he behaved in a peculiar way: after a while he refused to pay the bill. When asked to do so, he said to the therapist, "At what point will you sue me?" The therapy was terminated with little benefit. This man had moved so far away from the analytic ideal that there was little more that could be done for him.

The Workaholic. Dynamic psychology has brought many new words into our vocabulary; among them is *workaholic*, the person who throws him- or herself so wholeheartedly into work that nothing else counts—like the alcoholic, who values alcohol above all else. The word *workaholic* carries the connotation that the devotion to work is excessive and warps the person's whole life. It is this excess that the psychotherapist is often called upon to treat.

A simple case of a workaholic is that of Stanley, a twenty-five-year-old resident in medicine. His father, also a physician, was a brilliant but erratic man. Stanley finished medical school, then could not make up his mind what specialty he wanted to go into. Because of this indecision, he took residencies in two specialties: internal medicine and family medicine. The two residencies combined took up 110 hours a week. His schedule was so heavy that he could see his wife, a seventeen-year-old girl, only on Friday evenings. Not surprisingly, she left him after a short while.

Other typical problems were seen in the therapy of Walter and Adele, both college professors, though in different fields. Walter had been born in Europe, the only son of a bitter woman who conformed to the character type of the overprotective mother. Although Walter's father lived only a few blocks away from him, he took no interest whatsoever in the boy, which of course intensified the tie between Walter and his mother.

When the family arrived in this country, Walter was about eighteen. Because of their financial circumstances, Walter and his mother slept in the same room. With such near-incest forced on him, it was not unexpected that he continued the sexual fantasies about his mother that had been occupying his mind since he first reached puberty. Nor is it unexpected that Walter was only too eager to leave his mother, while she was only too eager to hold on to him.

The army gave Walter the chance to leave. Drafted, he was sent immediately to another city. Because he was drafted at the end of World War II, however, he saw little active service. Once mustered out, he went to a distant college to resume his studies. There he met Adele, fell in love, and soon married.

Adele came from an intact family but was equally repressed. The couple were both virgins when they married. In the course of time, Adele withdrew from sex more and more, while Walter retreated into a vivid sexual fantasy life; he even had a large collection of pornography. Sex became less and less frequent. Both were very bright, however, and both succeeded in their respective fields. In fact, both immersed themselves in their work so much that contact became almost a rarity.

Then one day Walter woke up to realize that he had not had sex for almost six months. Adele had never protested. She had earlier had some treatment with a questionable analyst who had assured her that "sex and children are of no importance in life; you just have to feel good about yourself." With such assurances it was only too easy for her to avoid intimacy.

Walter, however, spurred on by his sexual drives, fell in love with a much younger woman, one of his students. Now he finally began to have an active sex life. In fact, she was more sexual than he, and demanded sex more often. But at least his libido had finally come into his life.

Walter and Adele were eventually divorced. He married his new-found love but encountered discord in that relationship as well. After a very long analysis, Walter was able to find himself and reach a satisfying mode of living, which this time included an active sex life. Adele, however, remained bitter about the divorce and never remarried.

In both Walter and Adele, work was in great part a defense against sexuality. Most of Walter's analysis was devoted to a discussion of virtually paranoid ideas about what everybody around him in the university was doing to him. It was only when these could be overcome that he could enjoy a woman.

Walter's early love for Adele was a chance to get away from mother; the later love for the second wife was a chance to have an active sex life. Adele's love for Walter was equally an escape from her family. Paradoxically, she became more famous in her field than he in his, but this was scant compensation for the absence of a love life. Adele's love problem was made worse by her analyst's peculiar attitude that love and children counted for nothing.

It may be noted at this point that analysts and other therapists often force their own neurotic resolution on their patients. Adele's analyst was a German refugee who had lived under Hitler for several years. At that time, because of the disordered social conditions, he did not want to bring children into the world. Later, when the war had finished and he was safe in this country, he felt that he was too old for a family.

The Extramarital Affair

Although sexual relations are in one way or another regulated in all known societies, nothing arouses more interest, excitement, and conflict than the extramarital affair. Even anthropologists disagree about the simple question of how frequently adultery occurs. Thus Paige and Paige (1981, p. 177) state that no group in their sample condoned adultery, while Murdock (1949) sees our own society, with its strict code, as highly aberrant, stating that it seems unlikely that as many as 5 percent of the peoples of the earth have a general prohibition against sexual relations outside marriage (p. 264). For our own society, which is the most important for us, Kinsey found that it is probably safe to suggest that about half of all married males have intercourse with women other than their wives at some time while they are married (Kinsey, Pomeroy, and Martin, 1948). For women, Kinsey found that among married women, about 26 percent have extramarital sex by age forty, while between the ages of twenty-six and fifty, between one in six and one in ten have extramarital intercourse (Kinsey, Pomeroy, Martin, and Gebhard, 1953).

It is well known that in the ensuing years since Kinsey (some forty years), the strict taboo on adultery has been violated with increasing frequency. Blumstein and Schwartz (1983), in a recent survey, found that young women have increasingly adopted the idea of a sexual revolution and have changed their minds about monogamy, though the researchers do not offer any even approximate figures.

The question that concerns us is not so much the frequency as what all this means, how it affects the psychic happiness or unhappiness of the individual. These questions can be answered only by careful clinical study.

According to psychoanalytic theory, all human relations

are governed by ambivalence; and as a rule, the stronger the underlying desire, the greater the ambivalence. Hence it is not surprising that in the area of love and sexuality, a wide variety of customs has proliferated among various peoples, and a similar wide variety exists in our own society. We have religious persons who abstain entirely from sex, as contrasted with modern "swingers" who have sex with a multiplicity of partners. Within these two limits all kinds of variations occur.

Usually adultery is seen as a psychological problem. But withdrawal from sex is just as common, if not more so, and just as pathological. The analytic ideal is a proper combination of tender and sexual feelings toward some person of the opposite sex, but it is no secret that this is an ideal rarely reached. Still, therapists are guided by it in treating cases of marital discord.

Bartell, a sociologist, has done the most extensive research on swinging (Bartell, 1971). He interviewed 280 swinger couples in middle America. His conclusion was that except for the swinging, these people were typical of middle-class America. The swingers saw themselves as the leaders of a new sexual revolution. They saw swinging as a "way of life" and contrasted it with other, alternate life-styles. Bartell, however, did not agree. He felt that rather than being innovative, they were acting out an ideal image of American society as they pursued the cult of youth and the "in scene."

Swinging is not actually a modern phenomenon; it has occurred in virtually all cultures and at all times. The Romans were notorious for their orgies, which went beyond sexual promiscuity. They would eat till they were satiated, then vomit in order to be able to eat some more (what is now called the "binge-purge syndrome"); and they were highly sadistic, reveling in such "sports" as gladiator fights, in which participants were required to fight to the death.

Since the appearance of AIDS, more caution has been observed by many of those who like sex with a large number of partners. Other venereal diseases (for example, chlamydia) have also become more common, while the older ones (syphilis, gonorrhea) are still here. Thus swinging carries with it a considerable amount of risk to health.

Usually swingers argue that marriage is too "boring" and that this boredom can be changed only by switching partners. The complaint that marriage is boring is frequently heard, and not only from swingers, but it can be handled in therapy. After all, a constant round of different partners and indiscriminate sex can also become boring.

George, a forty-year-old lawyer who was married and had one child, lived in an open marriage—or rather, a *secretly* open marriage: he had sex with all kinds of women, while his wife had sex with all kinds of men, but neither had any direct knowledge of what the other was doing. They did not get along well; frequently they had violent quarrels in which both would scream at each other at the top of their lungs.

After some years of this, George developed severe headaches, for which he sought therapy. His childhood had been a highly restricted one; he was the son of Orthodox Jewish parents who would never let him have any fun. He married early, without any great love for his wife, primarily to have sex. Because of his headaches he entered therapy; some improvement resulted, but his way of life was not changed.

His wife led the same kind of promiscuous sex life, traveling from one resort to another (she did not have to work and did not want to) and having sex with any likely looking man who came along. She had one symptom that she disregarded: every afternoon she would lie down for a nap and wake up out of a nightmare, screaming with fear. Once she woke up, she was all right. Because this symptom did not affect the way she appeared to others, she simply left it alone.

Then one day she fell in love. The man's motto was, "Look ma, no hands," by which he meant that he avoided all attachments, including one to her. But she loved him passionately, and the suffering caused by this love led her to analysis. She told her therapist that in childhood she had undergone a constant battle with mother, who was still going to dance halls and picking up men when she was in her sixties.

Neither partner in this couple enjoyed the promiscuous sex after a while. There was the thrill of conquest, and there were constant new sensations, but both partners remained angry and dissatisfied. Eventually they sought analysis together.

Therapy ran in parallel directions for the two. The need for conquest, the need for excitement, the need to take revenge on the partner of the moment ("Love 'em and leave 'em"—the adolescent slogan), the neglect of their child, eventually helped both to give up their promiscuous way of life, settle down, and enjoy one another. Interpretations along the lines of the analytic ideal (for example, "You're looking for too much excitement") helped them to see what they were doing: acting out a frustrated adolescence. This analytic resolution led them to have another child and settle down to a less exciting but in the long run more satisfying kind of life.

Swingers like to boast that they are "freer" than other people, disregarding all the complications that having multiple partners carries along with it. Al, a thirty-year-old physician, after a period of sexual adventures decided to enter analysis. At this his wife, who had shared his sexual sprees, became furiously angry. He was going to reveal to strangers their most intimate secrets! She could handle their being together naked while he was having sex with another woman and she with another man, but when it came to talking out secret feelings, the jealousy mounted to rage in both.

Freud emphasized the close connection between love and sex—what is called "genital primacy" in psychoanalytic language. That is, the greatest pleasure comes from genital contact, but this is also accompanied by deep feelings of love and affection for the other person—feelings that cannot be spread out indiscriminately. Yet one swinger in Bartell's sample reported that at twenty-seven he had had sex with 8,000 different women. Obviously none of these contacts could have had any deeper meaning for him. Like so many social scientists, Bartell studied behavior carefully but left out issues such as love and warmth; the word *love* is not even included in the index to his book.

As always, sex, in whatever form, cannot be divorced from the emotional setting in which it occurs, as well as the total psychic make-up of the individual. At the simplest level, if married people are too promiscuous, the marriage sooner or later breaks up. The O'Neills, for example—early proponents of the open-marriage idea—eventually were divorced. But there are other consequences as well—for example, the effects on the children.

All of this should not be taken as an argument against sexual enjoyment. But there is a reason why all cultures find it necessary to regulate sex life. In the nineteenth century many anthropologists believed that primitive societies engaged in sexual communism, in which every person was available to every other. The more careful studies of the twentieth century have shown this to be a myth, however. There are no societies in which sex is completely unregulated.

Yet regulation can be taken too far. At the other extreme are those who, for religious or other reasons, either abstain from sex altogether or have very little, even in marriage. By now religion has lost its hold on much of the population, precisely because the restrictions it preaches are more than human flesh and blood can bear. Many members of religious groups even practice psychotherapy, thus gaining firsthand knowledge of the harm that the denial of the flesh can bring.

Some middle ground must be sought between the looseness of swinging and the harshness of religious fanaticism. In pursuing the analytic ideal, the therapist helps the patient reach this middle ground.

Joseph, a forty-five-year-old businessman, came to therapy originally because he was slacking off in his work. He was married, the father of five children. With the youngest, a boy, he had a long-standing quarrel. At one point Joseph put the boy out of the house and wanted to forget about him, but he was dissuaded from doing so by his wife.

At the outset of therapy, Joseph was consumed by the wish for an extramarital affair. His primary reason was that his wife more often than not simply refused to have sex because she "did not feel like it." Although this description of his wife was true, there were other, deeper reasons for his obsessive wish to have a mistress.

His parents had divorced at an early stage, so he had remained the only child. His father was a minister who lost his job because of the divorce and moved around in a rather aimless way, trying out various work alternatives but mainly employed by churches.

Father was an extremely domineering man. When Joseph

was about eleven, father induced him to write a letter stating that he would be happier with him than with mother, which the boy dutifully did. Father made the letter a part of a court battle for custody, but lost.

Mother was a rather weak and ineffectual woman whose only interest in life was her son. (Joseph's wife was similar, as might have been predicted.) Father remained the powerful figure who steered his life. At one point in his adolescence, Joseph found a girl with whom he felt he was in love. Father, who fancied himself something of a psychologist as well, spoke to the girl and decided that she was not right for his son. Joseph dutifully gave her up.

Joseph married at an early age, not so much out of any strong love feelings as because he wanted to get away from the constant battle between mother and father, and from his father's various manipulations. The marriage went along well for a while, but then the pressures of work, being a father in his own right, and some business reverses combined to make him depressed and seek out therapy. Actually, as in so many such cases, he consulted a vocational counselor ("headhunter") first, because he ascribed his problem to his job; the counselor advised him to enter therapy.

In therapy the need for an affair was unraveled. One part of it was identification with father, who had, to spite his wife and the authorities who would not employ him, taken another woman to live with him, without marriage (this live-in love affair was seriously frowned upon at that time, although today such relationships are commonplace). His Oedipal desire to have mother had been thwarted, and he wanted to make up for a frustrated adolescence, in which he had been seduced homosexually by an older man. He wanted to take revenge on this man, who still lived in his home town, but also prove to him that he was a real man who could have a woman of his own.

Thus the wish for another woman turned out to be a strong identification with a tyrannical father. Joseph came to see that in mistreating his oldest son, he was taking revenge on his own father as well as mistreating the boy.

The transference was a good one, and the explanations by

the analyst of his life history made sense to Joseph. Gradually the feelings of love for his wife and children came to the fore. When he finished treatment he was much happier than he had ever been. In the meantime his wife, at his urging, also entered therapy to find out why she was so averse to sex and so dissatisfied with her life.

In the case of Kenneth, a thirty-five-year-old salesman, the wish for extramarital sex was originally stimulated by his wife's illness. Most of her time was spent in bed, and Kenneth had to take care of everything: in the mornings he would have to prepare the children for school; in the evenings he would have to make dinner for everybody. Further, his work was very difficult. He was a "cold-turkey" salesman of medical equipment, a job that forced him to wait hours for his doctor clients. In revenge against all these pressures, Kenneth began to fool around with other women.

His background was severely deprived. One of twelve children from a ghetto area, he had vivid memories of all kinds of forbidden sexual activities as a child: sex with one sister; putting his finger in his mother's vagina when he was four and could get at it from under the table. Above all he was still angry at the Greek boarder who had seduced him while he was a little boy. He walked around town still looking for this man, swearing that if he found him he would kill him. Sometimes he would get on a crowded subway train at rush hour and push against women who were packed into the car like sardines. At times he would ejaculate against them; at other times he would merely feel them (unavoidable in crowded trains, but he chose those trains on purpose).

Kenneth could grasp his situation in the light of the analytic ideal easily enough, but he did not know what to do about the ever-ailing wife. On the one hand, he worshiped her because he felt that she was more gifted than he; on the other hand, her incessant illness was hard to take. For a while he became an analytic enthusiast, urging everyone he knew to try to resolve problems by going into psychotherapy.

In the course of the therapy, as the husband was making noticeable progress, his wife wrote the therapist a letter of complaint. They had married, she argued, on the basis of their mutual neuroses, and now his neurosis was being lifted while hers remained untouched. It was not fair. (This attitude, which many people take, has been called "mutual parentification." Some couples would rather remain ill, united by common suffering, than get well and enjoy life. This peculiar masochistic attitude, found in so many people, will be discussed in more detail in Chapter Five.) Eventually his wife did go into therapy, however. When she recovered from her physical illness, she made use of her talents by opening a store for antiques, at which she had had some experience. The store was really a better outlet for him than his sales work, so the two of them managed it together. They had had a strong love for one another before she became ill. This love came back once her illness cleared up, and they lived a happy life for many years.

There are many other motives that lead men into extramarital affairs. The simple wish for more excitement, or the cry that marriage is too boring, is almost never the real reason. The therapist, with the analytic ideal in mind, helps the patient to see the infantile wishes that he is acting out and move slowly or quickly toward a loving relationship with a woman. He experiences the truth behind Freud's remark that a man who does not love is bound to fall ill.

Regression in the Service of the Spouse

A *regression* is a falling back to an earlier stage of development. In some marriages one or the other spouse attempts to become a child, gaining or trying to gain the love of the spouse by infantile behavior. Such regression can take many different forms—drinking, illness, acting out, even psychosis or near-psychotic conditions—and is by no means infrequent.

The regression derives from a misunderstanding of love. To those who employ this defense, love means total submission to the wishes and desires of the other person. The other person may not want to be married to a baby, so the ploy often fails. But in many cases it does succeed, and the couple go through life with one completely dependent on the other—a variant of mutual parentification, mentioned before.

Such behavior highlights the need for a mature image of

love, which is such an essential part of the analytic ideal. In order to love, each person has to overcome his or her infantile conflicts, so that the love is experienced by both partners as a mature sharing of values, sexuality, affection, children (if and when they come), and everything else in life. This mature sharing results in what Cuber and Harroff (1965) call the intrinsic marriage—rarely seen, as noted earlier.

In a marriage based on regression, one or both partners abandon the analytic ideal and turn back to childhood to try to regain the love that was experienced as a child but that is no longer available, since neither is a child any longer. When the wish to become a child again is not gratified, a great deal of resentment is released. Hence these marriages usually fall into the category of the conflict-habituated.

A good example was seen in the marriage of Lou and Ellen. They met on a bus and instantly "fell in love." (Love at first sight is a fantasy more than anything else. To have a real love, two people have to get to know and value one another. In love at first sight, it is some physical characteristic that turns the other on.)

Lou was a salesman; Ellen, a housewife. The initial honeymoon lasted several years and produced two children. But then the regression began.

They began to play childhood games, such as looking at one another's feces in the toilet. Or Ellen would ask to be seduced as though their love affair had just started: she would sit on the couch and pretend to reject his sexual advances (this after eight years of marriage). He had to persist for three hours before she would give in. He in turn would retaliate for this infuriating behavior by masturbating three or four times before they went to bed, so that by the time she did feel ready for sex, he was temporarily unable to get an erection. Unconsciously, Lou and Ellen regressed with a view toward getting the other person's love, but in reality both became angry and fought frequently.

Lou, the youngest son of a wealthy family, could not really make an adequate living. What money he did make was supplemented by his family. Because he had always been supported by his family, especially his mother, the arrangement did not seem strange to him. The longing for mother and mother's love was powerful. Once he had a dream that he was walking on a beach that was covered with breasts.

As might be expected, Lou was constantly fantasizing about other women and extramarital affairs. But he did not have the aggression necessary to succeed, so that a lot of his love life remained at the masturbatory level. Occasionally he would "score" with another woman, and such incidents provided the greatest highlights of his life.

Ellen regressed in her own way. She began to overeat to get over her recurrent depressions (before therapy she had once attempted suicide—a harmless attempt in which she swallowed a number of aspirin tablets), putting on a great deal of weight, which made Lou call her a "big sloth." She exerted herself as little as possible; for example, to clean the bathroom she would sit on the toilet seat and manipulate the mop from there. She prided herself on her "freedom" in swallowing semen, as a result of which on the infrequent occasions when they did make love, she would perform fellatio on him. Unconsciously, she saw the semen as milk; she was still acting out the role of a baby taking mother's milk.

It is not difficult to see how the analytic ideal provides a useful guide in cases of this kind. Both Lou and Ellen came to therapy with a general dissatisfaction about life rather than with some specific symptom, although she was depressive to the point of suicide and he had a psychosomatic symptom (ulcers) for which he received disability from the government (on the grounds that it had been acquired while he was in the service).

Like their childish games, their love was a childhood kind of love in which each wanted the other to be a parent. The various games they played were the kind that children use to gain their parents' love. It took them many years to work out a more mature image of love, but they finally did when the children were grown up.

The mistake made by them was the idea that love is a childish clinging to the mate. A rather different pattern, involving violence and acting out, was seen in Max and Harriet, who were lovers, not yet married. Max was a German refugee who fell in love with Harriet shortly after they met. Thereupon his whole life began to center around her. In his background, to be romantic was to love the other person so completely that nothing else counted. He could hardly attend to his business, which was a retail store.

When he came to her apartment, he went through all of her possessions, which annoyed her. His attachment was so great that when she went to the toilet, he wanted to follow her in. A week after he met her, he demanded that she not see anybody else, which she refused to do because she had just come out of a bad marriage to a man who had been equally possessive.

When Harriet began to insist that she wanted to see other men and not commit herself yet, Max became wild. He got a friend to call her and threaten her with bodily harm if she kept certain dates (he had gone through her date book and had an approximate idea whom she was seeing). At his request the friend even called up some of the men and warned them of dire consequences if they did not stay away from her. At night Max would arrange disturbing telephone calls so that she could not sleep properly.

To Max, all of this violent reaction was a sign of true love. He wanted her to give up everything and everybody else in order to be with him. She felt so constricted and menaced by his actions that she finally had to report him to the police, get a restraining order, and defend herself in other ways. When she finally protested and forcefully told him to back off on one occasion when she was driving, he grabbed the wheel of the car and almost killed the two of them.

Eventually they broke up because of his insistence that she could have no life or even breath without him. I have called this the "glue love" (Fine, 1985), because it holds only when the two can be together all the time. This mimics the attachment bond of early infancy, in which the only safe place for the infant is either asleep or in its mother's arms. Gradually most people grow away from this excessive dependency as they leave childhood, but many do not, and they confuse it with love. Yet the analytic ideal sees love as a mutually gratifying relationship in which both parties enjoy a certain amount of togetherness and a certain amount of freedom.

Many men are quite fearful that the woman will desert them. To avert such a catastrophe, they resort to trying to convince the woman that she is inadequate. Such a situation was seen in Norman and Jill. They went together for years, but he did not want to commit himself to marrying her, and she in turn was convinced by him that no other man would have her. He had contracted herpes at one point, from a prostitute (according to his story), and spent much of his time researching the topic. It was, according to him, an incurable disease that had to be handled with the greatest of circumspection. She too, he said, had herpes, although she had no symptoms. (His research had led him to believe that herpes can exist without symptoms.) In therapy both he and she became aware that this way of life was based on fear, not on love. Though they called it love, it was at best a "glue love" similar to that seen in previous cases. When the analysis convinced them that neither really had any serious form of herpes, the fears were dissipated and the relationship broke up.

Love based on fear of the other person is seen quite commonly. The person feels terribly guilty about some past act and clings to the woman (or man) as protection against the "revelation" of this act to the world. In the case of Somerset Maugham, cited earlier in this chapter, his wife let the world know about his homosexuality, something he had been trying to keep secret for many years. This soured him so completely against women that he could never again relate to a woman—not even his own daughter. But guilt that binds is not love, and should not be confused with it.

Many times the regression takes the form of alcoholism (or sometimes drug addiction, as in the case of Peter in Chapter Five). Oscar was married to a woman who he felt was much superior to him. Oscar was the youngest of four children and had always been beaten down by parents and older sisters as hopelessly inadequate. His only sex experience before marriage was with a promiscuous girl around town, whom he called the "town pump handle."

When he married, Oscar felt fear and inadequacy more than love. But marriage was the thing to do, so he did it. Besides, he wanted sex and did not know of any other way to get it. He took a job as a clerk in a sporting goods store, even though his great ambition was to become a musician and song writer. Because of his low self-image, he could not bring himself to move in that direction, nor did his wife encourage him in any way.

The pressures built up to such a point that Oscar began to drink rather heavily. Added to this problem was the fact that his wife was sexually frigid and would submit to sex only on rare occasions. One day they were in a taxicab and Oscar, somewhat high, took out his erection and showed it to her. She ran to a psychiatrist she knew, who immediately diagnosed him as schizophrenic and put him in a hospital. In the hospital, because of his compliant personality, he produced some symptoms; for example, he claimed to be a twin (an obvious wish). His wife was eager to divorce him and used the hospitalization as an excuse. Once discharged and divorced, he went off on a long drinking spree. Dynamically, this spree signified an infantalization to gain his mother's love, which did happen in reality—only the mother was his *real* mother, who stood by him, not his wife, who deserted him.

In the course of the therapy, Oscar decided to pursue what he really loved, music. He found another woman, who really did love him and encouraged him in his ambitions. He became a competent musician, found jobs in the music field, and remarried. The second marriage was much more of a love match than the first.

Here too the drinking was a regression to gain his wife's love. When this did not work he was able, with the help of the therapist, to give it up and move on to a more mature way of living.

What is common to all these cases is the glue image of love: to love is to glue oneself to the woman (or the man). This glue is maintained by increasingly regressive actions, until finally the man acts like such a baby that something has to be done about it (for example, hospitalization, in the case of Oscar).

Working with the concept of the analytic ideal, the therapist gradually helps the patient to see that he has a mistaken image of love—an image that goes back to the nature of his family. The families that produce such dependent men vary in many ways, but what they have in common is the excessive infantalization of the boy. During World War II the term "momism" was coined for such men. Large numbers of them had to be rejected by the military services because they could not take the rigors of military life. (This World War II experience actually became the starting point for an enormous expansion of all mental health services.)

Psychosomatic Symptoms of Conflict

The discovery that emotional factors may lead to physical illnesses of various kinds is one of the major advances in twentieth-century medicine; it has given rise to the discipline of behavioral medicine in the effort to understand the cause-effect relationship. In many marital pairs, illness without ascertained physical cause is used as a way of avoiding the emotional conflicts that plague the couple. Because of the complexity of modern medical knowledge, it has become all too easy either to find some esoteric biological cause for symptoms or to ascribe them loosely to some vague "psychosomatic" trouble. A careful diagnosis by a competent physician is necessary before making a definitive judgment.

But it still remains true that a large part of what is called "illness" is closely tied to emotional factors that are unknown to the individual. In fact, *all* illness has come under careful scrutiny for emotional roots, even when the organic pathology is known (Kleinman and Good, 1985).

I have often noticed that in the initial stages of analysis, after perhaps several months, patients come out with some remark such as, "You know, my headaches are gone. I don't know why," or "My back pain isn't nearly as bad as it used to be." It stands to reason that in these cases, the physical symptoms were either psychically caused or psychically related.

In marital conflicts nothing is more common than to

cover up an emotional conflict with physical symptoms. This "mysterious leap from the mind to the body" (Deutsch, 1952), while it presents a theoretical puzzle, also represents a clinical reality.

Paul, a thirty-five-year-old artist, had led a stormy life. The only son of a divorced woman, his life had been dominated by the search for women. At sixteen he would skip school to stay in bed with his girlfriend all afternoon. An early marriage soon shattered on the rocks of his unwillingness to work.

Finally he found a woman who had equally severe problems; they fell in love and married. In the beginning things went well. Once the baby, a son, was born, however, the troubles began. Paul, who had always fantasized about writing the great American novel, began to be increasingly dissatisfied with his work. Fortuitously, his wife, Susan, at this stage inherited some money, on which they could live for several years.

Writing the novel was much harder than he had thought. He did not have any specific ideas—just wanted to write a book that would sell millions of copies. As time went on, the recognition dawned on him (and on her) that this was only a dream. The work simply did not progress. Both he and Susan had to go back to work.

However, Paul, who had been supported by his mother for a long time, persisted in the marriage. In despair about his behavior, Susan took an overdose of sleeping pills, for which she was briefly hospitalized. Clearly the marital arrangement was full of conflict for both.

Once out of the hospital, Susan went back to work and her salary, together with some income from her husband, was enough to support them for a while. As the boy grew older, however, bitterness increased on both sides. She had not really wanted a son and begrudged the time she spent taking care of him. Paul resented the drain on their finances, especially when the boy started school.

The result, predictably, was that Paul got sick. He developed stomach pains that defied careful diagnosis. The illness interfered with his work; long periods of sickness and unemployment followed. While there were many ups and downs in his condition, the illness in one form or another remained. The stomach problem was followed by a heart attack, mild in nature but devastating in its effects on his life. Susan could not take it any longer, so she left. He then found another woman—as would be expected, given that his whole life had been predicated on the idea of being taken care of by a woman (mother-figure).

A brief period of therapy resulted in some improvement. But then, in a fit of rage at the therapist, who suggested that he had some homosexual problems, he quit, never again to go back. On top of that, he told everybody that his analyst had dismissed him as a perfect specimen and that his only trouble was that he had married the wrong women. The novel, of course, was never written. He lived out his life, eking out a meager living, supported mostly by one woman or another.

In these cases there is always the possibility that the illness might be real. Modern medicine has made us very conscious of hidden illnesses that may come to the surface only when it is too late. And the heart attack was real, of course, though Paul recovered quickly. But he did have to be careful in reality, and he used the real restrictions to bolster his dependency.

In this case his wife could not tolerate the prolonged dependency; she had many problems of her own. But in other couples the wife not only tolerates them very well but unconsciously glories in them. It has been observed, for example, that the wives of alcoholics take some unconscious pleasure in their husbands' drinking; if the men do succeed in giving it up, the wives become very anxious. In this way a permanent mother-child relationship takes the place of a mature marriage.

In the therapy of Robert, a thirty-five-year-old upholsterer, the patient had come through World War II with a typical disability of pains of unknown origin in the stomach and chest, for which he received some compensation from the government every month. Treated at a Veterans Administration (VA) hospital for many years (on an outpatient basis), he was finally discharged after seven years with the verdict that he was an incurably dependent personality and should just learn to make the best of it.

Shortly after leaving the VA therapy, Robert fell in love

with a woman who was the opposite of everything he had known. June was exciting and vivacious, loved to enjoy the good life, and, as he later discovered to his chagrin, had a series of men on her string. June was willing to marry him because he was so obviously dependent on her; she could manipulate him in any way that she wanted. During their months of dating, she would take him to expensive night clubs, push him to buy her presents, even at times borrow money from him. But his love was unshaken.

Something warned him not to marry this woman, however, so he sought out more therapy. In this second therapy, which went much deeper than the first, he realized what a little boy he still was. One memory stood out in particular: one day in a quarrel with his mother, when he was nine years old, she had kicked him out of the house naked. Terrified, he had not known what to do until she finally let him back in. On another occasion, when he developed a skin eruption on his behind, she had tended to him faithfully, exposing his bare behind to her although he was already twelve years old. (As usual in such cases, the father stayed out of the picture.) His family background, that of a lower-class Jewish boy out of the ghetto, had left him with little self-confidence.

The therapy soon centered around the relationship with June, as her demands became increasingly exorbitant. He had saved about $6,000 from his army experience and soon saw his little capital diminishing at a rapid rate. If he did not do what she wanted, she became very angry, which he could not tolerate; so he remained obedient, knowing all the time that it was bad for him.

Finally he began to suspect that she was running around with other men. One night, after he had left her, he remained outside the apartment. He saw another man go upstairs, then come out a few hours later. When the other man left, he rushed into her apartment and found her half-dressed. In a fit of rage he put his hand into her vagina and found it wet. This was the crowning blow, and he broke off with her. She tried to coax him back with various excuses and promises, but by now he was strong enough to withstand her.

Now the analysis again centered around the nature of love. He came to realize that his physical complaints were a way of getting his mother's love. His love for June had been the admiration of a little boy whose mother could do anything that she wanted to (such as kicking him out naked). It was based on his own self-deprecating image: he saw himself as worthless and the woman as all-powerful. As the analyst pointed this out in various ways, and in many situations, his neurotic love for June became dissipated so that he could relate in a normal way to other women. The physical symptoms likewise diminished, and he finally became convinced that because the doctors had never been able to find anything wrong with him, he could forget about symptoms.

After the breakup he met another girl, who was much more suitable for him. Although he did not have for her the burning love that he had had for June, they did get along very well together, and she was anything but demanding. Marriage and children followed.

Various love problems of men have been passed in review in this chapter: among them, the man who idealizes women too much, the Don Juan, the man who retreats from love, the married man with numerous conflicts. Whatever the presenting problem is, an understanding of the analytic ideal soon brings the patient around to the recognition that his deepest problem is one of frustrated love.

How the analyst conveys to the patient the central importance of love varies entirely with the material that the patient presents. The idea of love's primacy, after all, is not new; it is rather the emphasis that counts. Primarily, what happens is that as the patient relates his story, he comes to see that what he thought was love really was not. In this way, rather than by any lecture or theoretical statements by the therapist, the various misconceptions of love are brought to the fore and corrected. Again, this usually takes a long time due to the significance of the working-through process.

4 | Sexual Conflicts

THE CONVENTIONAL IMAGE OF A MALE WITH SEXUAL CON-
flicts is of a brutal man who attacks women with callous im-
punity. However, we are surprised to find that the majority of
men suffer from many kinds of sexual conflicts. This is true of
all cultures but seems to be more true of Western civilization
than of others; Murdock (1949) lists only two other cultures
that have been as sexually repressed as ours.

When Freud began his work in the later part of the nineteenth century, many other observers had noted that the sexual
repression in Western culture was particularly harsh. Havelock
Ellis, for example, who wrote so extensively about sex, had to
acquire a medical degree before he could even ask his subjects
about their sex lives. What Freud contributed was the concept
that the prevailing sexual morality led to physical illness in both
men and women. This suggested the value of a change in the
public attitude toward sexuality, a change that has occurred in
considerable measure. In 1898 Freud wrote (SE III, p. 278),
"We see that it is positively a matter of public interest that men
should enter upon sexual relations with full potency. In matters
of prophylaxis however the individual is relatively helpless. The
whole community must become interested in the matter and
give their assent to the creation of generally acceptable regulations. At present we are still far removed from such a state of
affairs which would promise relief. And so here, too, there is
enough work left to do for the next hundred years—in which
our civilization will have to learn to come to terms with the
claims of our sexuality."

96

The almost one hundred years that have followed Freud's early discoveries have seen an enormous change in what is regarded as culturally acceptable in the realm of sexuality. Perhaps three-fourths of adolescents now engage in premarital sexuality. But the mere release of the sexual drive is not what Freud and other analysts had in mind. To be a full part of the good life, sex must be connected with love. And in the combination of sexuality and love (tenderness, affection), humankind is still struggling for a plausible solution (Fine, 1985); for most people it remains a far-off dream. So it need not surprise us that almost all men have sexual conflicts of one form or another. In the previous chapter I dealt with love; in the present chapter I shall deal with the actual sexual performance that men display.

The first large-scale examination of the sex lives of men was carried out by Kinsey in the 1940s (Kinsey, Pomeroy, and Martin, 1948). Several major conclusions emerged from Kinsey's work, which had a powerful impact. First of all, he confirmed that the theoretical sex code was widely flouted. As he put it, "It may be stated that at least 85% of the younger male population could be convicted as sex offenders if law enforcement officials were as efficient as most people expect them to be" (p. 224).

Thus to have an adequate sex life a man, especially the younger man (though this has since been extended to all ages), had to break the law—obviously an untenable situation, and one that explains the high incidence of neuroses derived from sexual causes.

Second, Kinsey confirmed that a great many men (he did not venture exact figures) suffered from some sexual problem or another: conflicts surrounding masturbation, illicit sex, and above all the inability to perform properly and to enjoy the whole sexual experience. While Kinsey, as a true entomologist, remained at the behavioral level, his data spoke for themselves. Thus with regard to premature ejaculation, perhaps the most common of the direct sexual problems of men, he wrote (p. 480), "For perhaps three-quarters of all males, orgasm is reached within two minutes after the initiation of the sexual relation and for a not inconsiderable number of males the climax may be reached within less than a minute or even within ten or twenty seconds after coital entrance. . . . The quick performance of the typical male may be most unsatisfactory to a wife who is inhibited or natively low in response, as many wives are, and such disparities in the speed of male and female response are frequent sources of marital conflict. . . . Nevertheless, the idea that the male who responds quickly in a sexual relation is neurotic or otherwise pathologically involved is, in most cases, not justified scientifically. . . . Far from being abnormal, the male who is quick in his sexual response is quite normal among the mammals, and usual in his own species."

In clinical practice we often find that men who consider that they suffer from premature ejaculation acquire this feeling because they live with women who are cold or frigid in their reactions. For example, the usual way of measuring speed of ejaculation is in terms of the number of thrusts of the erect penis while it is in the vagina. While exact figures are hard to obtain, it is usually estimated that the normal male will be able to thrust about 60 times in the vagina before ejaculating (this varies with age, health, and other factors). Because of the traditional notion that women are slow to respond, men may feel that they suffer from premature ejaculation if they ejaculate after 100 thrusts.

Ben and Madeleine, for example, told their therapist that Ben was a premature ejaculator. It turned out that he could thrust fifty or so times while in the vagina, while she could never respond. Upon closer examination it turned out that she was entirely incapable of orgasm. His image of himself as a premature ejaculator was thus based on myth and on her difficulties.

Kinsey's demonstration that perhaps three-fourths of all American men see themselves as suffering from premature ejaculation serves as a dramatic reinforcement of Freud's critique of our civilization. As far as women are concerned, Kinsey also maintained that vaginal orgasm, which had been stressed as a sign of maturity by some psychoanalysts (Deutsch, 1944), was a "biologic impossibility" (Kinsey, Pomeroy, Martin, and Gebhard, 1953, p. 224). Thus, putting both findings together, we find that sexually inadequate men are confronted by sexually inadequate women.

While a great deal has changed, especially under the impact of the Masters and Johnson studies in the 1960s, no large-scale studies of the magnitude of Kinsey's have been conducted since his day, and we have to rely on small samples, often inadequately interviewed or examined, to get more accurate information. In the largest study, Blumstein and Schwartz (1983) found a freer sexual attitude among the younger generation (as anyone on the current scene can see) but then concluded that "younger women are more interested in non-monogamy now. But we do not know if this will continue. It is possible that we are seeing the first wave of a new female sexuality; it is also possible that younger women will have a limited romance with non-monogamy and then return to more traditional female patterns" (pp. 282–283).

Blumstein and Schwartz also showed that by and large the traditional patterns, such as men being less faithful than women, tend to persist. They interviewed 12,000 couples, so their sample is a sizable one. They were so behaviorally oriented, however, that they did not investigate in any depth how much gratification and satisfaction the sexual relationship brought to the couple; like Kinsey's, their main focus was on frequency. But their study again shows that we are far from a real resolution of the sexual problem.

As was noted in Chapter Three, the male goes through a number of different stages in regard to women. First, there is the ambivalent relationship with mother. Then, at the age of fifteen to nineteen months, the male encounters his penis and girls. This is followed by masturbation, still a conflict. The rivalry with father (and/or older brothers) arouses in him various feelings of inadequacy. As a boy he is driven by the culture to fight with other boys, sometimes with harmful, rarely even fatal, effects (for example, ex-President Nixon's brother was killed in a rock fight with other boys when he was a child). In the school period, it would be "sissy" to go with girls; he sticks to the boys. After so much turmoil and hostility, when he comes up against the physiological changes of puberty, he has to overcome the homosexual life. At all these points, difficulties can and do arise. The man's growth to maturity is far from easy.

The sexual problems that prevent men from adequate

performance can be divided into three kinds: masturbation, premature ejaculation, and impotence (total inability to get an erection).

Because there are so many sex therapists around, a word should be said about the relative merits of direct sex therapy as opposed to psychotherapy. (For further discussion, see Kaplan, 1983.) Masters and Johnson, in their work in the 1960s, tried to do direct therapy with sexual problems, but their work was not illuminated by any great degree of psychological insight. The central role of love, for example, was completely neglected. To them, the need was for education and manipulation. Sex therapy centers have followed in their footsteps. While some manipulative devices succeed, the need is always for psychological understanding, and that requires psychotherapy. The medical aspects of sexual problems, where they exist, can be handled by a physician. There is a strong tendency to overestimate their significance, however; the great majority of sexual problems are psychological in nature.

Sexual Problems That Prevent Adequate Performance

Masturbation. For centuries both the Jewish and the Christian traditions severely condemned masturbation. As late as 1940 the U.S. Naval Academy at Annapolis ruled that a candidate would be rejected for any evidence of masturbation (Kinsey, Pomeroy, and Martin, 1948, p. 513). The most incredible practices were foisted on little boys for masturbation—tying their hands to the crib, spanking, operations on the penis, using foul-smelling substances, and the like. Together with that taboo on masturbation went a taboo on "excessive" intercourse, however that was defined; more guilt was thus created.

Why masturbation should have been so awful is in itself a subject worthy of investigation. René Spitz, in reviewing textbooks of pediatrics, found that up to about 1940 masturbation was listed as a disease—with etiology, prognosis, and treatment, like any other disease (1952).

In spite of all these moral and physical sanctions, boys have always masturbated and continue to masturbate, from earliest childhood on. Kinsey found that ultimately 92 percent of the total male population is involved in masturbation that leads to orgasm. More individuals educated to the college level are included (96 percent) than men who never went beyond grade school (p. 895). My own therapeutic experience is that Kinsey's figures represent an underestimation and that all boys (and men) at one time or another masturbate.

The traditional view that masturbation was "bad" for the boy prevailed until about 1940 (Spitz, 1965). Since then the tide has turned. It is now the boy who does *not* masturbate who is seen as mentally or emotionally disturbed. The boy who does not masturbate cannot avoid wet dreams (nocturnal pollutions), so that at some point in adolescence he is suddenly awakened by a wet dream that causes intense fright and guilt.

Masturbation provides a natural introduction to sex play. What boys (or girls) do to themselves, they later come to expect from their partners. In that sense masturbation may be seen as normal preparation for a normal sex life. In spite of this change in theoretical position, a large number of men who masturbate are filled with guilt and remorse about their actions.

A typical development was that seen in the case of Allan, a thirty-year-old school teacher. His childhood had been dominated by a powerful father who was almost entirely deaf. The father would take his frustrations out on the children, often beating them unmercifully. This changed only when Allan, at about the age of twelve, fought back against his father. But he remained a timid, frightened boy, even though he soon grew to be over six feet tall.

He could not remember any masturbation from childhood, which is the usual clinical finding. (The fear of masturbation tends to crush the little boy's ego.) In puberty he did begin to masturbate, but it was focused on his mother. Next door lived an attractive woman who was very much like his mother. The apartments were so arranged that he could see this woman dress and undress, and he would spend hours watching her. She took no real precautions to hide her body, either because she did not realize that she was being watched, or because she enjoyed it herself.

By adolescence Allan had overcome at least the surface fear of his father, but the underlying fear remained. This fear, together with the incestuous wish for mother, dominated his thinking. Not surprisingly, his relations with girls were limited primarily to occasional encounters with prostitutes. The few times that he tried to have intercourse with a "good" girl, he found himself completely impotent.

In the transference he was quite perturbed when he saw the analyst's eyes close at one point. He was now sure that the analyst slept through his sessions. In the individual sessions he would watch the analyst intently for any sign of sleepiness or waning interest. He was also a member of a therapy group. In the group he would stare fixedly at the analyst, occasionally calling out to the others, "You see, he's asleep. Why do you put up with it?"

Transference manifestations cannot be avoided and cannot be manipulated. Allan's extreme preoccupation with the analyst was noted and commented on by the other members of the group. They helped him to relate to them rather than focus so one-sidedly on whether the therapist was sleepy or not. (A number of papers on the sleepy analyst have appeared in the literature recently.)

Eventually, as his attention was drawn away from the analyst, he began to interact with the other members of the group, as well as with other people on the outside. Actually, he was a good-looking man, intelligent and attractive to women. As he shifted his interests to other people, his self-image improved, he was able to relate to women, and eventually he married.

Bryant was brought up in a very repressive Polish environment. His family had determined that he should become a priest, and for the first part of his life he went along with this determination. Masturbation was absolutely forbidden to him.

When he reached puberty, by which time the wish to become a priest had long since vanished, the whole sexual conflict erupted into an almost classical obsessional neurosis. It was "dangerous" to see a woman either nude or partially nude, so he avoided any situation that might lead to that. For example, when sitting in a bus, he would keep his eyes down, because if he looked up he might see a girl dressing or undressing. He also began to have tormenting sexual dreams. He was afraid to touch his penis with his hand, but his sexual impulses were too strong to resist masturbation; so he would rub his penis against the bed until he ejaculated. It took almost a year of analysis to convince him that nothing would happen if he masturbated in the usual way.

By the time he entered therapy, he had moved away from his family and made up his mind to relate to women. But the masturbation conflict remained uppermost in his mind. He could not rid himself of the thought that masturbation was somehow sinful and that he should stay away from it. He would masturbate for a while, then make up his mind to stop, then go back to it again.

The close connection he perceived between religion and sexuality continued even after he had decided to break away from the Church. Once he dreamed: "I sell my soul to the devil; the spirit of night, a woman, comes to me." Clearly, to go with a woman meant to sell his soul to the devil. In another dream he warded off sexual temptation: "I see Willie . . . talking to an Italian-looking woman. He is embarrassing her. She says, 'If you don't stop, I'll take my shift off.' I think she must be a prostitute. Her mother calls him in and offers him a drink. I excuse myself, saying I have to get up early." In this dream he is terrified of the woman who is ready to offer him sex.

The masturbation fantasies continued, with more varied content. He often fantasized a man on top of a woman and said to the man, "leave her alone." In one dream he saw two criminals, one on top of the other. The one underneath had an erection. He tried to get the fellow on top off by punching him, but couldn't do it. There were also a number of thinly veiled incestuous dreams about his mother.

The transference was always very distant; Bryant was clearly frightened of the analyst. However, he did have one clear transference dream in which he wanted the analyst to provide him with a woman. "I'm out with a girl who's been psychoanalyzed. I notice I'm a half-hour late for the session. I call up; then I realize I'll have to miss the whole session." In this dream he wants the analyst to provide him with a woman who will gratify him. The woman involved in the dream was one of the analyst's patients; she followed Bryant in analysis. He was free to wait for her and try to get to know her better, of course, but he was too shy to do that.

The therapy resulted in a loosening of his fears about women, together with much insight about his sexual fears. Unfortunately, as so often happens, the analysis had to be broken off because he took a job out of town.

The fear of masturbation is found in virtually every boy brought up in the conventional manner. Sometimes it reaches almost unbelievable extremes, as in the case of Carlos, a man who had masturbated a little but never ejaculated in the waking state. Sometimes he did have wet dreams, which convinced him that he was capable of ejaculation.

His case history assumes almost ludicrous proportions considering there was no childhood pathology. Carlos's main preoccupation for years was to be a good Boy Scout, and he succeeded in reaching the rank of Eagle Scout. When he was about twenty-one, he met a woman whom he liked and wanted to marry. They married and had sex, but he never ejaculated. Yet it seemed to make no difference to them.

Finally she decided that she wanted to have a child. They visited a physician, who cavalierly told her that her hymen was too thick. After waiting around with this diagnosis for several years, they went to another physician, who did find her hymen too thick and cut it surgically. After that, intercourse went more smoothly, but he still did not ejaculate. A visit to a third doctor finally led to a referral to an analyst.

What was surprising about Carlos was the absence of any gross psychopathology other than the inability to ejaculate. In masturbation he would fantasize a fight between a man and a woman, in which the man would put on the woman's clothes; the woman, the man's. Apart from that, however, the material he presented was completely ordinary.

In the analysis he produced little of any great consequence. He was the younger of two sons of a lower-middle-class Jewish family, and nothing unusual appeared in his background. He spoke about his life, his childhood, his Boy Scout history (of which he was especially proud), and the like. The analysis was conducted three times a week, with the patient lying down. After about six months of analysis, when the analyst came back from summer vacation, Carlos announced that he had been ejaculating in sex all summer, and that now the analysis was over. He knew that he had many other problems, he said, but did not want to work on them. He stopped therapy, and—truth being stranger than fiction—nine months to the day after he stopped, announcement came of the birth of a baby girl.

We know that the masturbation conflict arises in the boy somewhere between fifteen and nineteen months of age (Galenson and Roiphe, 1981). Most of the time the conflict is disregarded by the parents and other authorities, but as was shown here, it can have wide-reaching ramifications. Today enlightened parents permit or even encourage masturbation, but the traditions of the outer society still convince many boys that such actions are sinful.

Premature Ejaculation. Freud's clinical finding is that most men in our culture suffer from various sexual conflicts and are particularly concerned about premature ejaculation. Kinsey's work in the 1940s confirmed these findings.

The classic paper on the topic was written by Karl Abraham ([1917] 1955a), one of Freud's most distinguished collaborators, who begins with the remark that "no disturbance of male potency is so frequently observed by the nerve specialist as that of ejaculatio praecox (premature ejaculation)" (p. 280). He pointed out that premature ejaculation is an ejaculation with regard to the substance of the emission, and a urination with regard to the manner of it; thus it is a psychosocial fixation, in which the man confuses urination and ejaculation. Urination in this context is also a hostile act (as, for example, in the expressions "Piss on you" and "I'm pissed off"): the man is unconsciously urinating on the woman instead of trying to gratify himself and her by intercourse. Abraham drew a parallel with female frigidity, in which the clitoris has not yet given up its pleasure function to the vagina. (Although this formulation has been challenged in recent years, it remains essentially true.)

In most cases the man at first thinks that there is something wrong with his sexual apparatus, then corrects this impression by the recognition that he is fully potent in masturbation. In other cases the man is fully potent with prostitutes or women whom he sees as being of an "inferior" race but impotent with his wife or some other "good" woman.

Abraham divided men with this symptom into two types: men who are apathetic, inert, without energy, and passive, and overexcitable men who are in a hurry. Both are resentful of the masculine role, and in consequence are resentful of women. Abraham cited the case of one of his patients who was quite conscious of his hostility toward his wife. The slightest quarrel with her used to result in complete impotence on his part. On the other hand, whenever there was a reconciliation, his potency was good. He analyzed the variability as due to the presence or absence of the desire for revenge on his wife.

Underneath the symptom of premature ejaculation, as with all sexual problems, there is a fear of castration. Sometimes this castration anxiety takes the form of a fear of actual removal of the penis; more often it comes out as a vague or indirect fear of damage to some part of the genitals, or it may be displaced and come out as fear of a defect or loss or damage to some other part of the body. In any event, premature ejaculation is often only one aspect of any given man's fear of sexuality. His castration anxiety may take many forms, ranging from the superficially normal to virtually complete psychosis.

To the man suffering from premature ejaculation, the notion that he has hostility and contempt for women usually comes as a surprise. On the surface at least he loves his partner, sometimes passionately. Again this kind of love is illusory, however; the woman involved is unconsciously seen as a mother-figure (sometimes a sister-figure), so that in loving her, he must refrain from sexuality. Otherwise that love becomes incestuous.

Within this structure there are many variations. Often enough premature ejaculation is a surface symptom, easily remedied. Some men are able to remedy it by the simple device of having sex a second time; the second time the man's staying power, for purely physiological reasons, is much greater than the first. In addition, by that time he has overcome, to some extent, his initial fear of the woman's body. In other cases premature ejaculation disappears after the first few encounters with a woman. But frequently it may be masked in a sexually inadequate marriage; the man ejaculates too quickly, the woman is frigid, and both can blame the other for their own inadequacies. Here the educational process has brought about beneficial change; many women who previously would have tolerated the sexually inadequate man in silence now bring their complaints out into the open, either directly or in disguised form.

Daniel and Roberta had been married for many years, with three teenage children. Their sex life was limited to Sunday mornings, when the three children were in the parents' bedroom. Under the covers, with the children in the room, Daniel would enter her and ejaculate immediately. She went to one analyst, who told her to divorce him. However, she was reluctant to follow the analyst's advice. She went to another, on whom she let out all her fury—he was too young, his office was too shabby, he was not sympathetic (the first analyst had told her that she was being used as a doormat; the second did not agree). After some six sessions of this release of hostility, she bought herself a new diaphragm, put on some nice perfume, dressed more seductively, and arranged to have sex with her husband when they were alone. As a result, Daniel became much more potent and sex became much more enjoyable.

John (see also Chapter Six) was twenty-seven when he entered therapy. The immediate precipitating factor was his impotence and premature ejaculation with a woman with whom he had fallen in love. The primary relevant factor in his life history was a terribly depressed mother who had complained about her lot all her life, received innumerable courses of electric shock therapy and antidepressant drugs, and finally killed herself. For her depression she always put the blame on her only son, who, she said, "tore her apart" when he was born, a wound from which she imagined she had never recovered. To some extent she meant this literally, evidently thinking that her body was irreparably damaged. The father was a professor in a small college; he tolerated his wife's depression, remaining true to her to the end. He also encouraged his son to go into analysis and straighten out his life.

For many years John had drifted around, going from gambling to a short stint with a brokerage and other temporary means of support. When he met his beloved and became aware of his sexual problem, he went into analysis. Within two months his sexual problem had cleared up and he could move forward vigorously in his life, although he chose to remain in analysis.

Surprisingly, perhaps because of his father, the transference in analysis was extraordinarily positive. In some eight years of analysis, he never became angry at the analyst or critical of him in any way. Some would argue that he must have been concealing his hostility behind an idealizing transference, but this is more theoretical than empirical. The amount of hostility released toward the analyst varies widely from case to case. In the case of John, it was clear that the analyst had become a good father who was steering him in the right direction in life.

The quick resolution of the sexual difficulty was connected with this positive father transference. John accepted the analyst's explanation that he was confusing other women's bodies with his mother's. He also realized that he had drifted around for so many years because he was trying to get away from his mother.

Impotence. In his early years, Freud at one time surmised that man's sexual life is characteristic of his entire life. Although the concept of character structure has advanced enormously since Freud and the early 1900s, there is still some truth to this remark. The impotent man is often impotent in life; the potent man is potent. It is not surprising that ordinary language uses the same words.

Total impotence as such is rarely found in younger men (under the age of sixty). Usually it goes together with premature ejaculation and other difficulties.

Edward was a research scientist who found himself unable to handle the technical problems that were entrusted to him. In analysis he soon came out with a wish to perform cunnilingus on women. He was married and his wife permitted cunnilingus, but that was not enough for him; he wanted other

women as well. For some time he became involved in the following obsession. He would stand outside a well-known dance
hall that was frequented by many women who were there to
pick up men. When a woman came out, he would eye her up
and down to decide what it would be like if he performed cunnilingus on her. However, he would never speak to the woman; all
of this went on in obsessional thinking in his mind. In these
thoughts he was caught up in a dilemma: if he approached the
woman and eventually revealed that he wanted to perform cunnilingus, she would be offended and refuse to go along with
him; if he did not approach the woman, the same scenario would
be played out in his mind with the next woman. Eventually his
feelings about women's bodies were worked out in the analysis,
and he began to do better with his wife in their sex life. His
work also improved.

A problem commonly encountered in men with problems
of impotence is that of passivity. The passive husband is completely dominated by his wife, often a castrating, angry woman.
Because of his fear of her, the man's sexual functioning is impaired. Nathaniel Ross (1982) gives several illustrations of men
of this type.

One he describes as a man of fifty, married for many
years to a woman who had frequently admitted having lovers.
This man always felt like a child among his peers at successive
levels in his career. His relation to his wife was that of an under-
dog. She had a sharp tongue and was known for her formidabil-
ity in social situations. He frequently felt that she—like all wom-
en—was "big" and overwhelming, especially her breasts. He
suffered from serious sexual difficulties, never having had confi-
dence in his potency.

His background was that of the youngest of five children
in a family dominated by a father who had, according to the
patient, never brooked opposition by anybody, male or female,
and had never hesitated to express contempt and ridicule toward
his wife, children, and friends. The patient's mother was at his
beck and call, extremely passive and very proud of her meticulous, compulsive keeping of domestic financial records. Despite
the father's financial and social successes, he suffered a break-

down during the patient's adolescence. Although never hospital-ized or treated, he recovered and then retired, becoming increas-ingly wealthy through financial investments. This early type of retirement was to become one of the patient's principal ambi-tions, but he was never able to achieve it.

The family situation described by Ross is a familiar one. The man is crushed by a cruel, domineering father who gets his kicks in life by putting everybody else down. As the baby of the family, the boy is coddled by mother. But with such a back-ground, the man finds it difficult to complete the growth pat-tern from mother, to father, to the outside world. Inside he re-mains a frightened mama's boy, feeling hopelessly inadequate to meet the needs of society. Perhaps this was the kind of man Thoreau had in mind when he made his famous comment that most "men lead lives of quiet desperation." (Thoreau himself, from the little we know about him, was one of those men too.) The desperation derives from the feeling of being unable to identify with father, or to do what he has done, on the one hand; and on the other hand, from being pulled back to a warm, overkindly mother who gives him lots of what has been called "smother love," often as a way of compensating for the lack of sexual gratification from her husband. Caught between the cruel father and overspoiling mother, the man never fully grows up. It can be expected that sexual problems would be common; so-matic symptoms of other kinds are also frequent, because they symbolize the return to the nurturing mother (McDougall, 1985).

Symptoms and Character Structure

While the symptom is the most obvious aspect of the person's difficulties, it is embedded in a broader character struc-ture. In previous centuries attention was focused almost exclu-sively on the symptom. Then Freud grasped that the larger char-acter structure was really important. Today, as I noted earlier, we attempt to investigate the character structure as fully as pos-sible.

In the case of sexual conflicts, the topic of this chapter, the same symptom could have many different meanings, depending on the underlying character structure. Many apparently normal individuals suffer from serious disabilities that do not appear on the surface. In issues of sexuality people do not parade their troubles; what comes out comes out only in the privacy of the bed or in the therapist's office.

The conflicts underlying the symptoms can be divided into adjustment disorders and maladjustment disorders. Traditionally, psychiatry dealt only with the maladjustment disorders: those found in persons who were so markedly deviant from the average that it was obvious that there was something wrong with them. Today, as a result of psychological and anthropological research, it is known that many "normal" people have an adjustment disorder—that is, they are troubled (but not incapacitated) by various conflicts, sometimes quite deep-seated. Again, this is especially true of sexual difficulties, because no one parades these without a sense of shame or embarrassment. Our understanding of sexual conflicts thus rests more heavily on our therapeutic knowledge than on anything else.

Several case studies will serve to illustrate the interrelationship between symptoms and underlying conflict. Walter (mentioned in Chapter Three) entered analysis with two definitive statements: he would never become a father, and he would never allow himself to become dependent on the analyst. His refusal to become a father was at least comprehensible in the light of his background: his father had deserted his mother and Walter (who was an only child) and, although he lived only a few blocks away, had never again seen his son. The human being grows on models, and if the model of the father is poor, the boy often decides not to become a father. That was the case here.

With regard to dependency, the child is inherently dependent on his parents. Sooner or later he has to liberate himself. As was noted earlier, Walter liberated himself by entering the military service and then making a hasty marriage (which did not work out). This is not true liberation, of course; it is really a running away.

The analysis went along for a long time without any expression or feeling toward the analyst on Walter's part. Finally, however, his deeper feelings began to come out. In one session Walter brought a dream typical of many men: "I'm out in the fields with a psychiatrist, who is a woman. There are a lot of people around." The basic wish here was to turn the analyst into a woman, so that all his needs would be satisfied by her. In another dream: "I'm lying on my stomach, on a couch. A woman of about fifty is sitting in a chair watching. A girl dressed in black sticks a needle into my arm; I do not feel the needle but realize I am getting an injection. The doctor, whom I cannot see, cuts out a piece of my back, the upper back, and inserts a sponge into it." Again the analyst had become a woman, one who cut out part of his body—that is, castrated him. Then he had a directly homosexual dream about the analyst: "I am sitting across the couch from you. You play with my genitals." This dream frightened Walter; at the same time it encouraged him to talk more about his sexual fantasies, which remained extensive.

After these dreams the patient could allow more of his heterosexuality to come through. It seems paradoxical that by releasing homosexual fantasies, the man can become heterosexual, but that can be understood in the light of the childhood experience with the mother and father. If the boy cannot feel any tenderness for father, he falls back on mother and encounters the incest taboo. When that taboo carries over to other women, it keeps him away from them. Yet if he can now relate more warmly to father, he can identify with him and thus move on to heterosexuality.

Walter had a number of sexual conflicts: premature ejaculation, occasional impotence, a lack of desire for sex, and an obsessional preoccupation with pornography. In the course of a long analysis, he was able to work these out and move on to gratifying genital sexuality. Walter provides a good example of the difference between symptoms and character, and between an adjustment disorder and a maladjustment disorder. Outsiders would not know that he had any symptoms (and often wondered why he came to analysis); his deeper problems could be covered up by the facade of an achieving, sociable, good fellow.

The knowledge of the analytic ideal, which derives from the study of character structure, does not allow the analyst to be completely passive, but it indicates the direction in which his interpretations can move. Homer, a forty-year-old man, came back to analysis because his wife had left him. Not only did he suffer from premature ejaculation, but he was altogether afraid to touch a woman. Thus what his wife had had was an occasional quick sexual encounter accompanied by no tenderness—not even any kind of caress. It was for this reason that she left him.

It turned out that Homer had been in analysis with a man who had refused to talk about sex directly, feeling that the analysis of character would automatically resolve the sexual difficulty; in spite of seven years of this kind of analysis, the sexual problem was unchanged, however.

Homer was the older of two brothers. His mother was openly paranoid, literally fearing that the FBI would arrest her at any moment. A vivid memory of his childhood was that he was caught masturbating by his teacher when he was in the second grade. She had reprimanded him severely, warning him never to do anything like that again.

With such a background it was not surprising that his sexual life was extremely inhibited. He had had little sex in his life, concentrating instead on his long work hours as an accountant. In fact, there was altogether little pleasure for him; life was a duty to be fulfilled, not something to be enjoyed.

The second analysis was much shorter than the first. From the beginning he and the analyst both focused on the physical side of sex and on his lack of pleasure. He could not even dance with ease. To this more direct approach he responded favorably. The rejection by his first wife was overcome and he remarried, progressed in his work, and was able to enjoy life much more, including the sexual aspects. No strong transference was formed, and he discontinued therapy when the sexual problem was resolved to the point of no longer bothering him.

Many times sexual conflicts are bolstered by religious scruples or by a variety of irrational beliefs, such as the idea found in many men that if they have sex during the week, they will not be able to work properly. (This is similar to the notion seen among primitives that they must not have sex on the eve of a battle, because sex would "drain" them of their manly feelings.)

A strange obsession appeared in the case of Fred, a twenty-four-year-old clerical worker who came into therapy with a variety of complaints. He had what he called "anxiety attacks," in which he would be overcome by terrible fears. Sexually, he was completely abstinent; he had had sex only a few times, with prostitutes in Germany while he was in the army of occupation.

Apart from the anxiety, which troubled him, and the sexual abstinence, which did not, he had a variety of other problems. There was a severe fear of subways and elevators, which placed considerable restrictions on his movements; he was particularly panicked at the thought of being stuck in a tunnel in a subway car. To preclude such a catastrophe, he carefully avoided any subway line that went through a tunnel, always finding some alternate route even if it meant lengthening his trip by an hour. He also said that he had "delusions of grandeur," although he seemed to take the delusions as reality. He thought that he was a genius, a conviction going back to his earliest days in school, when a teacher had given him elaborate praise for a composition he had written. Although nothing in his adult life substantiated such a belief, he felt that sooner or later his real talents would blossom.

In one state of anxiety, he had made a private pact with God that if God would get him over the anxiety, he would never have sex before marriage. This pact had always prevented him from having any sexual contacts.

The pact with God did not yield to analysis; when pressed, he would only say to the analyst, "How do you know what God would do?" to which the analyst could not find any suitable reply. Not that Fred was in any way religious; he was a typical agnostic. But in this one respect, he feared God enormously.

The sex guilt was clearly tied up with fear of punishment by his father. Accordingly, he conceived the idea that if he went out of town for sex, he might escape punishment. So he went to Florida. There he paid a bellhop to send a girl to his room. The sex went well with her; the only drawback was that she specified that he could have only half an hour because she had another customer waiting.

Upon his return to New York, the phobia and the pact with God were as strong as ever. In spite of all evidence to the contrary, he insisted that "good girls don't have sex." Yet he did not want to go to prostitutes.

At this point the analyst tried out a behavioral technique. He said to him, "Let's see if we can test out your theory about God. When you dance with a girl, your penis is, say, four inches from her vagina. Obviously at that distance he does not strike you dead. At what distance then *would* he strike you dead?" Put that way, his phobia made less sense to him.

At a dance he approached a girl with whom he wanted to try out the theory. She was agreeable to sex. In their sex play during repeated encounters, he literally reduced the distance between the penis and the vagina inch by inch, coming to the analytic session each time for reassurance and understanding. Finally he was able to penetrate her. Even then he went in only a quarter of an inch or so at first, to see what God would do. When God did nothing, he had full intercourse.

Then, to his great consternation, after five dates the girl said that she was dropping him; she had found another man who was more to her liking. No doubt the cautious, frightened way in which he had approached her played a role in this decision. But he had broken the ice with "good girls," so he could go on. Eventually he married and made considerable progress in his work, becoming something of a writer.

These three cases—Walter, Homer, and Fred—illustrate the variety of ways in which sexual fears appear in the minds of many men. The classical symptoms of masturbation, premature ejaculation, and impotence tell only a small part of the story; the man's entire gamut of feelings about women have to be explored.

Particularly noteworthy, in light of the analytic ideal, is the man's capacity to love. Sexual inhibitions prevent him from loving a woman fully. However, the mere lack of sexual inhibition does not imply that love will follow. In order to love, the man must overcome the numerous inhibitions of his childhood, sexual as well as otherwise, and this is indeed a difficult task. But it is worthwhile.

Overt Homosexuality

The extreme of sexual rejection occurs in overt homosexuality. When psychologists talk about overt homosexuality, they refer to the exclusive choice of one sex as the sexual object, without concomitant rejection of the other. Because this book is about men, the discussion will be confined to exclusive male homosexuality.

By "homosexuality" analysts mean exclusive, compulsive sexual relationships with the same sex. As a man grows, he experiences both heterosexual and homosexual urges. A considerable percentage of men engage in some homosexual practices in their adolescence (Kinsey, Pomeroy, and Martin, 1948). However, the vast majority of men settle in heterosexual relationships. Many men also are bisexual, enjoying sexual relationships with either sex. While bisexuality, according to analytic theory, is inherent in the human condition (just as everybody has both male and female hormones), its continuation past puberty indicates some emotional conflicts.

Freud devoted the first of the three sections of his *Three Essays on Sexuality* (1905) to homosexuality, where he offered the first dynamic explanation of the subject, dividing the sexual goal into *aim* and *object*. The act toward which the sexual instinct tends is the sexual aim; the person from whom the sexual attraction proceeds is the sexual object. Homosexuality is a deviation of aim: homosexual men engage in a variety of what to the uninitiated are startling practices. For example, with the present fears about AIDS, two men may sit next to one another in a dark movie and masturbate one another through their trousers. Homosexual men often develop a kind of sixth sense about which men would submit to this and which would not.

Dynamically, the explanation of homosexuality is simplicity itself. It derives from the fear of sexuality, or castration anxiety. This in turn can be traced back to incestuous fixations. Many homosexuals, even in superficial conversation, reveal the extent to which they have been a mama's boy. The excessive attachment to a seductive yet denying and castrating mother is the essential mechanism that leads them to seek gratification with men rather than with women (Fine, 1987b). The more exact mechanism by which the various peculiarities of the sex are reached would have to be traced individually for each man, in much the same manner as it is traced for the heterosexual.

Socarides (1982) describes the pattern of abdicating fathers and homosexual sons. In the 212 pre-Oedipal patients whom he observed, specific distorting influences could be isolated—influences that led to emotional and cognitive difficulties characteristic of pre-Oedipal homosexuality. Invariably he found in his homosexual patients interlocking family pathology dating back to the patient's earliest years of life, profoundly interfering with the patient's capacity to resolve his primary feminine identification and producing severe ego deficiencies.

The passive husband is one step ahead of the overt homosexual man (although in many cases dissatisfied husbands leave their wives in order to go off with other men); his ego strength is at least great enough to marry and beget a family. Frequently after some years in marriage there ensues a bitter battle between the parents, each longing unconsciously for tender homosexual gratification, which they are unable to get in the conventional marriage.

It is by now well known that unisex situations, for both men and women, are conducive to a higher rate of homosexuality (consider, for example, the "fagging" that has always been so common in English public schools). In fact, the virtual disappearance of unisex schools can be traced to the realization that exclusive socialization with the same sex often leads to overt homosexuality; even the military forces in recent years have been willing to admit women in their ranks.

The core conflict within the homosexual man is his fear of the woman's body, coupled with the loss of superego prohibitions about touching the male body. One man who habitually performed fellatio on men and had them do it to him could not "by any stretch of the imagination" conceive how a woman could "do such a thing."

In more recent years a number of persons have argued that homosexuality is merely a normal variation, and that homosexuals are in no way more "neurotic" than the remainder of the population (Gonsiorek, 1982). I do not wish to engage in any extended argument on this point. It is in fact an argument rejected by the majority of the population, as well as by the majority of the professionals, although the American Psychiatric Association (APA) has had trouble making up its mind about where to classify the homosexual in the various editions of its *Diagnostic and Statistical Manual.* At first the APA (1952) called homosexuals "sexual deviants"; then it defined homosexuality as a "personality disorder" (1968). After much discussion it settled in 1980 on the classification of "ego-dystonic homosexuality," referring to homosexual feelings that are felt as ego-alien, or anxiety-provoking. It goes on to say that "the factors that predispose to ego-dystonic homosexuality are those negative social attitudes toward homosexuality that have been internalized" (p. 282). This represents the view that homosexuality—when it engenders no anxiety—is a normal variation, an attitude that aroused a storm of protest. Finally, in 1987, it dropped the term *homosexuality* altogether.

The trouble derives from misconceptions about what *neurosis* is, in the eyes of both the public and the psychiatric authorities. Neurosis should really be looked upon as the distance from the analytic ideal. A warm, close relationship between a man and a woman is part of this ideal. Since the advent of modern psychiatry and psychoanalysis some 100 years ago, numerous studies have been published about the treatment results with homosexuals. Kinsey found that a high percentage of men have transient homosexual experiences in adolescence, then move on to heterosexual lives in adulthood (Kinsey, Pomeroy, and Martin, 1948). Thus the vast majority of early homosexuals cure themselves without any pressure from the outside. From the time of Schrenck-Notzing (1895) to the modern studies by Bieber and others (1962), Hatterer (1971), and others, the average rate at which homosexual men move to heterosexuality is about 50 percent (Wiedeman, 1974), virtually regardless of the kind of treatment used. Homosexuality, after all, is a symptom (as is heterosexuality), and its dynamics have to be understood. Here are a few case histories.

Kim, a forty-five-year-old psychologist (now deceased),

had gone through a homosexual period lasting to about his thir-
tieth year. His homosexual activity was rather peculiar, in that
he was fixated on men between the ages of eighteen and twenty-
five. Occasionally he would pick up such men and have sex with
them. But his habit also took another strange twist. He would
get on a subway, find a likely man, and sit down next to him.
Then he would open his newspaper, and gradually get closer to
the other man's penis. Eventually he would give the other man
an erection. At this point he would get up and leave the train.

In analysis his life history revealed a domineering, seductive mother and an absent father (he had died when Kim was
six). Kim was an extremely anal person, giving himself an enema
every other day until he was well into his thirties. Mother, still
alive, dominated him. One of his most vivid memories was of
going to the store to buy her panties, which excited him immensely.

His first rather brief analysis was marked by his analyst's
anxiety about his subway habit. The analyst was always saying,
"You'll get arrested; you'll get arrested!" Somehow, though,
Kim was never caught; he must have had that sixth sense mentioned earlier. When he switched to heterosexuality and got a
girl pregnant, the analyst dismissed him with the admonition
that he should be a happily married man.

Kim did marry, had four children, remained satisfactorily (though not happily) married, and some ten years later
returned for a long analysis. The homosexual period was by
then completely in the past.

Lester was a thirty-year-old virgin who came from a farm
background in the Midwest. In his analysis he struggled with
homosexual feelings for a long time before he could reach a satisfactory heterosexual position.

Lester was the youngest of three children. The older two
were both girls; the oldest was thirteen years older than he. The
farm was in an isolated spot, so the family spent a lot of time
together.

Father was a hard-working farmer whom Lester feared and
admired. Father was one of four brothers and the only one who
married. One brother was reported to have made a girl pregnant

and then committed suicide. Another brother was quite ill and was said to have died at the Menninger Clinic. There were things about father that terrified Lester. Habitually he would castrate the cats around the farm to make them more docile. He would also beat the horses; he had even beaten a horse to death.

Mother was a down-to-earth farm wife. What Lester noted about her particularly was her big breasts. He had open sexual fantasies and dreams about both sisters. Because of the closeness of the living quarters, he had often seen them in their underwear as he was growing up. Both had married young.

In childhood he had both wet the bed and soiled himself until well into his teens. For this he was continually criticized by everybody, but he could not stop. His first and (before analysis) only sex experience was with a horse that he was driving around the farm.

In analysis he revealed numerous homosexual fantasies; in fact, for years they dominated his thoughts more than heterosexual fantasies did. Outwardly, however, he was always looking for girls. The one girl he had loved in college had rejected him, and he felt like a rejected lover.

Lester was extremely deferential toward the analyst. When he came five minutes late, he apologized profusely. He would often ask, "Am I doing this right? Is this the way I should be talking?" Once he sent the check (he was billed by the month) by mail, fearing that if he did not do so the analyst would drop him.

Lester's individual therapy was supplemented by group therapy. One woman in his group had had a lot of sexual experience. When she heard that he was still a virgin, she offered to be his first sexual experience. He accepted.

After this first sexual experience, he suddenly fell in love with a man. It was a violent, passionate romance that went on for almost a year. Preferably, they would perform fellatio on one another. During this period he did not go with girls; he even refused to go out with the woman who had given him his first sexual experience.

The working through of the sexual conflict went on for some time. In one dream he released an orgy fantasy: "I'm in bed, with one woman at the foot of the bed. Another woman is off to one side. A red rug is put down. I step onto it and into it in the presence of the women." In another dream he asserts himself with father: "My father and I are hoeing the fields; I tell him where to do the hoeing."

The working alliance was excellent. Lester was so enthusiastic about analysis that he would go home at times and lie down on the couch, free-associating on his own. Consequently, the working-through process saw few periods of stagnation.

The working through of the homosexual wishes was easily tied up with the numerous near-incestuous experiences of his childhood, as well as with the fear of his father. He advanced in his work and eventually married. Although the homosexual fantasies never disappeared completely, his marriage was a happy one.

Sexual Conflicts and the Gender of the Therapist

When psychotherapy started 100 years ago, almost all therapists were men. Naturally the literature, once Freud had called attention to transference, dealt largely with situations in which women were the patients and men were the therapists. In the last twenty years, however, many female therapists have been trained. A certain amount of information is consequently available on situations where the man is the patient and the woman is the therapist (Jones, Kerig, and Krupnick, 1987; Kulish, 1984; Orlinsky and Howard, 1980; Lester, 1985; Goldberger and Evans, 1985). Studies generally show that, in this relationship, as with the woman patient with the male analyst, there is a range of erotic transference manifestations ranging from the very constricted at one end to the very intense and florid at the other (Torras de Bea, 1987).

However, in my experience male patients feel somewhat more at liberty to display their sexuality to the female analyst than women do with men. As I noted in Chapter Two, the female therapist, like so many professional women, may be seen as a potential prostitute.

It may also be noted that male homosexuals are not averse

to entering treatment with a woman, but female homosexuals will almost never enter treatment with a man.

In terms of feelings, both discharge and interpersonal communication are equally possible with both male and female analysts. But in the area of sexuality, problems sometimes come up with men treated by female analysts: men may be terrified of revealing their sexual thoughts to a woman or, as has been noted, may look upon a woman as a kind of prostitute with whom they can do anything (Kulish, 1984). Here are two instances.

Herman, a twenty-five-year-old rabbinical student, was assigned to a young female social worker. One of his great fears was that he would get an erection during the sessions. He communicated this fear to his rabbi, who unfortunately advised him that it was not right for a young man to talk to a woman about such intimate matters. The patient quit treatment abruptly.

In another case, Mark, a twenty-five-year-old man who was virtually a virgin, insisted that he could get better only if he showed his bare behind to the therapist. She refused to allow it. He tried to break down her refusal in various ways, but eventually he simply stopped therapy. In this case he was trying to use the therapist as a prostitute.

There is still too little experience to warrant any significant generalizations. As time goes on and many more women practice psychotherapy, the reactions of their male patients can be appraised in a more comprehensive way.

5 | Pleasure and Pain

PLEASURE AND PAIN ARE THE POLES AROUND WHICH HUMAN
and animal behavior has always operated. Animals (men and
women included) seek to find pleasure and avoid pain. Yet in
our daily clinical work, therapists are confronted over and over
with persons who seem to do exactly the opposite; they pursue
pain and avoid pleasure. Technically, we call this "masochism"
—after the Austrian von Sacher-Masoch, who lived in the middle
of the nineteenth century and wrote a number of books about
pain and suffering. Originally masochism was seen as a partial
instinct, common to all children and connected with sexuality,
especially female sexuality. Later this view was abandoned, or at
least questioned, and the larger question became, What makes
people seek suffering and pain rather than gratification and
pleasure?

While the study of masochism began with sexual symptoms, they soon receded into the background. What became important was the masochistic character, or the wish to suffer.
Numerous papers and books on the subject appeared in the
1940s and 1950s. Perhaps the clearest exposition of the subject
is found in Theodor Reik's book *Masochism in Modern Man*
(1941).

Reik argues that upon closer examination, the reversal of
all pleasure values, and their transformation into a search for
suffering, prove to be fictitious. Masochists aim at the same
pleasure that others do, but they reach it by a detour. Intimi-
dated by threatening anxiety, by punishment, and later by unconscious guilt feelings, they find their particular way of avoid-

ing anxiety and gaining pleasure. They submit voluntarily to punishment, suffering, and humiliation and thus defiantly earn the right to enjoy the gratification denied before. Their basic formula is victory through defeat. In religious terms Christianity expresses it in the formula, "The meek shall inherit the earth."

Others have stressed the importance of the interpersonal situation in the masochistic personality (Berliner, 1958). Masochism is a pathological way of loving. It is the neurotic solution of an infantile conflict between the need for being loved and the actual experience of nonlove coming from the person whose love is needed. In other words, the masochistic attitude is the bid for the affection of a hating love object. It has also been called the "need-fear dilemma" (Burnham, Gladstone, and Gibson, 1969).

The difference between symptoms and the character structure must be considered in order to grasp the phenomenon of masochism. Some forms of suffering—for example, smoking—are pleasurable on the surface, and it is only outside instruction that convinces the individual that they are harmful. Others are obviously destructive; the extreme example is suicide. What the symptom means can be deduced only from a total knowledge of the person and the circumstances.

The analytic ideal involves the pursuit of pleasure as a positive good; yet it is often all too clear that the immediate pleasure (for example, alcohol or drugs) leads to ultimate harm. What psychoanalysis strives for (and adequate education as well) is a strong ego that can choose whichever pleasures seem suitable, discard those that make no sense, and rely on a healthy self-image and good sense of identity to find a gratifying way to live. But this is more easily said than done, because the childhood influences deriving from the parents soon enter the picture.

Every form of education involves placing restrictions of some kind on the child. Some are harsh; some are mild. Children are forced to do what their parents order them to. For psychological reasons the parental commands and prohibitions coalesce into an "introject," or "inner force," which ultimately leads to a superego formation that guides the activities of the child. The introject and the superego are both unconscious: the child can merely say, "I'm not supposed to do that," or even more simply, "That's a no-no."

Superego formation is interwoven with instinct and affect. Like all animals, humans are driven by a variety of urges that stem ultimately from their instinctual (or unlearned) nature. The basic urges for all animals are fear, love, and hate (or, in more technical language, anxiety, sexuality, and hostility). However, instinct per se is a theoretical construct; nobody sees or feels an instinct (Sandler and Joffe, 1969). What the person sees or feels is an urge to do something with the body—eat, run, engage in sex play, escape fear or punishment, and the like. Thus the emotions are the true springs of human action, while the instincts remain a theoretical biological construct. In a widely quoted theory, Tomkins (1979) lists nine innate affects deriving from the basic instincts: the positive affects are (1) interest or excitement, (2) enjoyment or joy, and (3) surprise or startle. The negative affects are (4) distress or anguish, (5) fear or terror, (6) shame or humiliation, (7) contempt, (8) disgust, and (9) anger or rage. While emotional experience branches out considerably from these so-called innate activators, Tomkins's list is as good a beginning as any.

In a useful clinical approach, Schafer (1964) lists eight general aspects and reference points for the investigation of affects: (1) affect existence, (2) affect formation, (3) affect stimuli (internal and external), (4) affect complexity and paradox, (5) affect location (in terms of time, layer, person, and zone), (6) affect communication (interpersonal and intrapsychic), (7) affect strength, and (8) affect history. It is obvious that the analysis of affects is concerned not only with feelings but with ideas, attitudes, fantasies, impulses, defenses, and all the other familiar major categories from which they are inseparable. In effect, affect analysis makes up the major portion of any kind of psychotherapy, because the patient usually does not have a clear comprehension of his feeling life, which emerges only slowly in the course of therapy. Thus it is also one source of the enormous resistance under which therapy has to be conducted.

In one session of group therapy, Ferdinand became furious and shouted at one of the other members; there were ten in all in the group. Shortly thereafter, when one of the others reminded him of his temper tantrum, he denied it completely. Even when all the other members agreed that they had seen his face become red and had heard him shout at the other person, he denied that it had happened. Instead, he said that the group was deflecting its anger at the leader to him. He complained that in this he was always the scapegoat for their rage. This gross misperception of the situation was characteristic of him; he also sometimes exposed himself to dangerous situations in which he would deny the other person's anger or hostile intentions. For example, several times he was mugged by men whom anyone else would have avoided. Clearly, considerable affect analysis would be necessary to counter Ferdinand's resistance.

Psychoanalysis is sometimes divided into the Freudian and the culturalist schools, each with its own list of emotions. But whatever list of emotions is used, it is important to note that the basic instinctual urges, which were originally conceived to be of a purely psychological nature, all turn out to be connected with interpersonal situations at a very basic level. Anxiety is usually seen today, in the light of Freud's work, as a fear of separation from the mother. As noted before, separation and attachment theories (Bowlby, 1980) have accordingly become an essential aspect of psychological discourse.

In earliest childhood the child is strongly exposed to the behavior of the mother and other significant caretakers. If mother rejects him, he may literally die; in the more usual case, he builds up defenses and becomes permanently warped or ego-deviant (Beres, 1956).

As time goes on, the introjects begin to form, as mentioned, and they consistently become stronger. Once the superego comes into existence, it becomes in all major respects the arbiter of the child's destiny. Where before the boy responded to the commands and prohibitions of mother and father, now he responds increasingly to the superego. While there are changes in the superego structure at later ages (Hartmann, Kris, and Loewenstein, 1946), the person remains motivated as much by inner as by outer considerations.

Pathology can best be understood as the result of a harsh

superego. If the parents are harsh, condemning, castrating, and the like, the boy will react accordingly and feel worthless, castrated, and inadequate. Once this self-image is formed, it is hard to break; in the more severe cases, it can be changed significantly only with psychotherapy. Here is to be found the riddle of masochism: to gain their parents' love, children are willing to accept pain and suffering.

At this early point in the development of a child's self-image, philosophical and social pressures begin to affect the child as well. Some families are obviously permissive, while others are highly restrictive. Whatever the society is like, combined with whatever the parents are like, becomes the superego of the individual. Children cannot escape this superego pressure; it is only later, when they are fully grown and away from their family, that they can use their own reason in a more independent way.

Gregg was told by his mother that it was normal to have three bowel movements a day. Consequently, he felt all through childhood that he was constipated. When he got to college, he discovered that his mother was uninformed in this respect, as in so many others. The stigma of constipation disappeared.

Our own culture is a composite of many different attitudes, so that it is difficult to describe one specific superego as common to everybody. But in addition to family and social pressures, there are legal constraints that the individual can handle most effectively by conforming. Those who succeed in handling all these problems still have many internal conflicts with which they grapple, but they function well in the external environment. I prefer to call such conflicts "adjustment disorders," as was noted in Chapter Four, because they are hidden, unconscious disorders that do not create any immediate trouble but may at some future time.

It is only the process of education and the growth of psychological knowledge that enable individuals to become aware of their adjustment neuroses and to try to change them, either with or without therapy (Veroff, Douvan, and Kulka, 1981a). It is as a tool of awareness that the analytic ideal, as described in this book, enlarges into a philosophy of living that has meaning for everybody, as well as a guiding framework for the psy-

chotherapist. Because of our complex psychological development, pleasures are rarely the simple pleasures that they are
imagined to be, and pain is rarely the simple pain that is felt in
a certain part of the body. The analysis of the symptoms is replaced by the analysis of the total character structure, and it is
only this larger analysis that has any deep and lasting effect.

It is often assumed that, in our society, men can live a daz-
zling life, full of success and women, and enjoy every moment
of the day. Men have so much at their disposal, it is thought,
that they have only to pick and choose what they want. Yet
over and over we find that they suffer, no matter how much
they have. Howard Hughes, the billionaire, became so reclusive
that he literally died as a result: his assistants could not get him
to the hospital in time to take care of his coronary thrombosis.
Many other examples could be cited (Fine, 1987a).

Among the problems of the masochist that will be considered are drug addiction, alcoholism, suicide, and self-damaging
acting-out disorders of various kinds. These problems arise from
the male's unconscious wish to suffer.

Drug Addiction

One of the major problems of our times is that of addiction to drugs—or "substance abuse," as it has come to be called.
It turns out that virtually all cultures ever investigated have had
some form of hallucinogenic drugs for habitual use: cocaine, for
example, comes from the coca plant of South America, where it
grows naturally and is chewed regularly by the people. However,
the mere fact that drug use is habitual does not make it normal;
in the analytic sense, it can become the adjustment neurosis of
that culture. Of the illicit drugs currently in use in our country,
the most important are cocaine, heroin, and marijuana. Drug addicts may, however, use one of a large number of other drugs.

In a classic paper, Rado (1928) distinguishes three types
of orgasm: the alimentary (early infancy), the genital, and the
pharmacogenic. In other words, drugs help the individual replace the genital orgasm with a regulation of pleasure based on a
drug rather than the natural bodily processes.

Further investigation has revealed that drug users, even though they profess to take drugs only for enjoyment, are in reality in a state of enormous anxiety. They are fearful that without the drug they will be literally annihilated or perish in some other way. Chein (1964), in a comprehensive study of heroin and heroin users, describes the three meanings of *H: H* is for heaven; *H* is for hell; *H* is for heroin.

Dynamically, the various states can be seen as a regression to an infantile period: the drug acts like mother's milk, soothing the infant and putting it to sleep. In one of the earliest approaches to addiction, Simmel, at his Tegel Sanitarium (near Berlin) in 1918, gave his addict patients an injection every four hours, in imitation of the four-hour feeding of milk to babies that was popular at that time. (This four-hour regimen of feeding was still in use in the 1950s, as is seen in the case of Peter, described below.)

Rado also notes that addicts are all too ready to give up their interpersonal relationships. They are fixated on oral-narcissistic aims and are, like infants, interested solely in getting their gratification, never in satisfying their partners or even in relating to them. Erogenously, the leading zones are the oral zone and the skin; self-esteem, even existence, is dependent on getting food and warmth. Patients will ask, "What can you offer me that the needle can't?" The addict is intolerant of tension; he cannot endure pain, frustration, any situation of waiting. He seizes any opportunity for escape.

This pharmacological image of pleasure—this pharmacological orgasm—has to be contrasted with the dynamics of the normal sense of pleasure. Normally pleasure is part of a cycle: the normal person, after enjoying pleasure, is able to rest. It is precisely this capacity to rest that is lacking in the addict. There is never any real gratification, just an overpowering need for the drug. All forms of rest—particularly sleeping, the normal restorative state—are foreign. Only the numbness produced by the drug offers any real gratification, and that does not last long. The need for immediate gratification is so great that addicted men become criminals and women become prostitutes just to get money for the drug. Here are several typical cases.

Peter, a thirty-three-year-old physician, was an extraordinarily difficult and interesting case. (Incidentally, the incidence of drug addiction among physicians and pharmacists is far higher than among the rest of the population.) Before seeing me, he had been to two other analysts. The first, a Freudian, had adopted a vigorous attitude toward the drug, which was methadone. Like Simmel, the analyst interpreted the drug as milk and insisted that Peter take the drug every four hours. Further, he informed the patient that he would be seen in psychoanalytic therapy three times a week and would sit up, switching to psychoanalysis and the couch when it seemed appropriate. Peter understood nothing of what seemed to him senseless jargon. The analyst was violating one of the first rules of therapy, which is to avoid any technical language, even with a professional in the field.

Yet in three months of this treatment, Peter made considerable progress. He recovered sufficiently to get back to work. At this point the analyst announced that the sessions would be increased to five times per week, and that henceforth the patient would have to pay for the analysis himself. (Previously Peter's family had been subsidizing him.) Because the increased fee exceeded his entire salary, he was justifiably annoyed by this demand and quit treatment.

Then he went to another analyst, a Horneyite. Unfortunately, this analyst tried to "technique" him too. He told Peter that he would not accept him for treatment unless he gave up the drug. To this, Peter reluctantly agreed. But the only consequence was that he would give himself an injection in the analyst's toilet before each session. Meanwhile, his addiction became worse.

Finally he came to see me. The analysis was conducted at the rate of five sessions a week, but no attempt was made to force him to withdraw from the methadone. As a rationalization for the addiction, Peter held on to the conviction that he suffered from pneumonia and colitis, which were masked by the drug. In the life history Peter presented, the illness of the mother was the major factor in earlier childhood. Father, a tailor, reacted to her invalidism by going out with other women, virtually deserting her entirely. "He never gave a damn about anything," Peter once said, "so he lived hale and hearty to a ripe old age."

The analysis went on in a straightforward manner for more than a year. A strong homosexual conflict was brought out in one of his few dreams. "I'm screwing a woman. Just as I'm about to come, I reach down, although it is very uncomfortable, and suck her penis." A marked feature of his actual sex life was an inhibition of ejaculation; he would sometimes fall asleep while having intercourse.

After a while what crystallized in the analysis was his third-night anxiety. He could withdraw for two nights, but the third night was intolerable. There was no way that he could be made to verbalize what his third-night fear was like—it was just awful. This sounded like the night terrors of his infancy, but no such therapeutic interpretation made any impression on him.

After about two years of analysis, a state agency caught up with him because of the excessive number of prescriptions that he wrote out. Because of the resulting legal pressure, I tried some unusual interventions. Ordinarily, social relations with a patient are avoided, but in this case I offered to let him stay in my apartment on the third night, in order to see what he was afraid of. He could get a physician friend to monitor any physical symptoms and a nurse to attend to his physical needs, and I would be available to probe into the dynamics of whatever came out. He accepted the idea several times. But each time he would back out at the last minute.

Because he kept on writing prescriptions, the state gave him the choice of going to jail or going to Lexington, Kentucky, to the National Center for Drug Addiction. In the meantime he had found another woman, and his marriage had begun to break up.

He chose to go to Lexington. There he was appalled by what he saw. There were men there who had been in and out of the hospital for twenty-five years. Some swallowed a condom filled with drugs to smuggle them into Lexington, retrieved it from their bowel movement, and managed to find a needle with which to inject themselves. That a man of his stature could have reduced himself to such a place was horrifying to Peter.

Upon release he looked up an old friend from medical school, Dr. L., who had begun to act out in the wildest possible sexual manner. Through him Peter also found another new woman. Once he had sex with her in the presence of Dr. L., which made him more aware of his homosexual wishes.

About two weeks after his release from Lexington, Peter tried withdrawal in Dr. L.'s office. He stayed there day and night, with his new girlfriend present all the time. I visited him there four times a day. Finally he lived through the third night uneventfully. None of the dire consequences that he had so long feared came true. He felt liberated.

While the therapeutic working alliance was good in some respects, in others it was not. In spite of that, the working-through process led to significant changes in Peter's character structure. It might even be said that with the working through of the third-night anxiety, he worked out an infantile psychosis.

After the liberation, he was divorced and eventually married the new woman; he also resumed his medical practice. I maintained contact with him for about ten years. There appeared to be a steady integration of the analytic work that had been done, although analysis per se was not resumed.

Although at one time drug addiction was regarded as virtually incurable, in more recent years views have changed. As with so many forms of pathology, the deep oral regression that is manifested by addicted patients does yield to analysis if systematically pursued.

Dynamically, Peter's drug addiction could be traced to several different roots. There was first of all the identification with the dying mother, to whom he had given many injections as a child. Then there was his collapse after marriage and independence from his parents, because adult activity was too threatening to him; his superego would allow him to go so far but no further. Yet the oral narcissism that required constant supplies to be nourished would not allow him to flourish in his role as an independent physician, where he had to do the nurturing. And finally there was the masochistic streak in his nature: pleasure was taboo; he had to suffer.

Less dramatic, but in some ways more typical, is the case of Stuart, a twenty-year-old college student who flunked out of college for poor grades and involvement with marijuana. He came back home to New York and entered treatment.

The family history was full of mental illness, but even more important was the crushing father, who blamed his own failure in life on the boy. In his youth the father had been an opera singer, but unsuccessful. So he gave it up, married, and had one child, Stuart. When the father was seen in conjunction with Stuart's therapy, he complained incessantly about the boy. His own father had been hospitalized for manic-depressive psychosis and had died in the hospital. Other relatives had also done poorly. Why, the father queried, did the therapist insist on treating the boy? He was obviously crazy and should go into a mental institution right away. But he agreed to his son's psychotherapy for a while.

Stuart was being seen at the time of the Vietnam War. Among other things he was afraid of being drafted, and therapy offered a way out. (Men who were in therapy at that time generally were not taken into the service, which provided more motivation for therapy than he would otherwise have had.) But even with that motivation, he was not eager for help and a really effective working alliance was never set up. In general, when therapy is being paid for by a parent or some other relative, there is an additional resistance to be overcome.

Stuart never seemed to take the therapy seriously. He came on time and he associated, but much of the material centered around the battle with father. He did grow enough to give up drugs and to get into one of the local colleges, however. At that point the therapy was discontinued by him.

In this case the patient was dominated more by fear of the external punishment than by any inner drive to get ahead and succeed in life. Such an attitude is rather typical of the drug addict. In the extreme, it merges into a kind of paranoid state in which the main objective is to defeat authority figures, who are seen as persecutors. This dynamic factor played a role in Peter's treatment as well.

Alcoholism

The history of the American struggle with alcoholism is a long and tortuous one. In the nineteenth century the Women's Christian Temperance Union attacked saloons and their accompanying vices, finally managing to pass the Prohibition Amendment. But Prohibition proved even more disastrous than the saloons. The era from 1919 to 1933, when Roosevelt put an end to Prohibition, was an extraordinarily lawless one. Because alcohol was so easy to get, "bootleggers" and "speakeasies" abounded. It was argued then that the high crime of the era was due to Prohibition. The high crime of the next era was not foreseen, nor were the psychological consequences of alcohol consumption.

In 1965 a federal task force was appointed to study the topic; they came up with a comprehensive treatment program in 1970. The task force stated flatly that alcohol is the most abused drug in the United States. "The extent of problems related to alcohol abuse and alcoholism is increasing and has reached major proportions" (U.S. Secretary of Health, Education, and Welfare, 1970). (Among American Indians, for example, the alcoholism rate was found to be 20 to 50 percent.) They presented a long enumeration of social problems connected with the use of alcohol: impaired health and work capacity, automobile fatalities and other accidents, and many other disabilities. Various measures recommended by the task force were undertaken to combat the drug, but they have not led to any meaningful reduction in the overall incidence of drinking. It is generally estimated that there are about 100 million persons in the United States who at times use alcohol to excess, though only a small percentage are confirmed alcoholics.

Although women are drinking more than before, it is still men who form the preponderant percentage of alcoholics: estimates of the ratio of men to women range from eight to one to four to one (Chafetz, Hertzman, and Berenson, 1974). For a long time, alcoholics were considered "bad" or "sinful." In 1960 Jellinek published a well-known book in which he labeled alcoholism a disease, which has been the prevalent view ever since. In spite of extensive research and numerous therapeutic experiments, however, the treatment of the alcoholic man remains extraordinarily difficult.

Many men drink with no harm done; they are able to drink in moderation, even if they go in for an occasional binge. These men are treatable like anyone else, because they can keep the alcohol under control. The real problems are those severe alcoholics who go off on extensive drinking bouts, sometimes for several weeks, often with disastrous consequences. The columnist Heywood Broun, well known in his day, was an alcoholic; one winter night he passed out in the street and died of the effects of the cold.

Efforts to treat the alcoholic have ranged from the religious to the psychiatric to the cultic to all kinds of psychotherapeutic—none with marked success, though with the patient's cooperation some progress can be made. Because the disease does respond to a better self-evaluation, the patient's participation is still the primary factor, no matter how severe the drinking is.

Of the numerous attempts to treat alcoholics, two are especially noteworthy for their success rates. One is use of the drug Antabuse (disulfiram), brought to this country in 1948 from Denmark. If combined with alcohol, it makes drinkers sick; consequently, they stay sober for some days after treatment. The trouble is that they may quit the drug. When its effect wears off, they often start drinking again. The other is Alcoholics Anonymous (AA). Certain psychological principles are operative in AA: alcoholics are given two quarters, and when they feel the urgent need to call someone, they always have two numbers available. The chance to talk to another human being helps with the loneliness that overcomes them if they do not have a drink. AA militates actively against psychiatry, trying to impress its members only that they are guilty and should give up drink.

In the long run the effects of both Antabuse and AA are limited, however. Flexible measures must be undertaken, including a conscious urging of the patient to give up drinking once the psychodynamic factors that led to it have come to light.

A common finding is that during a state of intoxication,

the patient may engage in homosexual acts or may fly into terrible tantrums that are unmanageable by outside forces. Not infrequently, hospitalization to control the drinking has to be resorted to.

Psychoanalysis, or psychoanalytic therapy in the pure sense, rarely is effective with alcoholics, because they are not conscious of the interpretation or miss so many sessions that no consistent work can be done. But there are exceptions. The following case was reported by Dr. George Daniels in 1933. The patient was an unmarried man of thirty-three. Social adjustment and work were both satisfactory. Drinking did not become a serious problem until the suicide of his younger sister two years before the beginning of his analysis. After her death he stayed away from women. He felt so guilty about her suicide that the onset of the analysis brought a further exacerbation of his drinking. Then came a most revealing dream: "He was in an office resembling his own, in which one door leads into a corridor and the other into the main office, where the clerks have their desks. The door into the corridor had been locked for some time by order of the office manager. A girl, apparently a secretary, came in from the main office and to his astonishment passed out through the corridor. The thought occurred to him that perhaps this door, which he had supposed was locked, had been open all the time. He went to the door, tried it, and sure enough he could open it without difficulty. He did so, passing into the outer corridor where he waved to an office colleague whom he saw there" (p. 129).

Throughout the first months of analysis, the patient had repeatedly denied interest in the opposite sex and had preached homosexuality (though he did not practice it). The dream showed the deeper unconscious feeling that the female genitals had been permanently closed to him, and his surprise on discovering through the dream that this was not so, that the door was still open. Associations brought out that the night of the dream he had attempted intercourse with a woman of his acquaintance and had been able to insert his penis, though he could not complete the act. He also revealed that before this night he had had no physical contact with women since the death of his sister.

The dream literally "opened the door" for him to a life of heterosexuality and a diminution of his drinking.

This case highlights many of the characteristics of the man who drinks too much, whether he becomes a severe case or not. The sexual fantasies are so guilt-provoking that either he cannot perform adequately, or if he performs cannot form any binding relationship to the woman. If his homosexual and incestuous trends are overcome, however, the drinking may fall into line.

Gordon, a twenty-seven-year-old bisexual who was married but had sex with men as well, had been a severe drinker. The drinking started in his teens, when he was the head of the Young Men's Temperance Union in the church where his father was a deacon. On the surface he seemed like a model leader, arranging tea parties, excursions, and the like. He started going out with a girl, Thelma, whom he saw every day but with whom there was no sex or even much physical contact. Then one day she suddenly said to him that she had met another fellow, one who was more attractive to her; she gave up Gordon.

In retaliation he held a meeting of his church group, ostensibly to have a tea party. At the meeting he ostentatiously pulled out a bottle of liquor, drank it, and became terribly drunk. The consequent scandal forced him to leave the city and move to New York.

In New York he lived a life of alternate binges and homosexual and heterosexual acting out. In the midst of this he married, though neither partner took the marriage too seriously. Because he had specialized skills, he could always get a job, so he worked on and off, his working punctuated by the binges.

Then Gordon encountered Antabuse and a friendly psychiatrist, both of which helped him to bring his drinking under control for a while. But this control did not last long. He soon discovered that after staying away from the Antabuse for seven days, he could drink again without suffering any unfavorable consequence. So back he went to the drinking-sex-work pattern.

In the meantime he found another analyst, to whom he formed a strong attachment and to whom he always returned after one of his drinking bouts. He remained bisexual. The dynamics were easy enough to see: he was the son of a very strict religious family that had offered him no outlets for pleasure. It was a puritanical atmosphere that he could not tolerate too long.

In spite of his acting out—heterosexually, homosexually, and with drinking—Gordon managed to continue his therapy on and off for about five years. Then suddenly his wife became pregnant, which made a great deal of difference in his life, because he had never thought he could become a father. He wrote to his therapist, "But things are so much brighter, and suddenly nothing seems futile anymore."

Several years later the therapist had another letter from him, stating that he had settled down with his wife and new baby and, while he drank occasionally, it was not nearly as bad as it had been. The underlying depression hinted at in the letter had been with him all his life.

It may be questioned whether any real therapeutic progress had been made. (That question can always be raised.) On the surface at least, considerable change had occurred. Even if Gordon regressed later on, he had gone through a period where life seemed more meaningful to him. The major dynamic factor in his drinking, a protest against an excessively strict family, had been absorbed by him.

Not infrequently alcoholics go through some positive experience that induces them to give up drinking. In the above case, it was the positive transference that carried Gordon through. A somewhat similar dynamic was present in the case of Harold, a thirty-eight-year-old accountant. Harold was also the son of an extremely strict family. He was the middle of three children—the other two, girls. Mother was terrified that the girls would let themselves go sexually, so she would secretly have her husband follow them whenever they went out on a date. Harold was discouraged from going with girls, so he rarely went out.

A vivid memory was the frequent beatings he got from his mother for being disobedient. He would freeze himself to the point of not crying when she beat him, which became a matter of pride with him. In school he just drifted around, doing nothing in particular.

Then came the service, which brought an enormous change in his life. But there all his defiance and disobedience came out.

He would not march when told to, would not clean his gun, would not obey orders. Finally he was hospitalized and eventually given a section 8 (neuropsychiatric) discharge.

In the hospital he cried incessantly. All the pent-up emotion of his childhood finally came to the fore. He was not given any psychotherapy; a psychiatrist merely spoke to him a few times. When he was discharged, he was advised to go to a VA outpatient clinic, but he would not do so.

At this point he met a writer, whom he came to worship. The man was brilliant, thought Harold; he was an unknown genius. He would follow the man wherever he went. This writer was also a homosexual and drank a great deal, and Harold followed him in these habits too. They were constantly drunk together.

Then Harold recognized one day that his writer-friend was not all that he was cracked up to be. Their sex play, mostly mutual masturbation, no longer satisfied him. So he came back to New York, unsure of what he would do.

Harold took some courses to improve his accountancy skills. In one of the courses, one of the instructors mentioned vocational guidance to Harold. Unsure of what kind of help he wanted, he consulted a psychologist instead, who suggested psychoanalysis. At first he was reluctant, afraid to entrust his life to anybody, but he accepted a trial period. (The trial period was a device used by Freud in the early days of his practice to make sure that he was not dealing with schizophrenia; the differentiation between neurosis and schizophrenia was very difficult at that time. Today the trial period is rarely used, except for special occasions such as the present one.) After the two-month trial, he was an enthusiastic advocate of psychoanalysis. His life began to make much more sense to him, and he began to see that there were ways out of his various dilemmas.

During the first year of analysis, Harold's attention was focused almost entirely on the analyst, with whom in effect he fell in love (just as he had with the writer in the earlier period). He came to see that because of his fear of his mother, he was running away from everything, which got him nowhere. The positive transference carried him along.

In New York he still had a few friends with whom he socialized occasionally. One was a woman he had once had some contact with in his travels. A divorcée with a nine-year-old son, she indicated an interest in him. The relationship blossomed; even the fact that she was five years older than he was meaningful. Not unexpectedly, he fell in love with her, and they soon moved on to marriage. When the analyst met him on the street some years later, he was still deliriously happy.

An amusing incident brought him back for a statement from the analyst. He had applied for a driver's license, and one of the questions was, "Have you ever been in psychiatric treatment?" Proudly he said yes, even specifying that it had been very successful. The blasé clerk merely noted that he had been in treatment, which meant that he was refused a license until he had a statement from a qualified professional that he was emotionally "well enough" to drive a car.

Many men have periods of alcoholism of longer or shorter duration. The psychodynamics of their drinking has to be explored, as well as their entire life situation. When that is done, many of them, often unexpectedly, give up the drinking and take up a more normal life. The decisive factor is generally whether the transference is positive or negative. In all the cases mentioned it was positive, which carried the patient along to a good conclusion.

Suicide

More than 20,000 suicides are recorded each year in the United States, and Dublin, a noted epidemiologist, estimates that the true number is closer to 25,000 (Weiss, 1974). Death by suicide thus represents about 1 to 2 percent of all deaths occurring in the United States. Suicide has ranked among the first twelve causes of death in most European countries and in North America for many years. Generally, it is held that women *attempt* suicide more often, while men *commit* suicide more often (especially older and single men). Thus suicide is more of a male problem than a female problem.

With such statistics it is understandable that considerable research would be directed at the topic, but until Edwin Shneidman came along in the 1950s, the research was generally sporadic and unreliable. The sociologist Durkheim wrote a famous book about suicide, but his interest lay in the collapse of the social surroundings, which he called "anomie," a word that has entered our vocabulary.

It is the isolation or alienation felt by individuals in many societies that leads to the suicide. However, because the subjects are no longer available, an examination of their psychodynamics is obviously impossible. After a lifetime studying the subject, Shneidman (1985) came up with ten common characteristics of suicide. These are worth quoting (p. 121):

1. The common stimulus in suicide is unendurable psychological pain.
2. The common stressor in suicide is frustrated psychological needs.
3. The common purpose of suicide is to seek a solution.
4. The common goal of suicide is cessation of consciousness.
5. The common emotion in suicide is hopelessness-helplessness.
6. The common internal attitude toward suicide is ambivalence (i.e., loving and hating the same person).
7. The common cognitive state in suicide is constriction.
8. The common interpersonal act in suicide is communication of intention.
9. The common action in suicide is egression (escape).
10. The common consistency in suicide is with lifelong coping patterns.

Working with thirty men from the Terman longitudinal study of gifted children, Shneidman reports that he was able to predict, when a subject was age thirty, that he was a likely candidate for suicide at fifty-five. However, so many variables may intervene in the course of an individual's life that prediction of suicide is at best a highly dubious procedure.

The psychoanalytic hypothesis has always been that no one kills him- or herself who has not first wanted to kill someone else (Freud, 1910: SE XI). That aggression is internalized. But obviously there are many people who have murderous wishes and do not kill themselves, so the picture is not complete. Henry and Short (1954) show statistically that suicide increases with downturns in the business cycle—that is, it seems to have economic causes as well as psychological.

In a well-known study, Hendin (1964) compared suicide rates and dynamics for the three Scandinavian countries, where suicide has notoriously been high. He found that high rates in Sweden and Denmark were associated with rigid self-demands for superior performance (with subsequent self-hate for failure) in the former, and a "dependency loss" in the latter. The lower rates in Norway, on the other hand, were associated with persons reared to be externally aggressive; they became suicidal when that aggression was inverted toward the self. In this country the studies of Paffenbarger, King, and Wing (1969) of 40,000 American male former university students revealed that early loss or absence of the father was the dominant distinguishing characteristic of their subjects who committed suicide.

Clinically, the case of a forty-nine-year-old dentist who attempted suicide, recovered, and then attempted it again is typical. Ike was very unhappily married. Totally impotent with his wife, he found a mistress (a psychotherapist) with whom he was quite potent. He had falsified his tax returns for many years, by his estimate doubling his available capital. He was constantly fearful that the IRS would uncover his various schemes and send him to jail. Interestingly, the fantasy about jail was that he would become a dental assistant there and work his way out (he was a practicing dentist, it may be recalled). Both times he made preparations for suicide by carefully dividing his assets among the various members of his family. Both times the suicide was averted by enforced hospitalization.

One aspect of this case is revealing. Although he was worth a considerable amount of money, because of his fear of the IRS he felt totally impoverished. Before his second suicide threat, he went to see an analyst, but he found the analyst's fee too high. The analyst, in sympathy with his plight, then agreed to accept part of the fee in cash, with the remainder to be paid after the crisis was over. When he was released from the hospital the second time, he refused to honor this agreement, even reprimanding the analyst for requesting the agreed-upon fee. Thus the wish to get even was obviously a part of the whole suicide complex.

One of the most important findings reported by Shneidman and other researchers is that no one commits suicide without giving a good deal of advance warning. The suicide itself is a cry for help. But before that cry materializes, there are other, often verbal cries for help, many of which are disregarded by those in the surrounding environment.

In 1968 Shneidman helped to found the American Association for Suicidology. In the wake of his work, numerous suicide prevention programs have been set up all over the country. These have helped, though there are both successful and unsuccessful cases. Hatton, Valente, and Rink (1977) cite the following unsuccessful case from Shneidman's Suicide Prevention Center.

The patient, C. T., was forty-one years old when he first called the center. At that time his relationship with the man whom he had lived with and loved for fourteen years had just ended. Twenty years earlier C. T. had made a suicide attempt with an overdose of sleeping medication following a broken love relationship. During the past fourteen years, his life with his roommate had been stormy, with frequent fights and separations. He worked as a designer of women's clothing but for the past few years had experienced difficulty in finding and holding a job.

A year and a half before his first call to the center, C. T. had sought outpatient therapy at a psychiatric hospital but had discontinued treatment after a few months. When he first called the center, he was experiencing suicidal impulses but had not yet formulated a suicide plan. He reported that he was depressed and had trouble sleeping, despite the use of tranquilizers prescribed by his physician. Although the caregiver encouraged

C. T. to reestablish his previous therapeutic relationship, he did not follow through.

During the next five years, C. T. called the Suicide Prevention Center forty-eight times. He accepted a referral for psychiatric help and was hospitalized on two occasions. During this five-year period, he experienced recurrent depressive and suicidal states. His love relationships were transient and of short duration. He was unable to obtain employment. After one psychiatric interview he was designated as emotionally disabled and began receiving welfare. He complained of a variety of physical ailments, including stomach ulcers, a disintegrating spinal disc, rectal bleeding, and severe insomnia. He was eventually found dead by his apartment manager, his body having remained undiscovered for four days.

In both these cases, as in the vast majority, the suicidal individual suffered a terrible loss of love. This may take the form of an outright rejection or of intense internal guilt. Again the analytic ideal, with its emphasis on love, is of great value in therapy.

A patient who has attempted suicide and recovered presents a greater risk of another suicidal attempt than a person who has not. As already noted, one principle that I have found useful is that a patient in therapy will not regress below that level previously experienced in life; that is, if he has attempted suicide, he may try it again, but if he has not, it is highly unlikely that he will. Similarly for psychosis: if a patient has been psychotic, he may during therapy become psychotic again, but if he has not, it is most unlikely that he will.

When a man who has made a suicide attempt and recovered enters therapy, my major therapeutic effort in the beginning is to help him understand the dynamics of his suicide attempt. Inevitably, this leads to the nature of his love life, with all the consequent ramifications of the feelings of rejection. After the dynamics of the suicide attempt have been cleared up, at least in verbalizable form, the therapy can proceed on its usual course.

Two mass suicides in modern times have attracted the attention of mental health professionals. One was that involving a bizarre religious cult in 1978. Led by the Rev. Jim Jones, about 1,200 Americans emigrated to Guyana, leaving all their belongings behind in the United States. They set up an isolated community over which Jones had complete control. He was, for example, the only man who was permitted to have sex (Fine, 1986). Then suddenly, for no apparent reason, Jones ordered all of his followers to commit suicide by drinking poison. Almost all followed his command.

The other event is the mass suicide of Japanese kamikaze pilots during World War II. Perhaps 7,000 pilots actually committed suicide. Some 9,000 more were standing by in training and would undeniably have committed suicide had the war lasted longer.

The dynamics of this enormous number of suicides, for which there is no parallel in any other modern country (the Nazis and the Communists swore to die for their country but did not commit suicide in any significant numbers), involve total self-debasement. One Japanese wrote a song that could be seen as a symbol of the psychodynamics of suicide for the Guyana episode as well as the kamikaze situation. He wrote, "Insignificant little pebbles that we are, the degree of our devotion does not falter, as for our country we move toward our final rest" (Hoyt, 1983, p. 118).

It is clear that in both cases the individual had submerged himself completely in the community: in the case of Guyana it was the Rev. Jones who dominated; in Japan it was the emperor. Thus in general the suicidal person seems to be immersed in some larger mass, where he loses sight of his own individuality. Clinically, suicide, with that loss of the self, poses a great problem for the clinician, and every precaution, including enforced hospitalization, should be taken in handling such a patient.

Self-Damaging Acting Out

It is difficult to restrain the impulses; analysts speak of the "tyranny" of the drives. Some people retain their control for quite a while, then suddenly break out of the pattern and let themselves go. Referred to as "acting out," this behavior usually takes the form of sexual or aggressive actions that are clearly inappropriate to the situation and have a destructive effect on the person. It can best be defined as an action, usually repetitive and compulsive, that serves the unconscious purpose of resolving the repressed internal conflict by external means. Acting out and action are so close (Freud himself did not distinguish them clearly) that they are often hard to keep apart. A common mistake made by therapists is to become moralistic in such instances, and preaching takes the place of analyzing—a danger to be avoided.

Jim, a thirty-five-year-old businessman, was quite successful in his business, but he had always wanted to be an artist. Although he had little formal training, he spent a lot of his spare time painting. In spite of several attempts, he could not manage to sell his paintings or find a gallery to display them. Unable to find recognition, he became increasingly embittered. As so often happens, he took his bitterness out on women.

Although married at an early age, he had always had women "on the side." His wife was a completely self-effacing woman who loved him and would do anything that he asked. But nothing was enough for him. He came close to believing that there was a conspiracy against him to prevent the display of his paintings.

In analysis he made substantial progress, but a strong negative transference set in when he began to talk of his father, who had had a similar experience with writing (he had remained an unknown writer). In a rash move, Jim left his regular job in the hope that by devoting all of his time to painting he could get better results.

But in reality he was in full rebellion. In analysis he became increasingly irritated with the fee, which was moderate. He began to give the analyst checks that bounced, until the analyst would no longer accept checks at all, insisting on cash. Because Jim was short of money, a bill was run up which the analyst would not accept, and analysis had to be suspended.

He was confronted by one financial dilemma after another. For nonpayment of rent he was evicted from his apartment; for nonpayment of taxes the IRS kept a constant surveillance on his income. During this time he went from one woman to another, living on borrowed money.

Finally the interpretations that had been offered during his analysis about his self-destructive tendencies helped him to pull himself together. When the analyst sent him a typewritten bill for the overdue fees, he added a handwritten note: "How are you?" Jim finally felt that someone cared, so he began to rehabilitate himself. He paid his bill, went back to analysis, returned to work, and led a more reasonable life. Eventually he was able to make a better marriage with another woman and get past his self-destructive acting out.

Kermit seemed to be a model husband and father. He kept to his work, was faithful to his wife, and spent a lot of time with his two children, to whom he was very devoted.

In his youth Kermit had belonged to a left-wing splinter group, but this had never affected his everyday life. Then the family moved to a new neighborhood, where many people had the sort of cars that Kermit could not afford. Because there were so many cars, the parking space was limited and people began to park in forbidden areas.

This illegal parking incensed Kermit no end. Suddenly this meek, mild-mannered man appointed himself a one-man vigilante committee, heedless of the fact that he might be discovered and punished. He had a number of stickers printed with the message, "Parked illegally; get out." They were on an adhesive back that was hard to remove from the windshields of cars. He performed this chore of tagging cars late at night, when most people were asleep. No one, not even his wife, knew what he was doing.

The neighbors, annoyed by the inconvenience (they could not drive until the stickers were removed), banded together to find the culprit. Kermit made no effort to conceal what he was doing (beyond working at night), so he was apprehended fairly quickly. City officials brought him to court on criminal and civil charges.

The judge sentenced him to several months for damaging property but agreed to suspend the sentence if Kermit would pay for the damages done and go to psychotherapy. He agreed.

In therapy there was little that could be done with him.

He was completely unmotivated and found little to talk about. After a few months therapy was discontinued, with minimal results, if any. However, Kermit had learned his lesson and stopped his one-man vigilante activities.

Although the search for pleasure is built into the human being, many men, because of unhappy childhoods, turn it into a search for pain. Basic to this masochistic attitude toward life is a harsh superego, which is built up in an unhappy childhood. In therapy, the guilt and searching for pain are brought to the surface by the therapist, on the basis of the material presented by the patient, and a more reasonable way of life emerges as the patient sees more and more clearly what he has been doing.

6 | Feeling and Reason

THE PSYCHOLOGIST G. STANLEY HALL, THE FIRST PRESIDENT of the American Psychological Association, said a century ago that the intellect is but a speck afloat on a sea of feeling. With this proposition therapists are in complete assent: psychotherapy is a way of changing the world of feelings in which the person lives. In the emphasis on the analytic ideal throughout this book, I have tried to show over and over how real feelings emerge from surface rationalizations.

The Role of Feelings

It is particularly in the area of feelings that the changing male image makes itself felt in therapy. Women often complain about their husbands—no sex, no communication—a complaint that is often justified, because the withdrawal from sex (often with the idea or reality of an extramarital fling) and the inability to communicate feelings are part of the traditional male image. The analytic process tends to change this image in the individual patient and to attack the validity of this image in the culture at large.

Men in our society are brought up to be real he-men—macho, strong, never hesitant about what they are doing, secure, and so on. One need only consider the common image of what the man should be to see that a large majority are unable to live up to it. When a situation is unpleasant, a man denies it; in effect, he pretends that the quandary does not exist. Women, on the other hand, are more ready than men to face their problems

—that is, to recognize their feelings. Men *deny* their feelings, which proves to be a major resistance to psychotherapy.

Without going into too much technical detail, it can be said that there are three aspects to feelings: discharge (a kind of "letting off of steam"), interpersonal communication (for example, a cry for help), and physiological reactions. All of these have deep unconscious roots. One or all may be noted and misinterpreted by the individual experiencing them. The physiological reactions are often expressed in ordinary language: for example, "My heart jumped a beat," "He was shitting in his pants," "My stomach was tied up in knots," and so on—the list could be indefinitely continued. Beyond that, we also know that there are far-reaching effects of unpleasant emotions, including serious illness and even death. (In 1929 the physiologist Walter Cannon wrote a classic paper on voodoo death to explain the phenomenon of sudden death from fear sometimes observed in primitive groups; on rare occasions this phenomenon can happen in our own society as well.)

There are culturally approved outlets for emotion that are more acceptable to women and other outlets more acceptable to men. While there are many exceptions, it can be said that (1) women find it more acceptable to discharge their emotions, even in public; (2) women learn more ways of communicating their emotions than men, who consequently seem "affect-blocked"; and (3) historically, women have been regarded as weaker than men. In the nineteenth century this concept of the weaker sex became a medical doctrine, and physicians often regarded the woman as inherently frail, especially because of her reproductive system (Ehrenreich and English, 1978). Today our knowledge goes far deeper and shows that there are many illnesses of a psychogenic nature, some of them more common among women, some more common among men; even cancer has been implicated as having a possible psychogenic basis (Locke, 1985). It has been shown that there is a cultural universality in facial expression and that this universality is to some extent linked up with evolutionary considerations (Ekman, 1972). The differences between male and female facial expressions are obvious enough.

In terms of the psychology of men, these aspects of emo-

tional expression help to characterize what has been traditionally referred to as the "WASP" (white Anglo-Saxon Protestant)
personality, which has for a long time been regarded as the average or basic personality structure (Kardiner, 1945) of American
men. In his study of cultures, Kardiner includes an extensive
discussion of a town he calls Plainville, a typical American city.
The following is an abstract of the life history of a typical man
of his day, born in 1897.

James L. was born at Plainville in 1897, the oldest of four
brothers. He was inducted into farm labor when very young and
from age eleven to age fifteen had to do all the hard work on
the farm, because his father was ill.

After his father's recovery James went away to visit his
grandfather. During this first absence he felt very anxious, but
he denied it, saying, "People were good to me. I felt well treated
and understood. I wasn't lonely because I could always read a
book or something" (p. 379).

He left home at the age of fifteen, having a vague idea
that what he wanted was money, adventure, and a better life.
Later he changed his mind and wanted an education, because
he thought that would bring money. Then he conceived the idea
of becoming a writer. When he was eighteen, he wrote a movie
scenario, but he could not sell it.

Work on the farm seemed "dull," so in 1916 he enlisted
in the army. He thought it would be an adventure, wanted to go
to the Philippines or Hawaii. He also thought this would put
him in line for a pension.

In 1917, as a soldier, he found himself on the West Coast,
where he saw mountains and salt water for the first time. Here
his first marriage occurred. Shortly thereafter, he found his wife
in bed with another man and divorced her. This led to a period
of going after many women, of which he said, "I made many in-
nocent girls suffer" (p. 381).

After some adventures in the army, he returned to Plainville, where he began to be more tolerant of the failings of his
neighbors. He married again, hoping that his new wife would become a great romantic experience, but he felt disappointed. Several times he was unfaithful.

He felt no favoritism toward any of his children. He

wanted a companion to go fishing and hunting with him. His wife did not like to fish or hunt. He was by this time (age forty-three) quite disillusioned about all women and did not want to make another attempt at marriage.

The ethnographer states that James was a typical man of his town—affable, accessible, guardedly confidential, and "honest" within the limits of telling as good a story as possible. He could be taken as an average, well-adjusted individual with well-defined objectives and relative freedom from incapacitating neurosis. In the language of psychotherapy, he had an adjustment neurosis that bothered him considerably underneath but that he could readily cover up by a standard social adjustment.

Of his childhood he had many memories, especially of incidents of a sexual nature. The disciplinarian in the house was his father, but the executive end of the discipline was generally delegated to the mother. The severest aspect of the discipline was to begin farm work so early and so hard.

Subsequent statistical and clinical studies portrayed the same kind of personality structure, which is only now beginning to change. For example, in the Midtown Study of 1962 (Rennie and others, 1962; Fischer and Srole, 1978), the researchers found (1) a frequency of emotional disability far higher than had previously been estimated in any American population, (2) a huge gap between the unexpectedly large call for psychiatric help and the gross quantitative inadequacy of the services available, and (3) poorest access to such services for those most in need of them. One of the major findings of the study was that there is an inverse ratio between socioeconomic status and mental health: poverty is the greatest handicap of all, and it leads to all kinds of emotional disorders.

To handle this vast amount of everyday pain and unhappiness, an army of 300,000 therapists (Gelman, 1987, p. 70) has grown up in the United States and is expanding rapidly. They include psychiatrists, psychologists, clinical social workers, psychiatric nurses, and uncounted thousands of unlicensed counselors of varying levels of training and legitimacy. Bellah and others (1985), all sociologists, claim that there is a therapeutic revolution in progress: American cultural traditions define personality achievement and the purpose of human life in ways that leave the individual suspended in glorious but terrifying isolation—an isolation that therapy is increasingly being asked to assuage.

In all of these therapeutic efforts, individual or group, the major goal with men is to change their attitude toward their feelings. Men are being told every day that it is not "sissy" to have feelings, that it is all right for them to communicate what goes on inside them to some other person—whether a therapist, wife, or lover—that physiological reactions have an emotional basis that they have to take seriously if they wish to live longer and have a healthful, stress-free life.

The process of psychotherapy in its daily routine centers very strongly on helping the man become conscious of the feelings he has suppressed in the interests of presenting himself to the world as a fearless, macho man in the image of John Wayne. The major defense mechanism that men employ is denial. It takes a long time to pierce through this veil of denial and get to the real feelings behind it. Often enough the denial is mixed with projection, in which the alleged root of a man's troubles is externalized to some other person. As a rule, men who employ this defense mechanism come to therapy only when pressed to do so by some urgent loss or threat of loss in the front that they put up to the world, not because of internal feelings of dissatisfaction.

Many therapists make the mistake of complicating the therapy unduly with difficult and far-reaching interpretations; it is as though they were more interested in impressing their supervisor than in helping the patient. The feelings that are repressed by men are the basic ones in human existence: fear, anger, homosexual fears, heterosexual fears, the need to suffer, and the like. These feelings are encased in the symptomatology, and the task of analysis is to separate them out and to help the patient to see that they *are* his feelings. Once that is done, their roots can be traced back to childhood. Eventually a patient sees that he is dealing with the ghosts of his childhood rather than the reality of his present life. This is the working-through process, which may and often does take a long time, unless the patient is particularly gifted for therapy.

The patient almost always covers up his feelings by reference to reality, and the analyst has to penetrate the reality to help him bring out the underlying feelings. Here are two case vignettes, one of which worked out successfully while the other did not.

Derek, who had already become an analyst himself, felt anxious about the summer vacation (the famous "August"). In the last session before the vacation, he had a dream: "I'm downtown in a restaurant. Stuart, a former patient, comes up to me and shakes hands warmly. He is with a woman."

Stuart was a patient who had come to him for a number of years, then suddenly dropped out without notice. Several follow-up calls got nowhere; the patient had quit for good. Derek had been very bothered by this incident. He was still in supervision when it happened, and he had discussed the case with a number of supervisors to see where he had gone wrong. Nothing ever came out, however, and he regarded the case as one of his failures.

When an analyst dreams about a patient, it is plausible to assume that he is dreaming of his relationship with his own analyst. In this dream Derek identified with his ex-patient Stuart. At one level he too wanted to hurt the analyst by dropping out abruptly, making him feel inadequate just as he had felt when Stuart left him. At another level he wanted to find a chance to socialize with the analyst during the vacation. The meaning of the dream was obvious to him right away. In childhood terms he also wanted to regain his deceased father, to whom he had been quite attached and who had died in his arms.

In another case Larry, a professor at one of the local universities, came to analysis with a paranoid predicament. He had been married, with one child, but his wife had left him. Unwilling to put up a fight, he had acceded to the divorce, even paid child support for a while, and then gave up the child to the new man whom his wife married.

In spite of the fact that his ex-wife no longer had anything to gain from him, Larry was convinced that she had put detectives on his trail and was having him followed. Her purpose, he thought, was to prevent him from meeting any other woman. Typically, he would stand around in bars or social gatherings and identify some man, previously unknown to him, as the "detective." If he noted that the "detective" was looking at him when he talked to a woman, he would leave the woman and slip away quietly.

Larry had been through a number of psychiatrists. He had received shock therapy, tranquilizers, and various other drugs, but nothing helped. Finally he had consulted a detective agency on his own, to get the other "detective" off his back. The agency had charged him $7,500, which he paid—but of course nothing could be done for him. Then, at the suggestion of one of his psychiatrists, he went to a lawyer to see what he could do about getting rid of the "detective." The lawyer could see that he was dealing with a paranoid personality, so he referred him to a psychiatrist. Larry was caught in a kind of crossfire: the analyst had referred him to a lawyer, while the lawyer now referred him to an analyst.

Although little was learned about his childhood, the dynamics of Larry's paranoid constellation were quite clear. There was a repressed homosexual wish for another man that he could not bring to consciousness. Nothing could be done for him, and he eventually stopped treatment with an unknown outcome.

Many men grow up with this total denial of all feeling. In this way they go along with the cultural image of what a man should be like. Either they refuse to come to analysis, because that would mean sharing feelings, or they put up a tremendous resistance once they are in treatment. An extreme resistance of this kind was seen in Gilbert, a nineteen-year-old college student.

Gilbert lived in a dormitory, sharing a room with another young man with whom he had little contact. His life centered entirely on his studies; he did not date, had no hobbies, had no real friends, and lived away from his family, with whom he had little contact. His problems were completely intellectualized; in fact, he denied having any.

One time he ran out into a busy street out of sheer loneliness. In desperation he called his mother and said that he could not stand it any longer (it later appeared that he was even contemplating suicide). She referred him to an analyst, a referral that he accepted.

In analysis his total isolation and denial of all feeling

came to the fore very quickly. One extraordinary rationalization that he used was that there are, after all, no happy people in the world (including both his parents and his grandfather, a physician) and no happy people described in books. His mother, a book lover, plied him with tragic novels in which the hero usually came to a bad end.

Yet shortly after the analysis began, he brought in a collection of notes discussing the philosophical question of whether happiness was possible, and if so, how it might be possible for him. At one point he told the analyst that he had stopped masturbating because it was essential that he should have no feelings; he was going to be a pure scientist. In spite of this denial of feeling, a good working alliance was established fairly quickly, perhaps because Gilbert could see how extreme his position was and how senseless it was in the eyes of the world.

After a while the material began to center on his body and his sex life. He had never really had a date in his life, and he began to wonder what it would be like. Dreams were prolific and frequently centered on girls. Once he dreamed: "I'm in the lockers naked; a bunch of girls come along. I don't care." He could see that there was a wish to show himself naked to girls.

After a few months he realized that he was becoming dependent on the analyst, which frightened him. His immediate association was that it was like the dependency on his mother when he was a child, which was shattered by the birth of a younger brother when he was five years old and the move to a new location, where he no longer had any friends.

Slowly, under the impact of the transference, Gilbert began to move toward people. Because he was living on a college campus, it was easy enough to make some friends for the first time. Girls were available on the campus, so he began to do some dating. Gradually his mask of denial of all feeling began to break down as a result of more favorable life experiences and the good feeling that he built up toward the analyst. Although there were many ups and downs, the case eventually worked out very well. He went on to a graduate degree, found a wife, and started a meaningful new life for himself.

This case (although highly telescoped) is a good example

of how the analytic process works. First a relationship had to be established with Gilbert, which occurred because he felt the need to get out of his desperate loneliness. In this relationship he presented his own ruminations on life, which could be discussed as they never had been before. Slowly the childhood roots of his isolation came out. He could see that because he was no longer a child, he did not have to keep himself so far apart from people. At his age the natural pleasures of growing up—sports, dates, and socialization—were all easily accepted. Based on the positive transference to the analyst, he went through an education about life—in part from comments by the analyst, in part from his own thinking, and in part from the prodding of his friends.

The Role of Reason

Aristotle's dictum that humans are rational animals has been a mainstay of Western thought. Yet those of us who study people often come to doubt it. Irrationality seems to be as common, if not more so, than rationality.

On the surface psychotics seems to be totally irrational; their ideas are strange, their behavior is odd, and often even their words are unintelligible. Hence it was thought for centuries that such people had lost their "reasoning capacity." They were, it was held, not really human, and hence should not be treated as human. This was the prevailing opinion until Freud came along.

While Freud himself did little work with psychotics, he laid the basis for understanding them. Today we see them not as totally irrational but as living in a state of terror that goes back to their childhood. Human beings live by attachments—first to the mother, then to the father, then to the outside world. If these attachments are broken or fragile or inadequate, the ensuing terror leads to all kinds of strange behavior—behavior that is more typical of the child than of the adult. So psychotics do not violate the statement that the intellect is a speck afloat on a sea of feeling; they merely hide the feelings more effectively.

There are some psychotics who are so far gone that nothing can be done for them, whether by physical or psychological means. But for most there is much more hope today. Usually patients present a mixture of rational and irrational material that can be treated by psychotherapy, or at times by psychotherapy with drugs.

The analytic process is frequently described as one in which a pact is made between the analyst and the healthy part of the patient's ego. This pact allows the ego to hunt down the unhealthy aspects of the patient's life and make some sense out of them. Sometimes the mere assertion that the behavior has a cause has a healing effect, as a patient once told me. When I said to him, "There are reasons for what you are doing," he was relieved and excited, because he could finally find out what was driving him.

While the basic problem in the severely disturbed is almost always a fear of separation, coupled with difficulties in forming and maintaining attachments to other human beings, it is usually difficult to tackle these problems directly. Instead, they are covered up by the patient by a variety of rationalizations that he clings to with firm determination. Thus the criterion for normality becomes not conventional behavior as such, but the capacity to engage in a rational discussion rather than stick pigheadedly to one distorted perception or point of view. Some examples will illustrate this point.

Nathan, a twenty-five-year-old schizophrenic (introduced in Chapter Two) who had been hospitalized twice for making violent attacks on his stepfather, complained that he was unable to walk on the street without running into people—implying that people were always running into him deliberately. To understand this curious idea better, I went for a walk. I gradually came to see that people walking on the street make an unconscious pact with a person approaching them that one or the other will get out of the way. Nathan could not make such a pact. Underneath his wish to jostle people were his deep loneliness and sense of inadequacy, of course, but these emotional factors he was not well enough to discuss.

One incident in his life presents a revealing example of how delusional or semidelusional ideas can become fixated. Like so many other men, Nathan was afraid that his penis was too small. He went from one doctor to another, begging them to give him an injection that would make his penis grow. Finally he hit upon a doctor who, probably to humor the poor man, gave him an injection of some harmless substance, whereupon Nathan convinced himself that his penis had grown. Somehow, in his mind, a little later it had shrunk again. Whereupon he began to go to doctors all over again, telling them that an injection had once made his penis grow and that he wanted to have such an injection again.

In his background was a dominating mother who had been through a terrible shock when her first husband (Nathan's father) had suddenly died of a heart attack at the age of thirty-five. She compensated by keeping the boy at her side (though she did later remarry) and telling him that no girl would go out with him until he had his nose straightened. In accordance with her wish, he did wait until he was nineteen and had his nose straightened before he dared to ask a girl for a date.

Neurosis is likewise built around a series of fixed or semi-fixed ideas that do not respond to reason immediately. (If they responded, the person would not be in need of therapy.) Thus, paradoxically, one of the major goals of therapy is to help the patient to think more clearly. Human behavior is always rational, but the rationality often exists at the unconscious level, absent from the conscious. By making the unconscious conscious, the person regains conscious control of his reasoning power. As Freud once put it, the voice of the intellect is soft, but it persists until it gets a hearing. The process of psychoanalysis or dynamic psychotherapy may even be defined as one in which the voice of the intellect is allowed to get a hearing. Consequently, the basic principle of all therapy is that the unconscious roots of seemingly irrational behavior must always be uncovered.

The mother of a young college freshman, Oliver, called in panic to ask for help with her son, who "refused to eat his food." When the young man was seen, he was about fifty pounds overweight. He gave the following explanation for his eating behavior: In the first place, he had not refused to eat; he had merely cut down to one meal a day. The reason for this was that his mother had overstuffed him with food from the day he was born, so that he was seriously obese. She delighted in serving him, even preparing a menu in writing for him. As long as he was in high school, he was not bothered by this treatment. But when he entered college, he took health and hygiene courses and learned that his diet was not wholesome (too much fat, too few salads) and that it was not good to be overweight. When he told his mother about this, she refused to listen. Because he had no independent resources by which to feed himself, he hit upon the idea of limiting himself to one meal a day. It was at this point that his parents became panicky and called for help.

This case illustrates one of the basic principles of modern therapy: every disturbed patient has a disturbed family background. Bleuler (1978) describes the childhood of his schizophrenic patients as "horrible," though the nature of the horror varies from case to case. It is clear that Oliver's parents were emotionally ill themselves; otherwise they would have paid attention to the everyday knowledge about nutrition that has become routine in our society. Since the work of Lidz, Fleck, and Cornelison at Yale (1965), and many others, it has been well established that the families of schizophrenics have either overt or borderline pathology themselves. Likewise, by now it is well accepted that any kind of neurosis runs in families—in other words, people imitate the emotional patterns of their family. For various reasons, including social, certain persons are scapegoated and become "patients," while others with the same or worse pathology consider themselves "normal" and stay away from therapy. The expansion of psychological knowledge is gradually bringing changes in this picture.

In the process of clarifying seemingly irrational behavior, psychotherapy seeks first to make the behavior ego-dystonic (that is, make it incompatible with the ego, so that it creates anxiety), if it is not already, then relate the behavior to the man's personality structure, and finally trace it to its infantile roots. This can also be expressed as the process of acquiring insight (Richfield, 1954).

As a general rule, it is best to leave an irrational behavior alone until it has crystallized into a pattern that the patient can identify. If some symptom is analyzed too early, the patient may simply leave treatment in a fit of anger.

An alcoholic reported that he had consulted a psychiatrist

who, during the first session, asked him to lie down on the couch. He found this too "sissyish" and left treatment. It was later learned that he then went to an allergist who regarded alcoholism as an allergy. This somatic explanation was more acceptable to the patient than a psychological one. In a culture that abhors real intimacy, psychological explanations are bound to be terribly frightening to many men. Again, as psychological understanding expands, these fears are bound to diminish.

Because the emotional experience is so basic, the analysis of any seemingly irrational behavior always comes down to some feeling that the patient is trying to hide. The technique of therapy involves allowing the man to keep this hidden—but to explore the reasons for this behavior—until the patient feels free enough to bring it out himself. Herbert Strean (1984) reports on the case of a man who would not reveal his name. This patient, whom he calls Mr. A., was in analysis with Dr. Strean four times a week for close to four years, but he would not reveal his name for a year and a half. "If you insist that I give you my name," he told Dr. Strean in the first session, "I will be unable to be in treatment with you." Dr. Strean accepted the restriction and allowed the analysis to proceed.

The dynamics of Mr. A's secretiveness become quite clear through his dreams, fantasies, and transference reactions. Like most patients, he projected his superego to the analyst and feared his disapproval. He enjoyed teasing the analyst. In effect, he was playing a popular game from childhood: "I've got a secret, but I won't tell. You've got to try to make me tell." For Mr. A., keeping secrets was in many ways the equivalent of keeping his fantasies hidden. His secret murderous wishes coupled with his incestuous wishes (his Oedipal conflict) seem to explain his wish to keep secret his academic accomplishments and his intellectual potential. Eventually the big secret came out: he wanted Dr. Strean to rape him. In spite of these resistances, however, the therapy proceeded very successfully and ended on a happy note.

Every patient has some secret that he is reluctant to reveal, although few are as dramatic as this one. In the course of a psychological examination I once conducted on a hospitalized patient, the patient fell into a catatonic stupor from which it took him two days to emerge. (The stupor was prompted by card 11 of the Thematic Apperception Test, for those who know it.) I asked him to tell me the secret if he could. He said that the scene reminded him of an episode on Okinawa during World War II. He was walking along and saw two figures in the distance. Taking them to be Japanese, he shot at them, killing one (a man) but missing the other (a woman). Fearful that she too would be murdered, the woman offered herself to him sexually. He accepted. Then he found out that they were both Okinawans, not Japanese at all. The memory of this incident, which he had never revealed to anybody, had stayed with him for years and had been revived by the psychological test material that was presented to him. It may be noted that a short time later he broke out in an overt schizophrenia for which he required long-term hospitalization.

Because there are always parts of the personality that are irrational in greater or lesser degree, in the therapy of every patient various irrational beliefs are brought to the fore and overcome through the therapeutic process. It is important not to avoid the patient's secret, but it is also important not to press too hard. Therein lies part of the art of psychotherapy.

John (mentioned in Chapter Four) had been told by his mother that he had "torn her apart" when he was born, thus making him responsible for her lifelong depression. Although he was too intelligent to accept this at face value, he knew too little about women to be able to deny it completely. One major root of his withdrawal from women was the fear, taken over from his mother, that if he got a woman pregnant, the birth of the baby would tear her apart. Thus intercourse became equivalent to murder, which naturally had to be avoided. This came out only much later, when many of the details of his life had already been brought to the fore.

Not infrequently, irrational beliefs come out that simply have to be bypassed for the sake of therapeutic progress; nothing on earth will convince some patients that a given belief is untrue. A belief of this kind came out in the treatment of a homosexual man, Philip, who seemed to be moving toward heterosexual activity. But the woman he was pursuing, a psychologist, moved out of town to further her studies. Philip thereupon found another young lover in his homosexual encounters (as is so often the case, the younger man was supported by the older), who Philip said had the largest penis in New York. When this was questioned, the query was pooh-poohed with the argument that he, Philip, had seen many more penises than the therapist had (which was true enough but irrelevant) and that he knew when one was big and when one was small. This was really a fantasy to compensate for his own penis, which he, like most men, looked upon as small. Argumentation and years of analysis could not budge this conviction. It was only years later, when the younger man revealed that he had only been using Philip and his money to get through school, that Philip's notion about his lover's enormous penis disappeared.

A final word may be said here about the psychotherapy of schizophrenia. It has become customary nowadays to treat schizophrenics with drugs, because of the conviction that they are too far gone to understand any kind of rational discussion and because they are generally full of delusional ideas that cannot be discussed. This has become a rationalization for the widespread use of drugs, even though the outcome of the treatment of schizophrenia has not changed in 100 years (Warner, 1985). To some extent this rejection of the schizophrenic derives from the therapist's failure to understand the psychotic part of his own personality (Karon and Vandenbos, 1981). Following the precepts outlined in this chapter, however, in which it is noted that in many if not most schizophrenics there is a mixture of rational and irrational elements, the therapist who wishes to work psychologically can be much more optimistic about the outcome than the one who uses drugs and sees the whole process as determined by purely organic factors.

A word may also be said here in comparison of dynamic psychotherapy and those treatments that rely most heavily on cognitive or rational factors (for example, those of Beck and Ellis). Discussion of cognitive conflicts can certainly lead the patient a certain distance, but unless the deeper feelings involved are brought out, the result is bound to be less effective in the long run. Irrational cognitions are always tied up with deeper feelings of which the man is unaware.

7 | Family Role

THE FAMILY IS THE BASIS OF ALL KNOWN HUMAN SOCIETIES and, as recent research indicates, of many primate groups as well. And yet, as Anthony and Koupernik (1970) point out in *The Child in the Family,* in spite of an incredible amount of study, our knowledge of the family remains fragmented and unsystematized. (See also Gordon, 1978.) This is especially true of the role of the man in the family, a topic that has only recently come into focus (Lamb, 1986). No attempt can be made here to sum up the literature on family dynamics. Rather, my major goal in this chapter is to trace the development of the man in the family until he himself marries and forms a new family, particularly as it comes out in the therapeutic situation.

Two questions are primary in considering any family situation. First, how much love is there in any given family? This question is obviously crucial, given that love leads to happiness, while hatred leads to misery. And second, what is the role of the man (or boy) in any given family?

It has long been known that all psychopathology is related to the family environment (Grotjahn, 1960). At first Freud and his immediate group thought that the conflict within the family derived from the fact that society accorded the parents the role of socializing the child, which meant taming his impulses; from that point of view, the family of a troubled child was found to be "bad," and reform was necessary (Flugel, 1921). In the period between the two world wars, there was a strong movement in all areas of living to release people from the prewar inhibitions that had led to such disastrous massacres.

But while this release had some positive effects, there were also negative consequences. Children not only had to release their impulses (the id); they also had to develop control (the ego and the superego).

In line with this recognition of a need for control and the findings about maternal neglect and separation in infancy, the pendulum swung the other way, so that the family came to be seen as the major source of every individual's security, not merely the child's. From then on the intrapsychic life of the child has been understood only by grasping the family environment as well as the biologically determined impulses; in fact, impulses themselves seem to be related to parental comfort and stimulation (Ackerman, 1958; Brazelton and Als, 1979).

This change in orientation led to a family therapy movement, which seems to be increasing in numbers and weight. Still, the value of family therapy as opposed to individual therapy is highly variable. However the neurotic result comes about, it is crystallized in introjects that are increasingly immune to any influence except intensive psychotherapy. While the shortage of therapists, and their heterogeneous training, make for a bewildering variety of "schools," I have already indicated my conviction that the analytic ideal remains the underlying philosophy of all schools (Fine, 1979b). Yet the problems of people can be understood only in the context of their families, even if the therapy takes them away from immediate family concerns.

In the course of the history of psychotherapy, men have been treated at every age, from infancy to senility. To order the case material and theoretical knowledge most appropriately, instances will be given from a variety of age levels. It should be remembered that we are in the midst of a social revolution, in which the roles of men at all ages, as well as of women, are changing rapidly.

The Infant Boy

Boys have been treated from earliest infancy—in a sense even prenatally, because many pregnant women are treated through their pregnancy. Selma Fraiberg (1980) initiated child psychiatric consultations for infants in the first year of life with excellent results. One of her cases can be summed up as follows.

Leonard was referred to Fraiberg at five months of age in a grave nutritional state. The baby was starving. He vomited after each feeding and had not gained weight in three months. At birth he had weighed eight pounds; now he weighed only fourteen pounds five ounces. No organic causes for his growth failure could be found.

Examination of the family revealed that the mother was a timid, sad-faced, seventeen-year-old girl, while the father was a gaunt young man of twenty-one. The family was in a state of great stress and deprivation. They were living in poverty, supported only by the father's small earnings and food stamps. In addition, they had lost the support of their extended families by moving to another city.

The therapy was carried on by home visits twice a week. The mother, Kathie, began to speak of deep revulsion at the feeding of Leonard. She was repelled by his vomiting, sickened by the sight and the messiness. Further exploration revealed that the decline in Leonard's weight curve had started at three months, when solids began to enter his diet. Neither of his parents knew exactly how much food the baby needed.

The initial assessment provided a psychological picture: a baby who fed himself; a teenage mother who avoided contact with her baby, a mother who had a deep inner revulsion against messiness and possibly against her own destructive rage, a mother who was an adolescent with unsatisfied bodily and psychological hungers.

The therapy focused on an unwanted child handled by a frightened mother; the therapist treated both the mother's needs and the child's needs. By the time Lenny had reached his first birthday (that is, after seven months of treatment), the major part of the therapeutic work was done. Therapy itself continued until the family moved to another community, when Lenny was eighteen months old. As is so often the case, the therapy was literally life-saving. (See also Provence, 1983.)

The Child

Emilio Rodrigue (1955) describes the treatment of a mute psychotic boy of three. The child, Raul, did not speak, having lost the few words he had once mastered more than a year before treatment began. He did not utter any articulated sound, only an occasional guttural scream. He was first described as a quiet baby, neither crying nor laughing much, who worried his parents only because of his persistent lack of appetite. A deep and sudden regression took place after his sixteenth month, when his mother became pregnant again, and further worsened when, a few days after his second birthday, she gave birth to a second boy, the child's only sibling.

Raul was four months old when the mother went back to work. He was left alone so much that he could not become attached to anyone. However, later on, the author adds, the mother changed and was "helpful beyond expectations," and the father was also cooperative. After some five months of analysis, in which the analyst consistently interpreted, without noting any real sign of comprehension on the part of Raul, the boy began to speak; his first word was "Mummy." Here once more the basic needs for contact and communication are brought out. At first Raul had no real role in the family; later, when he was given a role, he responded.

In our Center for Creative Living, a two-and-one-half-year-old boy was brought in because he could not sleep. At night he would cry out for either mother or father, and one of them would go in to him. Even then he would not sleep but would wander back into the parents' bedroom. Louis, the baby, could keep them up all night.

Both parents had been previously analyzed, so they were perplexed and bothered by the problem. It turned out that both had had considerable sexual experience before marriage and that in childhood both had gone through intense Oedipal conflicts. It was as though the boy was now repeating what his parents had been through.

When Louis was brought in, in the playroom he turned

the mother doll over and pointed to her anus. Clearly he was still concerned with his toilet training and with what his mother's body looked like. The parents also reported that he would get into bed with his mother, put his head between her legs, and order his father to get out. The unconscious fears, part of which came from the parents, aroused by this excessive stimulation prevented him from sleeping.

Therapy involved some manipulation and advice. The boy was brought into the parents' bedroom and allowed to sleep at the foot of their bed. Apart from the Oedipal conflict, he suffered from severe separation anxiety (nor are the two so far apart). Some joint sessions with the parents also brought out their various conflicts about the boy. They learned to reassure him that mother would not go away and leave him (she did work) and that he would be allowed to play with mother, but not sexually. After a few weeks of this reassurance and manipulation, he was able to go back into his own room and sleep adequately.

The first child therapy case in history, reported by Freud in 1909 (SE X), has been affectionately named "Little Hans." Hans was a five-year-old boy who developed such a fear that a horse would bite him that he refused to go outdoors. The child's father was an adherent of Freud's and came to him with the problem. Freud treated the boy through the father, seeing the boy only once.

The dynamics of the phobia were traced by Freud to the Oedipal situation. The father brought the various productions of the child to Freud, who interpreted them, and these interpretations were then given back to the child by the father. It turned out that the phobia had started when Little Hans was three and one-half years old, after the birth of a sister. Her birth started the child on a train of thought about where babies came from, the differences between the sexes, and related questions. Hans was much preoccupied with his penis, which he called his "widdler." (This peculiar translation is itself a sign of the times: the German word is *wiwamacher*, which translates quite simply as "pipimaker" or "wiwimaker.") Actually, the interest in his penis was tied up with castration fears as well as with curiosity about men's and women's bodies. Eventually these fears led to the horse phobia, which made him afraid to go outdoors for a while, partly because of the fears generated about men's and women's bodies. The phobia was directly derived from the Oedipus complex; the horse was equated with the father, who, Hans thought, would castrate him for wanting mother. For protection, Hans stayed home.

The therapeutic result was excellent. The child got over the phobia completely. His interest turned to music, which was his father's profession, and he later pursued a musical career with distinction. According to all reports he led a comparatively normal life.

Fourteen years after the therapy, Little Hans, then nineteen, appeared in Freud's office and announced himself: "I am Little Hans." He had forgotten the whole incident completely; he no longer recalled anything of his phobia or his treatment.

The case is important historically because it is the first time that infantile sexuality was demonstrated to exist in a child directly. Freud noted that, although strictly speaking the case taught him nothing new, he was able to show directly in a child the suppositions that he had derived from the analysis of adults. It is surprising that Freud saw the case only as an exception and did not utilize the opportunity to make this the beginning of child analysis.

Sexual material by children can now be read like an open book. I have often told my students: don't argue with theory, just have a few children and see what you can see.

In the psychological examination of a five-year-old boy by a male psychologist, the child unexpectedly demanded that the examiner should take down his pants. When asked why, he replied that he wanted to see the examiner's penis. This example shows that analytical material is so readily available that it can be picked up almost anywhere. But a proper openness to human beings is essential. Freud (1920: SE VII, p. 133) once commented: "If mankind had been able to learn from a direct observation of children, these three essays could have remained unwritten."

In therapy the following incident occurred with Malcolm,

a ten-year-old boy in our clinic. He was referred because of his fear of rock-throwing fights, which went on all the time in his neighborhood. In his anxieties he had pulled out so much of the hair on his head that he was bald in spots; his mother covered the spots with black pencil.

Once during the play therapy, Malcolm and the therapist were shooting rubber-tipped darts at one another, a common enough activity in such therapy. Malcolm pointed to his penis and asked the therapist to shoot him there. The therapist shot at his shoes. "No," Malcolm insisted, "shoot me *there*," pointing directly to his penis. Naturally the therapist did not do that, but this led to an exploration of his castration and sexual fears.

Melanie Klein and Anna Freud both began the practice of child therapy in the 1920s, with somewhat different theoretical perspectives. Melanie Klein insisted that the young child could be treated in exactly the same way as an adult, except that instead of free association, she used play materials, such as little wooden men and women, carts, and the like. She strongly insisted that the analysis of children should probe resistances and transferences according to exactly the same principles that governed the analysis of adults. Anna Freud, on the other hand, argued that because the child was still so highly dependent on the parents, a full-blown transference such as occurred with adults could not be expected. The controversy still goes on, though the extreme positions have been modified on both sides.

Melanie Klein offered a number of examples of her technique. Here is one taken from a paper in 1932 (Klein, 1932).

Melvin, almost four, was very difficult to manage. He was strongly fixated upon his mother; at times he would be aggressive and overbearing. He got on badly with other children, especially with his younger brother.

At the very beginning of his first hour, Melvin took the toy carriages and put them first one behind the other and then side by side, alternating the arrangement several times. He also took a horse and carriage and bumped them into one another, so that the horses' feet knocked together. Later he said, "The horses have bumped together too, and now they're going to sleep."

The basic interpretations all went back to the notions the boy had about his parents' sexual intercourse, together with various fantasies about his internal life. In spite of the controversies surrounding Klein's view that infants have at their disposal a full range of sexual fantasies, she and her followers have reported consistently good results.

The other early approach to child therapy, that of Anna Freud, involved less of an emphasis on transference and more of an emphasis on being a real person to the child. For example, in one case of a ten-year-old boy with an obscure mixture of many anxieties, nervous states, insincerities, and childish, perverse habits, she tried to make herself interesting and useful to the boy (Freud, 1946). First she did nothing but follow his mood and humors along all their paths and bypaths. If he was cheerful, she was cheerful; if he was serious and depressed, she was the same. She followed his lead in every subject of talk, from tales of pirates and questions of geography to love stories and comments on stamp collections.

After a while she brought in another factor: to prove useful to the boy. She wrote letters for him on the typewriter during his visits, was ready to help him with the writing down of his daydreams and self-invented stories, of which he was proud, and made all sorts of little things for him during his hours.

Then came something she called "incomparably more important." She made him notice that being analyzed had very great practical advantages; for example, punishable deeds had an altogether different and much more fortunate result when they were first told to the analyst, and only through her to those in charge of the child. Thus the boy got into the habit of relying on analysis as a protection from punishment and claiming her help for repairing the consequences of his rash acts. Once, for example, he got her to restore stolen money and to make all the necessary but disagreeable confessions to his parents. Thus she became a very powerful person in his life.

Anna Freud related a later amusing incident about this boy. She shared her office with her father. One day the boy got into a conversation with one of her father's adult patients in the waiting room. This man told him about a dog that had killed a fowl for which he, the owner, had to pay. "The dog ought to be sent to Freud," said the boy; "he needs analysis." The other patient thought this was crazy. But what the boy meant was that the poor dog wanted so badly to be a good dog, and yet something inside him forced him to kill hens.

Although both of these methods produced results, subsequently the role of the parents in the child's neurosis was given increasing importance. Generally speaking, in well-run child guidance clinics children are not accepted for treatment unless the parents, especially the mother, also enter treatment. Otherwise there is the ever-present danger that as soon as the child shows some sign of improvement, or some behavior of which the parent disapproves, he will be pulled out of treatment. Here is a typical case.

Noah, an eight-year-old boy, was brought to our clinic because he had bowel movements in the classroom. When the teacher said to him, "Noah, go home," he would reply, "Let the others go home." He had no anxiety about the way in which the smell offended everybody.

When Noah entered therapy, he showed the following behavior. He was almost always aggressive with the toys in the playroom, and on more than one occasion he threw toys at the therapist and had to be physically restrained.

At the end of each session, he did not want the therapist to leave. He would state that he was going to jump out of the window (the playroom was on the third story of a brownstone). The therapist, sure that the boy would not do anything of the kind, went off to another room. Then Noah would come down to the receptionist and write letters to the therapist, telling him how much he loved him. After about a year and a half of therapy, however, the boy, as might have been anticipated, became extremely anxious about the alienation of all his classmates.

Unfortunately, Noah's mother was not cooperative in her therapy. After one or two sessions, she revealed that a physician had told her that her husband had some hereditary nervous trouble, so she had nothing to do with it. It turned out that there was also a fair amount of love play between the mother and the boy. In the afternoon she would be tired and "take a nap," which he would be invited to share, and did. When it was recommended that this practice be discontinued, she stopped therapy.

Again this case brings out the role the boy played in the family. The mother, unhappily married, wanted to play with her son instead. When this goal was interfered with, she broke off the entire relationship. In spite of everything, however, the boy did stop having bowel movements in his pants.

To some analysts the ideal solution is that where both parents and the child are in individual treatment. However, for many reasons this is rare. But no matter how difficult the circumstances of treatment, it should not be thought that no progress can be made with the child; he becomes increasingly independent as he grows older, and some children have an almost incredible ability to get past the parents' emotional difficulties (even psychosis).

A six-year-old boy was brought to the children's hospital suffering from stomachaches in 1946. The physicians could find no organic cause and referred him to a staff psychologist.

It turned out that the mother, a recent refugee from Poland, felt that Hitler's agents were after her because she was a representative of the Polish underground (a delusion). Every once in a while, she claimed, they would get to her and poison her food, at which point she would keep the food from the children for several days, then suggest to them that they had stomachaches. It was obvious that she was a full-blown paranoid schizophrenic, so she was hospitalized immediately.

The remarkable feature of the case is that in spite of her blatant psychosis, the boy was not so seriously disturbed. When asked whether he really had bellyaches, he said frankly that he did not but had said so because his mother wanted him to. The father was a mild-mannered, seemingly patient individual who gave the children the nurturance they could not get from the mother. It often suffices to have one adult person be a warm, nurturant figure to help the child grow up in the face of the worst obstacles.

Because of the problems connected with family management of the child in therapy, many therapists have turned to family therapy as a way out. There are innumerable approaches to family therapy (Green and Framo, 1981). Some are analytic, some supportive, some manipulative, some educational, some encouraging of acting out. It would take us too far afield to discuss all these various schools (wherever one turns in psychology, it seems that schools sprout up). Suffice it to say that under the proper circumstances, family therapy can be of help; often enough it can be combined with individual therapy as well. If the patient is suitable, however, the deepest changes, in my opinion, are brought about by intense individual therapy.

In principle, the therapeutic approach to children is the same as that to adults: establish a relationship (whether a classical transference or not—Sandler, Kennedy, and Tyson, 1980), uncover the dynamics, let the patient gradually become aware of what is going on, and find a resolution in terms of more mature behavior that is closer to the analytic ideal. It could safely be said that these principles govern all effective therapy, though the actual working out may vary in many different ways.

The Adolescent Boy

While treatment of the young child necessarily draws the family into the picture (though to different degrees), the adolescent has more freedom and more flexibility. It is still desirable to pull in the family, either for consultation or for psychotherapy, but adolescents are already able to make their own way to some extent. After all, adolescence itself is an invention of the twentieth century; even the term is new (after 1900). In former times, and in many other cultures today, most individuals went directly into an adult situation almost as soon as they hit puberty.

However, while adolescents are more independent, they are also more rebellious. Furthermore, they have a difficult psychological task, in that they have to distinguish between the real parents and their superego, which, after all, was derived from the real parents. It can only be expected that the therapy of the adolescent will be a stormy affair, with numerous disruptions, abrupt terminations, rebellious behavior, and the like.

For a long time analysts believed that adolescents should

not be treated at all, because of the extreme turmoil in which they find themselves. As one writer has put it, adolescence presents a normal psychosis. Others, however (Offer, 1981), present a contrary opinion, arguing that the image of severe adolescent turmoil applies only to certain deviants. Offer states (p. 129), "Throughout the ages, adults have created a 'generation gap' by systematically distorting the adolescent experience. This has clearly been a disservice to normal teenagers since distortion forestalls effective communication. But it is also a disservice to disturbed and deviant teenagers, since they are denied needed help by adults who blithely assert that adolescents are just: 'going through a stage.' Our message is simple. Teenagers are persons—persons whose feelings, thoughts and behaviors are as varied and as rich as those of adults. The portrait of the adolescent is best drawn by him/herself."

Offer's denial that the normal adolescent goes through considerable turmoil is denied by many others. But it is agreed that certain problems occur in adolescence that are not found earlier or later in the life cycle.

Laufer and Laufer (1984), in their work, stress the importance of physical maturity in the adolescent, thus reemphasizing Freud's initial point that for the first time in their life, adolescents have to deal with actual body products from their genitals, rather than fantasies. Everything depends then on the parental reaction to these body products (semen, menstrual blood). In the traditional family they were seen as sources of derision or scorn; in the more modern family they are seen as signs of healthy maturity.

Whatever attitude the adult takes toward the adolescent's physical changes, physical maturity leads in adolescents to what Laufer and Laufer call the "central masturbation fantasy"—a fantasy that usually takes some time for the adolescent to reveal. Consider, for example, one patient, whom they call Mark (p. 11), who was sixteen when he initiated treatment. His behavior during masturbation conveyed to him that he was either mad or perverted. Most often he masturbated in the nude. He liked to have his anus exposed and his buttocks very tensed. Sometimes he hit himself on the back. At other times he crawled about on the floor growling, with the pleasurable idea that somebody might enter his anus; or he masturbated in the living room while his mother was ostensibly asleep in one of the armchairs, placing himself either behind or beside her.

More typical than the fantasy cited above is that of a pirate ship full of women, or a house with a cellar full of scantily clad women. The patient who had the former fantasy, a boy who had had practically no sex education, was told by a friend when he was about ten years old that there were houses to which sailors would go. In these houses there were women lying around on couches, the friend said; men would get up on top of them. When this boy reached puberty, he went back to this fantasy of the women on couches; he was so poorly informed that he did not even know that ejaculation was supposed to take place after intercourse; he even masturbated for several months while the pleasurable sensations involved in orgasm remained incomprehensible to him; he knew only that it "felt good."

Masturbation also gives the boy a sense of power (Nydes, 1963): he can have all the women he wants; he can be a king, or emperor, or commander of pirates, and the like. Further, the erection itself and subsequent ejaculation may fill him with a sense of strength that is missing in the preadolescent boy.

Masturbation is only one aspect of the sex problem of adolescence, albeit a very important one. In the wake of the sexual revolution, it is generally estimated that sexual intercourse begins much earlier than was previously the case, especially since women have cast off many of their inhibitions. Some authorities state that three-fourths of adolescents are having sporadic, sometimes regular, intercourse. Nowadays marriage is generally delayed until the twenties, but this can exacerbate problems such as teenage pregnancy (as in the case of Kathie, cited earlier in the chapter). Intercourse carries with it various health dangers as well. Many of these, such as syphilis and gonorrhea, have long been known. But the appearance of AIDS has created a new and extraordinarily difficult problem. Advertisements for condoms have become routine, even though the condom does not offer absolute protection.

Many boys choose the alternative of "going steady" from an early age (fifteen or sixteen). But this too has its drawbacks;

for example, the boy and girl may later go off to different schools, which keeps them separated for long periods of time. There is no easy solution, so the adolescent boy just has to make the best of it—which means cope with his internal conflicts. Under the present circumstances this seems to be one of the healthiest solutions.

External conflicts also increase as the adolescent's sense of self grows; rivalry with other boys intensifies. That boys fight a lot is obvious enough, but the potential intensity of adolescent rivalry requires emphasis. In former times these fights could lead to bodily damage or even death (for example, in the duel), but the civilizing process has at least brought the violence down to a less lethal level.

Patrick, a nineteen-year-old seaman in the navy, took to walking around town with a chip on his shoulder, daring anybody to knock it off. He was a tall, husky young man, weighing over 200 pounds. But one day he came home with a black eye— he had met a man taller and stronger than he, and in the ensuing fight had gotten a black eye.

If boys do not fight directly, they identify with fighters or sports figures who fight in one manner or another. Games sublimate the wish to fight, and I scarcely need to emphasize how significant games are to the adolescent boy. In fact, if the boy in his teens does *not* engage in sports, a problem is already present.

Intellectual development also moves ahead rapidly in this age bracket. Those who go on to college and higher degrees often show enormous early intellectual ability; mathematicians, for example, frequently do much of their best work before the age of thirty. The French mathematician Galois, who solved the theory of equations, wrote down his solution the night before he was killed in a duel at the age of twenty-one. When the boy is not moving up the educational ladder, however—whether because of a lack of ability or some other cause—he loses interest in intellectual questions, falling far behind in his knowledge of the world, of history, and of other areas of enlightenment. In a recent book by Diane Ravich (1983), the author found in young people an appalling ignorance of some of the most elementary facts. For example, one-third of the students surveyed did not know what the *Brown* v. *Board of Education* decision had to do with, 75 percent did not know when Lincoln was president, and 70 percent could not identify the Magna Carta. More and better education was called for.

Primary in the boy's psyche is the question of liberation from his parents. It is in adolescence that many young men leave home to wander around the world, with little positive in mind (compare the story of James L., cited in Chapter Six, who in another generation did the same thing in his own way). Most of the time, however, the boy stays home and has to fight out the liberation battle on his own turf. Here he has to distinguish between the superego and the actual parents, often a very difficult distinction to reach.

Erik Erikson, who has written so wisely on the topic of adolescence, coined the term "psychosocial moratorium" for this phase of the boy's life. He wants a period when there are no demands (or none of any consequence), when he can enjoy himself without fear of the consequences, and when he will not be faced by too much pressure from the parents and from society. A trip around the world or to some distant place is a typical form of the psychosocial moratorium sought by young men today. One young man had decided that he would sail down rivers on rafts until he was thirty. It is in this period that many boys also resort to drugs.

Another significant development in adolescence is the attachment to groups. Human beings, like all mammals, are group creatures, and once liberated from the parents they seek out groups of their own age. Sometimes these groups are destructively inclined, and we call them gangs; at other times they represent a harmless form of socialization.

Levine (1980), in his study of the sixties, found that quite suddenly large numbers of young people began an exodus from the cities to form noncreedal rural communes. While no reliable statistics are available, various authors have estimated that approximately 3,000 communes, mostly rural, were formed between 1960 and 1970. The estimates of those who joined range from 40,000 to 80,000. Those in these communes were seeking the true goal of social life, whose realization had been thwarted by urban society. Another authority, Zablocki (1980), who also made a careful study of communes, found that the preeminent value in all these communes was love. Thus the commune was a reconstruction of the family, but one in which love was dominant.

Ralph, a fifteen-year-old, was the third of five children of a minister. Once his father caught him smoking marijuana and gave him a severe thrashing. But then the father, in his fifties, met a woman in her thirties of whom he became enamored. He left his wife and went to live with the other woman. Ralph had a severe reaction. After much soul searching, he found and joined a cult in Chicago. There he took on a new name, different dress, different habits, and an altogether new identity. Psychologically, it was clear that he had joined a new family. When his father reproached him for what he was doing, urging him to return home and finish school, Ralph replied that he was only doing what his father had done by leaving mother. The group he had joined was planning to go to India and settle there. Ralph's commitment to the group was not a matter of religious conviction, although religion played some role; it was the wish for a new world, where he could live in a different kind of family structure.

This flight of youth to cults has become a burning issue; parents often even resort to legal measures to get the child out of the cult. What they overlook is that the cult is part of the boy's search for a new identity *because the old one is much too painful.*

Erikson has also written extensively about "identity diffusion" (Erikson, 1974), the ability of adolescents to find some identity that can help them move on to a more adult way of living. The adolescent boy tries in various ways to find a new identity but often cannot be satisfied with whatever identity he has chosen—student, lover, wanderer, vagrant. Frequently in this adolescent identity confusion, the man is pulled out of his depression by identification with some older, more famous man. It is one of the ways in which the psychotherapist plays a significant role.

The example of the young William James, later to become one of America's greatest psychologists, is used by Erikson to illustrate identity diffusion. James suffered in his youth and into his manhood under severe emotional strain, for which he vainly sought the help of a variety of nerve cures. His letters attest to the fact that he was also interested in his friends' crises and that he offered them passionate advice that betrayed his own struggle for sanity.

He came to maturity quite slowly. At twenty-six he could still write, "Much would I give for a constructive passion of some kind." This is a nostalgic complaint that we find again and again among the young college men of today, epitomized in the question, Who am I?

James wandered in and out of various fields for a long time; he did not "find himself" until shortly after he turned thirty. While studying in Germany in the 1860s, he suffered a breakdown, with thoughts of suicide. When he returned home in 1868, he was still ill. He did take his M.D. degree at Harvard in 1869, but he was unable to begin practice. Between that date and 1871, he lived in a state of semi-invalidism in his father's house, doing nothing but reading and writing an occasional review. His depression and panic were relieved by the reading of Charles Renouvier, a Kantian philosopher, on free will and decision. He came to the decision that "my first act of free will shall be to believe in free will" (McDermott, 1978). From then on he could function—as a teacher, researcher, philosopher, and psychologist.

The adolescent search is brought to an end when the boy reaches a state of identity that can form the basis for the man's future life. He has found himself, often by identification with some older man, and from then on can function in a socially normal and useful way. In this process the familial environment and behavior play a dominant role.

Barry, a seventeen-year-old, originally went to his physician for help when he reached puberty and recognized that boys were giving him erections but girls were not; he sensed something wrong. The doctor sent him to a psychotherapist. An investigation of his situation revealed that he lived in a two-bedroom apartment with father, mother, and grandmother; there were no other children. But he had to share the bedroom with his grandmother, who suffered from recurrent bouts of depression so serious that she was given electric shock treatment in the home —treatment that Barry watched.

When the boy came to therapy, it was suggested to the mother that she should find an apartment in which the boy could have a room of his own. The mother quite naively asked, "How would that help him?" It was clear that his parents had little feeling for Barry's conflicts.

After a few months of therapy, Barry decided to join the army, for which he needed (and was given) his parents' permission. Once he was in the army, he had a negative reaction and wanted to come home. The mother tearfully approached the therapist, asking him to write a letter saying that the boy should not be allowed to come home; if necessary, he should be hospitalized. In this case it was quite clear that the boy was unwanted by either parent.

A different family situation was seen in the case of Tony, who came to an analyst on his own, asking "to have my personality changed." He was the older of two boys, but he also had an "adopted sister" Susan, whom the family had befriended and who spent a lot of time with them. He was seventeen; she was nineteen, and had a boyfriend. He had begun to have sexual fantasies about her, which worried him. The central masturbation fantasy came out fairly quickly: that Susan was in the next room "going all the way" with her boyfriend. Later this was tied up with fantasies about his parents. For example, at one point he took forty Librium tablets in an effort to kill himself. This was done because he could not sleep; he would pace the floor all night. This night pacing represented the adolescent boy's curiosity about his parents' sexual activities.

When mother was interviewed, she revealed that when Tony was born, she could not understand what was meant by "mother love"; for the first four months of his life, she had no feeling for him at all. Then she had another child, and a postpartum depression for which she consulted the family physician. He advised her to leave the children and go away for a while, which she did. When she came back, after a few months, she felt better but had made up her mind that she would avoid any deeper attachments to the children, fearing that they would make her sick. She herself had been deserted by her father when she was a little girl. (This is an example of the typical poor advice that does so much harm when the therapist [or physician] is insufficiently educated.)

Not surprisingly, Tony grew up rather isolated from other children. He said that he had always felt closer to father than to mother. The year before he started analytic therapy, he had fallen in love with a girl, Janey, and had wanted to have sex with her. She refused and broke off with him, leaving him feeling badly hurt. After that there was little that he did except study; he wanted to become a physicist.

When the situation was discussed with the parents, they both reacted positively. The mother joined a therapy group for her own problems; father was solicitous and cooperative. They joined together in trying to uncover the errors they had made in bringing up their children.

Once in therapy the boy moved ahead rapidly. He recognized his isolation, his fear of girls, and his fear of sports that involved physical contact with other boys. After about three years of therapy, he went away to graduate school, where he received his doctorate. About ten years after termination, in connection with some other matter, the mother sent the therapist the following letter: "To bring you up to date—Tony has married and has a three-month-old daughter. He is still at a research institute and is happy and achieving. We have been in frequent contact (even before the baby was born). I guess we all did some growing and we enjoy each other. Many thanks, again and ever."

The major and obvious differences between this and the previous case of Barry were the interest taken by the parents and their willingness to undo some of their past mistakes. Again, love moved mountains. Had the parents rejected Tony in the manner in which Barry's parents rejected him, there is no telling what would have become of him.

Thus the adolescent boy's need to free himself from his parents and his attempts to reach an independent identity of his own become the crucial questions that will determine the boy's future.

The Bachelor

The further development of the man in the family centers around his own marriage and its consequences—happy or unhappy marriage, children, divorce (when it occurs). Love (as embodied in the family) and work remain the major sources of happiness and unhappiness throughout life.

Some social scientists present alarming statistics of the terrible state that marriage is in. Yet the percentage of people who marry remained incredibly constant for a long time: from 1850 to 1860 it was 93.1 percent of men and 94.2 percent of women; from 1960 to 1970 it was 91.9 percent of men and 95.1 percent of women (Caplow and others, 1982, p. 388). However, since 1960 or so the marriage rate has been falling and the divorce rate, which had been fairly level, has accelerated its historical trend upward (Blumstein and Schwartz, 1983, p. 30). There is little knowledge of the *kinds* of marriage that existed in the 1900s and earlier, however, although the evidence points to severe strains even if the partners did not break up as often as in recent years.

The availability of women to men has always been high, so that the reasons for men not marrying have always been intrapsychic. The higher percentage of women in the population, which increases with increased age, works more of a hardship on women than men; thus in the forty-to-forty-four age group there are 141 single women to every 100 men, and if separated and divorced people are included, there are 233 unattached women for every 100 men (Blumstein and Schwartz, p. 32). Most men still marry; late in 1980 94 percent of all men aged fifty were married (Blumstein and Schwartz, p. 32). Thus if a man does not marry or marries very late (what we consider "late" varies with the social circumstances), it is pertinent to inquire what has held him back.

Orson came to therapy when he was about thirty, because he could no longer tolerate his lonely life without love. He was a scientist working at a highly abstract level, so even in his work he did not have much human contact.

His mother had died when he was born. Father, a transit

worker, then took in a woman to help him raise the boy, which he felt unable to do on his own. She devoted herself whole-heartedly to Orson. Father was so impressed by her devotion that he married her. The trouble was that both married for the sake of the boy, not because they had any great love for one another. The marriage was a cold one, what Cuber and Harroff would have called "devitalized" (see Chapter Three).

As Orson grew up, his stepmother wrapped her life around him completely. Once he reached puberty, she began to warn him about girls. She told Orson that many girls had syphilis (AIDS had not yet entered the picture, otherwise she might have brought that in, too). Because she was a nurse by background, Orson believed her. His stepmother also told Orson that girls were out to "hook" a man into marrying him and that they cared for little except money and the children that marriage could bring (reflecting, perhaps, her own life picture). Orson believed this, too.

Once an adult, Orson began to experiment a little with girls. With one whom he found attractive, he began a sexual relationship. She was willing and responsive. But once when they were having sex, she said to him, "Wouldn't this be so much nicer if we were married?" Frightened by this fulfillment of his stepmother's warnings, he immediately broke up with the girl.

Not long thereafter he consulted an analyst. The transference was almost immediately positive; Orson had found the kind, understanding father whom he had never known. Encouraged by this father-substitute, he began to experiment with other girls as well as to work out the pernicious effect of his stepmother's dire admonitions. His work went well and did not involve him in any romantic entanglements.

Toward the end of his therapy, the father had a kind of nervous breakdown and had to be hospitalized. The chief symptoms were severe depression and suicidal impulses.

It took Orson a long time to find a woman whom he could love and with whom he could find happiness. But eventually, at the age of thirty-six, he did. With their marriage the therapy could be ended.

In many ways this life history is typical of the man who

remains a bachelor until late in life. In childhood there is a strong attachment to mother, who prefers him above all else, including her husband. The parents do not get along well, he cannot marry mother, and he cannot identify with father, so a bitter battle ensues. As a result, he cannot find much purpose in living and moves around from one interest to another, or from one place to another. One is again reminded of the life history of James L. (see Chapter Six), whose sexual discontent was handled by casual affairs, while Orson's was handled by immersion in hobbies of various kinds.

One could well ask why the transference became and remained so positive in Orson's case. There was a powerful identification with the analyst, whom he saw as an omnipotent father-figure, quite unlike the beaten-down, meek, suicidal father he had known in reality. This homosexual identification with the strong father is an essential element in the growing boy's heterosexuality. If there is not a strong father, or if there is no father at all, the boy's heterosexuality will not be based on any positive identification and will accordingly be much weaker and less gratifying. Without such an identification figure, Orson would have drifted around much longer. In this way, unless analysis steps in, one generation of weak men produces another generation of weak men.

It is generally believed that psychotherapy is limited to the more affluent, better-educated part of the population. No doubt that is true as a general proposition, but the basic common sense of therapy is rapidly filtering down into those less well favored by fate or endowment. The following case is a good example.

Ted, a thirty-one-year-old postal worker, came to analysis at the suggestion of one of his friends, who said that "psychiatry helps." He was the older of two brothers; father was dead, and mother had remarried. In the first session he revealed that he drank too much; however, the drinking apparently did not interfere with his work. He drank when off duty, never while working.

Although he had left school at fifteen and could not grasp some of the psychoanalytical concepts, he turned out to be a good patient. A satisfactory working alliance was established fairly quickly. At an early stage it was agreed that one of the main goals of therapy was to help him get married; he admitted that he was afraid of girls who were too pushy or wanted him too much.

His brother was five years younger, and Ted had vivid memories of the time of his birth. When his brother was one, Ted began to bully the baby and was stopped by his parents. He was fond of his father, who "took me places and did things with me."

When the brother was born, his Aunt Sally, mother's older sister, came to live with them. She lived there from the time Ted was five until he was eight, and he slept in one bed with her. When he was eight, she married and moved out. Evidently there was quite a bit of seduction; he remembered how he had danced with her once when she was wearing nothing but a slip.

Ted was overweight and had always liked to eat too much. He had one uncle who owned a grocery store, where he had worked. On two different occasions the store had been held up at gunpoint. One of the robbers had held a gun to Ted's head, which left him terrified of ever working in such a store again. While he was dissatisfied with the post office, he was afraid to try anything else.

Ted had sex occasionally (one-night stands were the mainstay), but there were frequent fantasies of orgies and watching women dress and undress. The analysis showed that the drinking served as a defense against the sexual fantasies. He had many fears too, such as that if a woman performed fellatio on him, she would "suck him dry."

He was a prolific dreamer, and much of the therapy centered around his dreams. The split between sex and tenderness came out very soon. In one dream: "I was in love with this girl and we couldn't get together. I was shot and she was waiting for me to die." Here he felt acutely the hostility of the woman toward him.

Transference material was sparse, as is common with men from Ted's socioeconomic background (the doctor is too awesome a figure to allow familiarity). But in the twentieth session, he produced a direct transference dream: the therapist came to his house for a visit, and Ted offered him a pickle. Here his wishes to help other people came out.

Homosexual material also came out in various ways. He reported that when he was given a rectal examination by a physician, he felt squeamish and wondered how the physician felt.

After verbalizing his fears of affectionate women, and diminishing his drinking considerably, he was finally able to find a woman whom he could like and have sex with. After about three years he married and brought the therapy to an end.

In this case the various defenses against getting too close to a woman were systematically brought to light and analyzed. It was helpful that Ted was a prolific dreamer and had reasonably clear memories of his childhood. Even though he was in the beginning totally unsophisticated analytically, and even rather paranoid about the whole process ("It was like a racket"), he could produce the material and succeed at reflecting on what it meant. What came out was the sibling rivalry with his brother, the incestuous relationship with his aunt, the anger and sexual desire for mother, the homosexual play at puberty, and the sharp split between the virgin and the whore from adolescence on, which created so much anxiety that he covered it over with his drinking. The therapy had to convince him that not all women were money-grubbers out to get him, and that an exchange of mutual affection with a warm woman could in the long run be more gratifying than the one-night stands with pick-ups and prostitutes that had been the mainstays of his life before treatment.

Thus the major dynamics of Ted's bachelorhood came to the fore: a deeply felt sense of inadequacy about himself, including much castration anxiety, homosexual wishes, and a great deal of hostility toward and distrust of women. These are the factors that in general keep men bachelors, though the degree of the childhood attachments causing the "symptoms" varies from one to another. In the following vignette, similar dynamics were also apparent, but it appeared to be too late for the patient to change much.

Ulysses was forty-three when he first applied for therapy at our Center for Creative Living. He was an unemployed actor

—as the trade puts it, "between engagements." He was referred by a former roommate, who had had a spectacularly successful analysis.

The life history was horrendous. Ulysses had been taken to eastern Europe in July 1914, shortly before World War I broke out, by his mother, leaving his father in this country. (It was not a breakup, merely a visit to mother's family.)

Then war broke out, and mother and son were stuck in a little European town for seven years. They went through all the horrors of war and revolution, including pogroms. The town they were in changed nationality four times. A number of times the Cossacks rode through, trying to kill all the Jews they could find. Ulysses was a blond boy who spoke like a native; when the Cossacks rode through asking him where Jews were hidden, he said that he did not know—although he knew that his Jewish grandfather was hiding in his own home.

When mother and son came back to this country, father had remarried, having obtained an Enoch Arden divorce (that is, a divorce allowed in the unexplained absence of one spouse). Somehow this proved to be illegal, and mother had father jailed for bigamy. He succeeded in escaping to another state, one from which he could not be extradited, so Ulysses never really saw his father at all.

After Ulysses became an actor, his mother continued to support him until he was almost fifty, when she died. He did make a stab at Hollywood, where he met an older woman who was a well-known actress earning a high salary. She wanted to marry him; the only trouble was that she was given to recurrent depressions so severe that she was frequently hospitalized. He found the idea of spending the rest of his life with her intolerable.

Although he later went through various therapists, mostly young, pretty social workers, no change could be effected in his life patterns. He remained forever aloof, unattached, bound up in the horrors of his family, always making fun of himself. Had he become involved with anyone emotionally, he might well have developed more severe symptoms; the distance protected him. He remained a lifelong bachelor.

In this case what seems to have been most decisive was

the total absence of a father. If the two cases (Ted and Ulysses) are compared, the fathers are quite different. Ted's father, a cab driver, was very nice to his son, so there were many pleasant memories. Not so with Ulysses. The total absence of his father made him even more dependent than ever on the mother. He never developed any workable transference to any of the half-dozen or so therapists whom he saw. He spent his life running away from the Cossacks who had terrorized him and his relatives when he was a child.

As has been noted, the course of a man's life may be viewed as a series of interpersonal experiences, from mother to father to peers to the outside world—and eventually to women, on the basis of identification with father. If any one of these experiences is too traumatic, many problems follow. One of them is bachelorhood, the prolonged inability to commit oneself to one woman. Bill's case illustrates how bachelorhood can result from early traumatic interpersonal experiences.

There was a time when children who for one reason or another could not live at home were sent to orphan asylums. Bill was one such child. (These asylums are largely institutions of the past, because of the findings of modern psychology that a family atmosphere with some love and interest is as vital to the child as food.) The institution in question was run along quasi-military lines; the boys were even dressed in uniforms adapted from those used in the American Civil War (this was in the 1920s).

Bill was not an orphan, but he was sent to the asylum during his mother's prolonged illness. After the mother's health improved, Bill was forced to remain in the asylum for economic reasons. In his later years Bill had many fond memories of the asylum—its regime, its routines, its strict form of discipline—but there was no one person there to whom he could become attached except in a negative way. He hated with immense passion the director. When he first came to therapy, in his twenties, he swore that he would kill the director if he ever had a chance to do so, but he was deprived of the chance by the director's death; otherwise Bill might have acted on his intention.

Drafted into the army during World War II, Bill was stationed in Italy. Because of a physical disability, he remained a paramedic and did not see actual combat, but he still spent more than three years there.

While in Italy he met one woman with whom he formed a long-lasting liaison. But he could not bring himself to marry her, even though she was quite willing. It would have meant never coming back to the United States, and even though he could have managed in Italy, it seemed too risky to him.

Upon his return to this country, he found a civil service job that supported him well, with additional benefits accruing to him as a veteran. He would not return to his family, whom he hated, but went to live on his own. His father, who was a Talmudic scholar, made his living as a toilet-room attendant in one of the larger hotels, which left Bill with a deep sense of shame.

The psychological anxieties resulting from his break from his family led him to a therapist, with whom he formed a deep attachment—one that actually lasted all his life. In the course of the therapy, he met one woman with whom he fell in love. But, as in the case of Ulysses, the woman was mentally ill. A number of times she had such screaming fits that he had to call the police to calm her down; on a number of occasions, she spent brief periods in a mental hospital. Although he saw her almost every day for two years, he could not bring himself to marry her, and finally the relationship broke off.

For a long time after that, Bill cherished the fantasy of rescuing a prostitute. He would seek out prostitutes for his sexual enjoyment, then fall in love with them and try to get them out of the "life." Needless to say, it never worked. The women were always alcoholics, or drug addicts, or man-haters, or simply unreliable.

When he was in his fifties, Bill began to turn to young girls—in their early twenties or even younger. These girls found him too old, which he could not accept. He insisted on trying to form a relationship with them; they consistently refused.

In the meantime he continued the break with his family; he felt too far above them. He had many acquaintances, was a jolly fellow with a vast array of songs going back 100 years, but in any intimate situation he felt so frightened that he would break it up quickly.

When his therapist suddenly died, Bill began to seek out others; he went from one therapist to another, but none could satisfy him. His resistance took an unusual form: he believed that analysis had not yet caught up with his type of problem, so he was doomed to lead the kind of lonely life he was leading. One of his favorite amusements was to go to the public library to read, knowing no one around him, merely to assuage his terrible loneliness. After his relationship with the woman who was mentally ill, the question of marriage never came up again. He remained a lifelong bachelor.

One factor here is typical: Bill fell in love with a woman and pursued her for two years. But her mental illness was too severe. He felt rejected, even though he had done the rejecting. Thereafter he could never trust himself with a close relationship to a woman again, because he could never tell when the woman would show signs of craziness.

This history of previous rejection is typical of the bachelor. The biological urges are so strong that the vast majority of men find some girl in adolescence who arouses a feeling of love in them. If a lasting relationship does not work out with this girl, as is so often the case, the boy, later the man, feels eternally rejected. Many will not even trust themselves to seek out intimacy with another woman; these men remain bachelors. Many do try to make a marriage, but then one thing or another intervenes and the marriage turns into a source of bitterness rather than joy; the love is missing. (See the discussion of marital conflicts in Chapter Three.)

Throughout the lives of such men, if the probing goes deep enough, there is a history of rejection by women: by mother, early girlfriends, sometimes sisters, then partners in adolescent relationships. If the early traumas are too severe, the man can never again find a satisfying love.

The question is not marriage: many men marry without having any great love for their spouse (as do many women). But without love, that most essential component of the analytic ideal, they do not find happiness in marriage or in life.

8 | Social Role

IN ADDITION TO HIS FAMILY ROLE, THE MAN ALSO HAS A broader social role to play. Apart from the relationship with his wife, he has to relate to the children, he has to carve out a career for himself in business, and he has to represent the family in many other ways in the wider world. With the advent of the women's liberation movement, and the reevaluation of all family values that has been going on for the last twenty-five years, all of these components of the social role have come under intense and renewed scrutiny.

While there is much talk of a new woman created by the current upheaval in social relations, there is an equal need for a satisfactory definition of the new man (a topic that will be discussed more fully in Chapter Nine). The outlines of that definition have begun to emerge: in order to find love, a man must endeavor to find a happy marriage, with love and affection, and pleasure in his children. Men's various efforts to find happiness in the past, which emphasized success in the business (or professional) world, are inadequate without some inner affection and inner goals that are worth striving for.

Two questions are raised most often in this connection: what is the ideal role of the father in the family, and how should success and/or failure in the business world be evaluated for the man? It is these questions on which this chapter will focus.

The Role of the Father in the Family

Michael Lamb (1986), one of the foremost researchers on the father's role, writes (p. xi), "In 1975 I published a paper in which I described fathers as 'the forgotten contributors to child development.' Today, little more than a decade later, that description is clearly inappropriate." Lamb offers a relevant historical understanding of the father's role in conceptualization of the family in American history:

1. The earliest phase was one that extended from puritan times through the colonial period and into early republican times. During this lengthy period the father's role was perceived as being dominated by responsibility for moral oversight and moral teaching. By popular consensus fathers were primarily responsible for ensuring that their children grew up with an appropriate sense of values, acquired mainly from the study of religious materials such as the Bible.
2. Around the time of centralized industrialization, a shift occurred in the dominant conceptualization of the father's role. Instead of being defined in terms of moral teaching, his role came to be defined largely in terms of breadwinning, and this conceptualization of the father endured from the mid nineteenth century through the Great Depression.
3. Perhaps as a result of the Great Depression, the New Deal, and the disruption and dislocation brought about by World War II, the 1940s brought a new conceptualization of fatherhood. Although breadwinning and moral guardianship remained important, added to these was the father's function as a role model, especially for his sons.
4. Around the mid 1970s, the fourth stage was finally reached. For the first time there was widespread identification of fathers as active, nurturing, caretaking parents. Active parenting was defined as the central component of fatherhood and the yardstick by which "good fathers" might be assessed. Professional interest in the new fatherhood soon followed.

A fifth stage, which Lamb does not discuss, is under way now. People increasingly believe that the father should be able to derive some real pleasure from the various tasks of fathering, much as the mother has traditionally been expected to enjoy her role as mother—a pleasure derived from loving and being loved by his children. Again the various components of the analytic ideal must enter the whole description of the new family. It is not enough to keep the family together, as in the past; it is also essential that the various members should love one another and form a happy family. Because the man has been accustomed to deriving his greatest satisfaction from his achievements in the outer world (money, success, ambition), this notion of happy fatherhood involves the father in a new set of interpersonal ideals.

The first step toward a happier family, with the father devoting more time to duties at home, was the provision of paternity leave, an idea that first arose in Sweden but is now spreading all over the world. Minnesota has become the first state to require employers to offer parental leave to both the mother and the father of a newborn child ("Parental Leave," 1987). A federal bill with similar provisions is now (1988) before Congress, supported by representatives of at least twenty-eight states. Paternity leave as such will not produce any radical alteration in the internal dynamics of the family, of course, but at least it is a step in the right direction.

Psychological, sociological, and other research has conclusively shown that there is something radically wrong with the usual family environment in which people have been raised. What is wrong is not the family structure, but the feelings attached to it. Father was the breadwinner—and resented the hard work he had to do to support the family. In the lower classes this hard work was so unrewarding that large numbers of men simply deserted, and fatherlessness gradually became more frequent. In the United States today (Adams, Milner, and Schrepf, 1984), women head about one out of every five households. It is generally estimated that there are approximately eleven million children currently being brought up in the United States without fathers.

While the literature on father loss and father absence has burgeoned—there is no dearth of material on the harm done to the child brought up without a father—very little is said about the harm done to the father who is unable or unwilling to nurture his child/children. This inability or unwillingness comes from three sources.

First of all, most fathers have not been brought up from childhood to derive major or primary satisfaction from their children. They usually come from a family in which, as one writer puts it, "Daddy just didn't know how to make love. It was Mom who held the family together. He just went to work every day and came home and she'd have a list of sins we'd committed and he'd give us what-for about them" (Adams, Milner, and Schrepf, 1984, p. 2). Boys are not brought up to become fathers, either in our own or in other cultures. In the best extant cross-cultural study of child behavior (Whiting and Whiting, 1975), girls in six widely separated cultures were found to be more likely to be with infants and to show more nurturance generally than boys the same age, and this sex difference increased from age three to age eleven. Practically all cultures seem to have socialization practices that tend to produce such sex differences. Thus the man in our culture who attempts to get closer to his children is still more an exception than a rule. Nevertheless, it is this exception toward which mental health workers are trying to gear their clients and trying to revise the general attitudes of men.

In the second place, in the majority of divorces the mother develops such an intense hatred for the father that she makes it difficult or virtually impossible for the man to experience any great love for his children. So he takes the easier way out and simply abandons them. Psychodynamically, in most such families—which represent the majority—the woman's desire for children is greater than her love for her husband. So once she has the children, her only concern is to get rid of him and extract the greatest amount of financial support from him that she can.

And finally, the children in divorced families of this kind are caught up in a terrible dilemma. If they love father, mother will be angry; if they love mother, father will be angry. Many children take strong sides; others develop a variety of neurotic problems. Given that the number of divorces is already astronomically high and shows all signs of increasing, a new generation of neurotics is in the making.

It is here that the analytic ideal enters, not only as a guide for therapy but also as a blueprint for a different, more loving kind of society. As I have tried to show elsewhere (Fine, 1985), we live in a "hate culture," where the prevalent feeling of individuals toward one another is hatred more often than love. It is this hatred that has to be removed from family quarrels and parent-child relationships if the great epidemic of neurosis is to be overcome. It is here that the therapeutic revolution comes into play.

There is no simple formula by which the family can be reorganized. Veroff, Douvan, and Kulka (1981a) stress the change from exterior values to interior values that took place in the United States between 1957 and 1976. This change must be continued. The basic stress must be not so much on the effect on the child of the loss of father but on the absence of love in the father's life when he is isolated from the family or when he is forced back into the role of breadwinner or disciplinarian that he assumed in the past.

Carl, a thirty-five-year-old teacher, married with three children, was constantly on the verge of divorce. He and his wife had furious arguments, including physical attacks of a dangerous kind. For example, at one point she threw a heavy clock at him, almost breaking his leg.

In order to get ahead in his job, Carl began studying for a promotion examination. Unfortunately, he sought out a hypnotist to make him "remember better." The hypnosis did help him pass the examination, but it left Carl with the same serious problems in his social life.

In the meantime one of his sons had begun to stare into space for minutes at a time, which led them to take him to a neurologist for a careful checkup. All test results were normal, and the neurologist concluded that the child's symptom was psychogenic. He was left alone until they all entered family therapy.

When Carl entered individual and group therapy, he had a very positive response at first. But then his background intervened. His mother had been schizophrenic for many years, hospitalized as a hopeless case. She was so far regressed that he never even visited her, because she would not recognize him. Father had remarried.

After a period of therapy, and continued battles with his wife, Carl regressed further. He went into a paranoid episode in which he thought that people were staring at him with evil intent. This episode yielded in therapy to interpretations in terms of his wish to hurt the other people.

Obviously Carl was not being stared at as he suspected. The analytic ideal would see his suspicion as a paranoid symptom stimulated by his family troubles in much the same way that his son's staring was stimulated by the family troubles. Various materials he presented in therapy indicated that the trouble lay in his fear that his colleagues would be jealous of him for getting ahead, a feeling that might well have had some truth attached to it. In any case the interpretation that the paranoid episode was a reversal of his own hostilities had a positive effect on him, and the paranoid fears disappeared.

There then ensued a further period of regression, this one brought on by his wife's (temporary) refusal to have sex. At one point he went to a pornographic movie and masturbated in his trousers while watching the show. At home he began to masturbate more often and with more vivid fantasies. He was offered the interpretation that he wanted to regress to find his mother again, because his wife was temporarily unavailable. This too made an impression on him.

His wife also had many problems. It was suggested that they should try family therapy—father, mother, and all three boys. Carl accepted the suggestion, as did his wife. In the course of family therapy, he suddenly took much more of an interest in his sons. He wanted to know what each one was doing; he wanted to share their interests; he wanted to follow their school progress more closely.

Both parents, as a result of the family therapy, gave up their fighting and concentrated on the boys. The therapy was quite successful: after a relatively short time, the fights stopped, his son's symptom disappeared, and everybody seemed content —a happy family. Perhaps at some future time the conflicts would break out again, but of that there was no indication. It seems more likely that Carl, having acted out his fears about his mother, and his sexual fantasies, was now much more satisfied with his life. He had found his solution in a happier fatherhood, even though his relationship with his wife still left much to be desired.

It is well known that because of the harmful effects on the child of exclusive custody, joint custody in divorce is frequently a plausible solution. In some states (for example, California), joint custody has become the preferred disposition; in others it is recommended but left to the judge. In this chapter, however, we are concerned with the effects on the *father* of enforced separation from his children, a painful experience that is rarely considered in custody cases.

That men find it more difficult than women to form close friendships, especially in the later years, is a commonplace observation. If in addition the father is deprived of the love and affection of his children, his emotional difficulties multiply enormously. Reciprocity, trust, and the development of intimacy are crucial variables, yet males are socialized instead to be aggressive and dominant and to avoid intimacy (Stein, 1986). In Freud's work with the Oedipus story, the role of Oedipus's murderous father was ignored. Since Laius, the father of Oedipus, had originally put his son out to die, some have spoken of the "Laius complex" (Ross, 1979). This is described as a synthesizing metaphor for the body of hostile, destructive, and violent wishes that fathers harbor toward their offspring. Maladaptations arise when fathers give free rein to destructive aggression toward their children.

While this dominance and aggression figure strongly in the popular image of the father, there are a great many exceptions. In particular, under the impact of psychological research, there has been a strong and ongoing tendency in American society to diminish both the anger of men in general and the traditional punitive role the father was cast in in the average family. However, this considers only part of the picture. When in addition the mother in a divorce situation is highly antagonistic to the father, the father finds himself further isolated from his children. Many men, in their despair about this situation, give up on the children altogether, as was already noted. Many others, however, are willing to brave the storm, both for the sake of the children and for their own peace of mind.

Douglas, a forty-year-old college professor, is a good example of the struggles a man goes through to preserve his relationship with his children—in his case, a boy and a girl. After a long struggle with his wife, they had decided on a divorce. A seemingly amicable settlement was reached by consultation with a lawyer whom both respected. But after the agreement was reached, the wife pulled out and started an adversary action —something that is notoriously hard on both sides.

Douglas himself was the son of divorced parents. In his childhood his mother had done the same thing, but his father had responded by giving up entirely, so Douglas was brought up without knowing his father; he never saw him at all from the time he was three until he was sixteen. In the earlier years he had been filled with hatred for his father, but as he grew up his hatred diminished and he felt some sympathy for the old man who had had to live without children. The "empty-nest syndrome" applies just as much to men as it does to women.

The legal battle was violent, costly, and heartbreaking for Douglas, who had to stand by and watch his own childhood repeated. When the custody decision was finally reached, rights were given to the mother, as a matter of course, with only visitation rights granted to the father.

However, the mother would not respect the court order regarding the visitation rights. When Douglas was due to pick up the children, they would often not be there; or he would be told to come two hours earlier or three hours later than the agreed-upon time, which he could not always do. In the meantime the children went through a period of hating Douglas because he disrupted their lives to such an extent.

Douglas's own life was seriously disrupted as well. He devoted almost every weekend to the children, which interfered with his ordinary social obligations. When he saw the children, he had to spend time with their friends as well, thus interfering with his adult friendships and social contacts.

His ex-wife continued to try to "poison" the children's minds against him (*poisoning* is a legal term in these cases). She would paint him in the blackest possible light, making him entirely responsible for the breakup, describing him as a sadistic brute, frightening the children into thinking that he would beat them unmercifully, and so on. Finally her haranguing and repeated violations of the court order became so serious that she was found in contempt of court and admonished to obey the law.

While this legal intervention improved the external situation, it did not change the feelings of the children. Douglas struggled through many years of needless battles before the overt hostility of the children came to an end. But even as adults they retained a vestige of it, so that Douglas could never find the love and warmth in his children that he had hoped to. Legal decisions cannot change human feelings.

The courts today generally follow Michigan's Child Custody Act of 1970, making awards that are deemed to be in the best interests of the child. First and foremost among the designated factors to be considered are "the love, affection and other emotional ties existing between the competing parties and the child" (Slovenko, 1973, p. 370). Other factors are moral fitness, record of the child, mental and physical health, and so on. But as Slovenko says, these are all "sweeping, slippery words which say much and at the same time say nothing" (p. 371). Without a sweeping change in the feelings of the parents, custody decisions merely shift the battle from the marriage to the divorced state. Clearly the courts are aware of the hatreds engendered by a divorce situation, but they do not know how to effect a change without psychotherapy. Accordingly, it has become quite customary for a divorce to be accompanied by or followed by psychotherapy. Moynihan and Glazer (1975), who have written so extensively about the plight of the contemporary family, state that despite a generalized cultural piety about family life, the American government has been notable for a lack of social policies in support of the family as an institution.

Many families are held together, even though both parents want to split up, by the wish to safeguard the children from the ravages of divorce. This rarely works yet is often tried. Actually, the parents in these cases are protecting *themselves* against the hardships of divorce as much as they are protecting the children.

Everett, a thirty-five-year-old businessman, had an unhappy history. His parents had stayed together all their lives, but his father, suffering from a severe ulcer, had led a highly routinized life, going to work in the morning and coming back in the evening with seemingly no outlets for play or pleasure. With such a background it was understandable that Everett would decide not to repeat such a situation.

Everett was one of two children, both adopted. He never really could understand why he had been adopted, given that neither parent showed him much love or interest: the mother was home cooking and cleaning house; the father, off at the office.

Still, especially because he was a pious Catholic, he decided on marriage at an early age. Both he and his wife were virgins at the time of their marriage. Their sex life was miserable. Because of a deep sense of obligation, the couple adopted two children, also a boy and a girl. He found a business at which he could succeed.

The home life remained bad, however. There was no sexual pleasure; there was little social life; there was little love between him and his wife. Nor did he care much about the children, although he was closer to the boy than to the girl. Finally he obtained a divorce and went off to another city to make a new start. His daughter went with him.

In the new city he found another woman, much more sexual and exciting to him than his ex-wife. They were soon married, and life seemed to open up for him. But the effects of his pious childhood could not be overcome so easily. In addition, the business brought with it many headaches; it had its ups and downs. So he began to drink rather heavily, stopping off at local pubs on his way home. Naturally he met other women there, and he would occasionally have a one-night stand.

His daughter, in the meantime, had reached puberty and begun to act up in all kinds of ways, especially sexual. She said openly that she would go with any man who would take care of her; she even spoke of becoming a prostitute. When she got into trouble in school, he washed his hands of her and she went back to live with her mother.

His new wife had two children, both girls, and Everett in spite of himself developed some affection for them. But after a

while these two children, whom he adopted, were likewise experienced as a burden. Finally he entered therapy, where he began to understand himself better.

In the therapy what came out was his sense of defeat and
hopelessness about life. The only thing that had seemed to matter was money; so he had focused on the business, where he did
well. With his new wife, the drinking, running around, and
moodiness that were so characteristic of him came out again.
But having been divorced once, he was unwilling to do it again.

While this second marriage was not ideal, he did eventually stick to it. The changes created by psychotherapy were of a
minimal nature; nevertheless, there were changes. Therapy was
discontinued prematurely, however, against the advice of his
therapist.

Everett was unable to relate to any of his four children,
all of whom were adopted. His feelings for women were also
weak. The one force that held him together was his business and
his wish for some kind of secure home life. He is a good example of the traditional father whom mental health workers are
trying to change. He was basically a depressed man, a potential
alcoholic, with little affection for other people. While on the
surface he said that he stayed with his new wife to give her children a home, in reality he was afraid of another divorce because
it would leave him on his own—lonely, isolated, and with no real
social life. Though therapy was really the only way out, he left
it because it aroused too many conflicting feelings in him.

Success and Failure: The Need for Achievement

Every society prescribes certain social roles for the man.
If he does not fit into them, he becomes a rebel, an outsider, in
the grip of anomie or, in extreme cases, schizophrenia. The
choice of role from among those prescribed is always a difficult
decision. For the boy it is made easier when he can fit into his
father's shoes. The trouble is that ours is a society in which the
wish to do better than father—or at least to be different—is
paramount in most boys.

Francis, a twenty-two-year-old law student, was the son

of a lawyer. Suddenly he dropped out of law school, took to drugs, and generally went downhill. When interviewed, he said that under no circumstances would he be like his father; he did not even offer any explanation of his defiance.

The social role is molded first of all by the psychodynamic constellations within the family, and second by the social conditions that prevail. If social conditions are relatively quiescent, the family dynamics will be decisive; if they are not, the social upheaval will take precedence. Jencks and others (1979), in their extensive work on inequality, show how in our society it is quite difficult for a man to get away from his family background. They note (p. 301) that family background, test scores, and years of schooling can explain 51 to 54 percent of the observed generational variance in adult occupational status. This means that more than half of the population remains at the socioeconomic status of their families, but it still leaves almost half who can rise above it. Jencks and colleagues maintain that luck explains as much of the variation in the individuals' income as competence. Thus the American rags-to-riches fantasy does not have as much validity as many people think, though it does have some.

Psychotherapy and the Socioeconomic Struggle. One major factor governing the psychotherapist's professional actions is that the lowest socioeconomic status is the least amenable to any kind of counseling or psychotherapy. This has long been a bone of contention between Freudians and social reformers, leading those who seek a social revolution to oppose the advance of psychotherapy. There is, however, no essential reason why social reform and psychotherapy cannot go hand in hand. To advance social reform, the psychotherapist must have a clear grasp of what is involved in the social milieu.

The historian Barbara Tuchman (1966), in *The Proud Tower*, points out that in the twenty years before the outbreak of World War I in 1914, six heads of state were assassinated, not one of whom could be called a tyrant. Their deaths were the gestures of desperate or deluded men to call attention to the anarchist idea. She describes the background of these assassins as follows (p. 64):

They came from the warrens of the poor, where
hunger and dirt were king, where consumptives
coughed and the air was thick with the smell of
latrines, boiling cabbage and stale beer, where babies wailed and couples screamed in sudden quarrels, where roofs leaked and unmended windows
let in the cold blasts of winter, where privacy was
unimaginable, where men, women, grandparents
and children lived together, eating, sleeping, forni-
cating, defecating, sickening and dying in one
room, where a teakettle served as a wash boiler between meals, old boxes served as chairs, heaps of
foul straw as beds, and boards propped across two
crates as tables, where sometimes not all the children in a family could go out at one time because
there were not enough clothes to go round, where
decent families lived among drunkards, wife-beat-
ers, thieves and prostitutes, where life was a seesaw
of unemployment and endless toil, where a cigar
maker and his wife earning 13 cents an hour worked
seventeen hours a day seven days a week to support themselves and their three children, where
death was the only exit and the only extravagance
the scraped savings of a lifetime squandered on a
funeral coach with flowers and a parade of mourn-
ers to ensure against the anonymity and last igno-
miny of Potter's Field.

For the men in these lower classes, life was even grimmer
than for the women, but for neither was it pleasant—nor is it
pleasant now. Oscar Lewis (1966) uses the term "the culture of
poverty" to describe the world in which the poor live. It is not
one in which the changes that can be brought about by psychotherapy are of any great consequence.

Yet just why does therapy stumble in its dealings with
the lowest socioeconomic classes in our society? After all,
Lewis's thesis about the negative culture of poverty has been
countered with the argument that there are many cultures that
are meager in resources where the people nevertheless maintain

a happy outlook on life. This is quite true, and presumably humankind can tolerate the extremes of poverty without a psychological collapse. But when rich and poor live together side by side, as in our society, the poor understandably demand social support. Here are some typical case vignettes.

Nathaniel was a discharged veteran with a diagnosis of schizophrenia, in remission, and a 100 percent disability pension, which at that time (1949) was worth about $180 a month. He worked as a lathe operator, earning $55 a week; thus his disability was almost as much as his salary.

Two weeks after entering the service during World War II, he had had a breakdown and attacked an officer with a rifle. He was hospitalized, got better, then relapsed. In his psychotic state he had become violent, throwing food out of the window and throwing other things around. The main form of treatment for such symptoms at that time was electric shock.

After he was discharged he married, raised a family, then relapsed again and was admitted to a VA hospital. Again he recovered fairly quickly, at which point psychotherapy was recommended.

In therapy he spoke first of some physical symptoms: tension, shooting pains in the head, excessive perspiration. He also spoke of his fear of another breakdown, accompanied by readmission to the hospital.

He had a special problem in his work. As he operated his lathe, from time to time someone would come around to check on how much he was doing. This made him very nervous, especially because the inspector was a woman. The therapist recommended that when he got nervous, he should simply go home, which he did.

Talking his problems out gave him a good deal of relief. He began to feel better and take more of an interest in his wife and children, though he remained very jealous of her because all she had to do was stay home and take care of the children, while he had to sweat it out at work.

After some six months he seemed to be much improved. The therapist presented him at a case conference run by a prominent consultant, who complimented him on the good progress made.

Then the therapist left the hospital staff. Because he was just starting a private practice, he offered to see Nathaniel free of charge. Nathaniel came for a few months; then suddenly one day he said, "Where are the papers?" He was asking how the therapist was going to be compensated, so that he could report to his review board and continued his disability payments. When the therapist explained that he was treating him free of charge, he stopped therapy abruptly. If the review board heard about his free treatment, he would have been considered "cured" and his disability allowance discontinued. Obviously the disability pension was more important to Nathaniel than the "nervous" problem.

Olaf was thirty-five when he applied to the VA clinic for therapy. He was told that he suffered from bronchiectasis, a term he did not understand. All he knew was that his physician had told him that he had "nervous" problems—his only outward symptom was a delusion that a woman was shooting an arrow at his chest—and should go talk to someone. Because he was on 100 percent disability, out of work altogether, he complied.

In the service Olaf had been in the navy, serving on an aircraft carrier most of the time, and he had seen some action in the Pacific. Before the war he had been a delivery man for a milk company, going from door to door in the mornings to deliver milk. After his stint in the service, he was so terrified that he could not work.

Olaf was almost completely apathetic about life. As usual, the denial mechanism was prominent. He had no problems, his marriage was fine, and everything was going well—it was just that there was something wrong with his "nerves." This explanation he took literally, thinking that the therapist would probe into his body.

It was virtually impossible to do any talking therapy with Olaf; he would not say anything. He was seen once a month for about two years. Surprisingly, even with only this minimal effort, the delusion about the woman shooting him cleared up. Here too the disability was worth more than the illness. Had the illness cleared up, he would have lost his disability allowance, as in the previous case of Nathaniel.

Neal was a forty-year-old veteran who worked as a garbage collector. He had chest pains and stomach pains with no known organic etiology—a symptom complex common among veterans. He had a 50 percent disability.

Because of the rapid turnover of therapists at the VA hospital, he was now with his fourth therapist, who became a little ambitious and started to inquire into Neal's childhood. At this Neal flew into a rage, saying that that was no concern of the therapist's and that he would report him to the chief psychiatrist, which he did.

Shortly thereafter the therapist left, discontinuing Neal's therapy. He later learned, however, that Neal had continued to go to the hospital clinic all his life. He would go for a few months, let off some steam, then stop. Nothing had any effect on him—neither therapy nor drugs. The VA hospital became like a second, supportive mother to him, a support from which he would not be budged.

On the other hand, there are many people from poverty-stricken backgrounds who do respond to therapy, in spite of their realistic material problems. The difficulty remains, however, that someone has to pay the therapist. To counteract this problem, Dr. Edward Hornick (1974), then chief of residency training at the Albert Einstein College of Medicine, opened a novel residency training program in the ghetto of the Bronx in 1971. When fully staffed, it was designed to train a total of thirty residents annually. Therapy was free. The program aimed at closeness to community, continuity of care, and the opportunity for residents to determine their own programs. His thinking was that in such a program the problems would force the experts to find solutions rather than the experts forcing their precut solutions on the population. After three years, however, he concluded that "Tremont [the residency training program] does not know where it is going" and that "the experience for all of them was 'mind-blowing' " (p. 231). His idealistic enterprise had come to naught.

To treat the large masses of low-income patients who are knocking at the doors of the mental health professions, current recourse is to brief therapy, drugs, and group-model HMOs (health maintenance organizations) (Goldensohn, 1986). Goldensohn, director of the mental health service of HIP (New York Health Insurance Plan), recommends that all such patients work with short-term therapy programs, preferably those that are flexible. HIP has averaged fourteen sessions per patient per year, but its range has been from a single visit to ninety sessions in the course of one year. Its mental health service has a revolving-door policy, and it provides lifetime care if one monthly visit is sufficient to maintain an individual's functioning. Payment for twelve visits per year is a reasonable expenditure to treat chronic mental illness, HIP believes, especially given that studies show that other medical costs are partially offset by psychological services (Goldensohn and Fink, 1979). However, there is considerable controversy about the effectiveness of these "quick-fix" procedures.

On occasion gifted therapists come along who can handle problems that everyone else considers insoluble. Schizophrenics today are generally treated with medication, as I noted in Chapter Six; those from the lowest socioeconomic classes are regarded as virtually hopeless, with drugs or without (Tissot, 1977), so they often receive a lower standard of care. Nevertheless, Karon and Vandenbos (1981), in a project at Michigan State Hospital, treated lower-class schizophrenics with psychotherapy with remarkable results. They used three groups: patients received either (1) psychotherapy without medication, (2) psychotherapy with adjunctive medication, or (3) routine hospital treatment, consisting primarily of phenothiazines. The patients were primarily poor, inner-city (Detroit), and black. They tended not to trust authorities, particularly white authorities. Those in the groups whose treatment included therapy were given rapid psychotherapy, which included one month of intensive, five-day-per-week psychotherapy. The median number of sessions was seventy over a twenty-month period. They found that with psychotherapy alone, the patients spent less time in the hospital, functioned better, and had less of a thought disorder. They agreed with Gunderson, Carpenter, and Strauss (1977) that "the reviewed results do however suggest that a variety of psychosocial residential treatments may obviate the need for drugs, or actually render them harmful" (p. 437).

Clearly this study by Karon and Vandenbos is unique. Like Sullivan's work in the 1920s, it shows that an extraordinarily gifted therapist can accomplish results with the most seemingly impossible patients. The field of psychotherapy for the poor remains wide open for such geniuses.

Psychotherapy and the Rich and Famous. While the poor and the unknown dream of fame and wealth, those who are famous and wealthy often lead lives that are miserable in the extreme. It sometimes seems as though the fame or the wealth has gone to their heads, but if we look more closely, there is always some psychological aberration, or many aberrations, that they simply ignore. However, had such people been less famous or less wealthy, they might have had much more out of life.

One such man was Howard Hughes (1905–1976), whose life was written up by Donald Barlett and James Steele (1979) in a book appropriately entitled *Empire: The Life, Legend, and Madness of Howard Hughes.* They write that "the public life of Hughes was itself enough to ensure the spinning of a certain mythology. He was a record-setting aviator cut from a heroic mold on the Lindbergh model. His amorous adventures with some of Hollywood's leading ladies and his eccentric life style were the stuff that sold newspapers. His fabulous wealth and his reputed genius at the business of making ever-greater amounts of money only heightened public curiosity" (p. 11). Hughes surrounded himself with a curtain of secrecy all his life, to such an extent that his second wife, Jean Peters, saw her husband only by appointment. Early in life he developed a fear of germs that was so severe that he had to reorganize every place in which he lived to avoid contamination. At the end of his life, he was living in Mexico. A heart attack required a flight to Houston, the nearest big city. Had he allowed himself more time to get to the hospital, he might have been brought through the attack. Without enough time, he died on the plane.

Hughes was born in Houston, Texas, in 1905. His father had acquired rights to an important drilling bit for oil and made a fortune with it, which he passed on to Howard, his only child. The boy's early life was transient and unsettled as his father followed the oil rush from one strike to the next. Accordingly,

Hughes hardly knew his father, who was either absent or had no time for him.

Like any ordinary narcissist, Howard was excessively devoted to his mother, who presents a good example of "smother-love." She forced him to take mineral oil nightly. She watched for the slightest change in his physical condition. If she detected any abnormality she whisked him off to a doctor for an examination. During outbreaks of infectious disease, the two of them often left Houston for some distant, uncontaminated place.

Not surprisingly, he had few friends. He did not spend a night away from his mother until he was ten years old and went to camp, where he did surprisingly well. The next year he went back, but thereafter he did not repeat the experience. Mother's hold was too strong.

Howard was a rather sickly child. Then in 1919, when he was thirteen, he suddenly found himself unable to walk. A specialist from the Rockefeller Institute for Medical Research was retained to come to Houston and see him but offered no cure. Yet after more than two months in a wheelchair, Howard was able to walk again. The cause of the illness remained a mystery. At that time the possibility of a psychogenic cause did not even enter physicians' minds, but it is not implausible given the severe emotional disturbance Hughes carried through his life.

School meant little to him, and his grades were mediocre. His only major interest was golf, at which he became quite proficient. As always, he was out to be the best in the world, but could not make it.

Then came the great shocks that drove him out of boyhood: in 1922 his mother suddenly died of an operation, when she was only thirty-nine, and in 1924 his father died at fifty-four. At eighteen Hughes was a millionaire. But the aftermath of the early death of both parents was a lifelong fear of death, germs, and contamination.

In 1925, at the age of twenty, he married Ella Rice, a wealthy young debutante from the Houston area. The night before his marriage he engaged in some eccentric behavior: writing his will. For the rest of his life, he was to write and rewrite his will—which then disappeared after his death.

Immensely wealthy, with no obligations, Hughes then went to California to get into the business of movie production. Shortly thereafter his wife left him. Although the biographers have little personal data to explain why, even in the playground that was Hollywood Hughes was "self-conscious with strangers and shy with intimates." Yet the ties to his mother are evident; he never got over her and apparently never really loved any other women, although with his movie contacts he dated many famous stars, including Katharine Hepburn and Marilyn Monroe.

After some movie failures, in 1932 he went into the aircraft business. Here he had to be the test pilot himself, and he suffered four crashes, one of them near-fatal. He did set two world records, however: for a transcontinental flight in 1937 and for a round-the-world flight in 1938.

In August 1944 he had some kind of nervous breakdown and vanished, working on his will during his recuperation. Already beset with numerous food phobias, he ascribed his recovery to the consumption of large quantities of fresh-squeezed orange juice.

Much of his life was taken up with numerous unimportant fights—with Washington during the war, against the Communists, against the income tax he did not want to pay. From about 1950 he seemed to be free from all intimate relationships, dealing only with paid subordinates. Even though he married again, to Jean Peters, another Hollywood celebrity, theirs did not seem like a real marriage; they lived separately from the very first. Around 1966 he became interested in Las Vegas and bought up a substantial number of hotels there, in an apparent effort to control the entire hotel space of Las Vegas. Legal action against him followed. Thereafter Hughes was involved until his death in endless moves from one place to another, and endless litigation that served no apparent purpose. His life revolved around his litigation, his will(s), and his business deals; he seemed to have no personal life worth talking about.

What are we to make of Howard Hughes as a human being? The pampered son of a peripatetic oil millionaire and a doting mother, both of whom died young, he was left a millionaire at eighteen. He was always a loner, always something of an eccentric. The pattern of grandiosity deriving from such a parental combination is familiar to us: he had to be the best in the world at anything he undertook, thus repeating the exclusive love of his mother, which he had enjoyed in early childhood. Had he gone to psychoanalysis at an early age, he might have created fewer headlines and gossip, but he could have lived a more normal life.

What Price Success?

Our culture is particularly obsessed with success, which William James called a "bitch-goddess" 100 years ago. The situation today is no different; a recent article in one of the popular magazines wrote that all ideals other than money are outmoded. But no man ever has enough money. And so there is a constant wish to do better, to make more money, to beat out the next fellow. Whatever social level the man is at, this push is noticeably strong.

One of the greatest problems of our time, crime, has an intimate connection with the drive for success. After all, if Nixon and his crew could be guilty of such an enormous list of crimes that all went to jail except Nixon (who had the good sense to resign in time), why should the average man hesitate? Every day brings new reports of high public officials convicted of various crimes, for some of which they are punished and for many of which they are not. With our frontier ways and our upwardly mobile strivings, it is no surprise that men are driven to get ahead by fair means or foul.

Paradoxically, with such an intense drive for success, we find that most men, when seen in an intimate situation, regard themselves as failures. What success is is defined more by the surrounding environment than by the inner needs of the individual, and because somebody around is bound to have more money or to do better or to have better publicity, each man sees himself as a failure.

Preston is a good example of the price paid for success by the average man. He was twenty-seven years old when he entered therapy, the oldest of three children (the younger two were girls). He had been divorced several months earlier. As his chief complaint he voiced the feeling that there was no zest in life for him; he had no capacity to enjoy himself.

He worked as an account executive for one of the larger advertising firms. While this had worked out well, he still regretted his "failure" at his first choice—to be a golf professional. From the age of thirteen to the age of nineteen, he had spent every day on the golf course—first as a caddy, then as a player. He practiced as much as he could. But try as he would, he could not lower his score below 80 (the pros commonly shoot in the 60s). So he had to give golf up. He went instead to business school and entered the world of advertising.

His marriage, a conventional one, had covered up a sex problem: difficulty in getting erections. This problem was still with him.

His first dream in analysis already revealed his great ambition: "I'm in a bar with a bunch of fellows, sales managers. They invite me to come and have a drink. I say wait till my company goes national; then I'll see all of you." Thus instead of socializing in a friendly way with the boys, he put himself into competition with them.

Preston's father had been a police officer, the cop on the beat. What struck him particularly about his childhood was that when father came home after work, he would just flop in a chair and do nothing. At work a big powerful man; at home a helpless lump of clay—the images still stuck with him. Naturally he was never close to father.

Preston now had a girlfriend next door, a model. They got along well; like him, she too had all her feelings bottled up. They spent much time together but did not have sex, but he was not sure what sex meant to him—especially after his failed marriage.

After about a year and a half of analysis, in which he made much progress, he was offered a tempting job at double his salary in London. Although the analyst advised him to refuse, because he was doing so well in his analysis, the lure of the money was too great for him, so he accepted. At first he was excited by the new city, but after about a year he wrote despairingly,

> Well, you were right. I didn't sleep well last night and so did a lot of thinking and by morning I was thinking very clearly. . . . You were right in your prediction that I would stop growing if I went to London and abandoned analysis for a year. [Actually, the patient had been advised to continue analysis in London and had been given several names but had not followed through.] I have stopped growing completely, and it is an awful feeling. I was beginning to get an inkling of what makes me tick. Just an inkling—but it was progress. I still am aggressive in the wrong areas; I still lack contact with others; . . . I still operate well below potential because I never come out of myself to seek things out. . . . Always the desire to please others or have them accept me, which doesn't let me be myself. . . . I look forward to seeing you again in June with more enthusiasm than I ever could muster for anything else.

In standard terminology Preston had a character disorder; in the terminology of this book, he had an adjustment disorder —no obvious symptoms, but life just was not full for him. Most of all there was no real love in his life. He managed to function, but the inner fears and conflicts remained underneath the surface. Yet to convince such men that they should seek out therapy is generally awfully difficult. That more people with such conflicts are going into treatment is part of the therapeutic revolution, or the "new rules" (Yankelovich, 1981).

Helen Tartakoff (1966) has coined the term "Nobel Prize complex" for intellectuals who are constantly dissatisfied with their achievements. She comments that the therapeutic scope of psychoanalysis has gradually broadened in the past fifty years to include conditions outside the sphere of the classical neuroses. The same activism, she says, that is responsible for much of the optimism and success in this culture, and accounts for the readiness with which many Americans accept psychiatric treatment, can become a serious source of resistance in psycho-therapy. In their more extreme form, socially sponsored atti-tudes to the effect that all things are possible if one tries hard enough represent Utopian illusions, whether they be religious or scientific in content, that have a long history on the Ameri-can scene. Actually, the very success that therapy has enjoyed in this country derives in part from the American feeling that anything is possible if you just try hard enough.

Some aspects of the resistance encountered in the "nor-mal" can be seen in the training analysis. On the surface it seems to defy understanding that people who are going to be-come analysts (or therapists) should require a personal analysis before they can perform adequately. It took almost fifty years for analysts to reach this position, and now the nonanalytic schools are following along, though they do choose other mo-dalities. However, in a paper in 1971 Arnold Lazarus, a promi-nent behavior therapist who interviewed twenty other behavior therapists on where they take their troubles, found that half of them went to analysts. All recognized that they had to talk to somebody to relieve their personal distress (Gitelson, 1954).

In the doctoral programs in clinical psychology, whether of the Ph.D. or Psy.D. variety, candidates are encouraged to undertake some personal exploration, if not a full analysis. Otherwise their own personal conflicts get in the way of their therapeutic work.

A sociocultural setting that emphasizes the goal of suc-cess may perpetuate into the adult years narcissistic and omnip-otent fantasies in therapists of being the "chosen" one, the "powerful" one, and color life in a manner that complicates development or interpersonal relations. The competition for money is thus replaced by a competition for number of patients cured. The subtler kinds of progress seen in the maturation of love, or improved creativity or communication, may easily es-cape attention.

Arthur Miller's two best-known plays highlight the ef-fects of the success ethic on men. In *All My Sons* the son finds out that father had been manufacturing defective planes during the war, which resulted in the death of many soldiers. Father justifies his behavior by saying, "I did it for you." The son spurns him. And in *Death of a Salesman* the hero puts up a front of great success and popularity ("It's not enough to be liked; you've got to be *well* liked") until his façade crumbles and he commits suicide.

The average man who is dissatisfied with his own achievement in life tries to make up for it by adopting a ball team, or some other favorite group, and projecting his ambitions onto them. The executive who does achieve a great deal finds himself suffering from "executive stress," for which innumerable prescriptions and nostrums are found on the contemporary scene, from Rolfing to Zen Buddhism. It is widely recognized by now that most men simply try too hard and do not know when to call it quits and be satisfied with what they have done. No doubt this is one reason why women live longer than men; the pressures for their achievement are simply not as great.

Pressure should not be used as an argument for not achieving, however. In cultures where pressures are minimal, such as communes (Zablocki, 1980), sooner or later rivalries develop that interfere with the smooth functioning of the culture. And even among animals, which display a dominant-submissive pattern that keeps their groupings running harmoniously, numerous fights erupt. The struggle for superiority is a very real drive that pushes everybody.

But this struggle need not lead to the terrible massacres, wars, and neuroses that have been such an essential part of the history of our civilization. It is here that the analytic ideal can enter—especially with its shift from success to love—to exert a moderating influence on the evils that exist in society.

In actual therapeutic practice, therapists must form some estimate of the capabilities of the men whom they are treating. Those whose ambitions run too high have to be brought down to earth; those whose ambitions run too low have to be roused to do more.

Yet I do not wish to give the impression that either of these tasks is easy. The self-image (see Chapter Nine), the man's evaluation of where he really stands and what he can really do in life, becomes fixed fairly early and is therefore hard to change. Furthermore, the man is strongly affected by what people around him think of him or will think of him, and these factors likewise affect therapeutic outcome.

Mention should also be made of the changes in the socio-economic climate. We have been living a state of unprecedented prosperity for the past forty years (since World War II), in sharp contrast to the depressed period of the 1930s. What can be done in a climate of prosperity is different from what can be done in a climate of depression. Hence the man also has the task of evaluating the nature of the times in which he is living—again a formidable question not easy to answer. To ignore these questions in therapy is a serious mistake, for without them the therapy becomes an exercise in abstract ideas rather than real goals.

9 | Self-Image

THE SELF IS INTRINSICALLY A COMMONSENSE CONCEPT THAT IS found in all cultures, in one form or another. Even the most primitive humans have some notion of themselves as distinct from others, noting some of their own and others' characteristics (Roheim, 1932). Yet because of the domination of the religious point of view, "self" was eventually subsumed under "soul." It was the business of nineteenth-century psychology to rid science of the notion of the soul; since William James ([1890] 1950), particularly, the concept has all but disappeared in scientific discourse.

Psychoanalysis and the Self

Psychoanalysts have approached the self in different ways. Freud used the term in the simple, commonsense way, in hyphenated form: self-esteem, self-reproach, self-punishment, and the like. The American tradition emphasized the self more than the European, partly because of linguistic differences, partly because of differences in philosophical attitudes. All the American thinkers have stressed that the self begins and continues in contact with other selves. Cooley formulated this in his term "the looking-glass self," Mead in his "generalized other," James in his "social self." By contrast, the German tradition led to such concepts as Jung's "superordinate self," Husserl's "being," Heidegger's "Dasein" (being here), Hegel's earlier "self-consciousness" (really equivalent to Freud's notion of primary narcissism). It was obvious that the American tradition went back to the *tabula rasa* (empty tablet) of John Locke, while the Germanic relied on the independent monads and their preestablished harmony, as postulated by Leibnitz. It was also clear that all these thinkers had something to offer.

Although psychology, following William James in the famous tenth chapter of his *Principles of Psychology* ([1890] 1950), had always studied the self empirically, the more orthodox Freudian school did not begin to discuss the self until the period after World War II, when the center of psychoanalytic thought was transported to the United States. James offered the simplest definition of self: "In its widest possible sense, however, a man's *self* is the sum total of all that he can call his" (p. 291). The definition given in the glossary of the American Psychoanalytic Association (Moore and Fine, 1968) is essentially the same: "The total person of an individual in *reality* including his body and psychic organization; one's 'own person' as contrasted with 'other persons' and objects outside one's self" (p. 88).

In the period after World War II, an entirely different approach was taken by Heinz Kohut (1971, 1977). His position quickly grew into a movement—some said dominated as usual by a charismatic leader. Like the bandwagon effect around other prominent analysts (for example, Kernberg—see Calef and Weinshel, 1979), sharp polarization and numerous contradictory arguments grew out of his movement. A Society for Self Psychology was formed. In essence, however, Kohut does not differ too much from other theorists (Rangell, 1982; Wallerstein, 1981). Kohut's main concept is what he calls the "selfobject," by which he means the inability to see oneself as an independent entity. This is much the same as the more usual psychoanalytic concepts of transference and projection.

In practice, the self can be dissected, analyzed, and changed without reference to arcane theories. At the beginning of analysis, the analyst may say to the patient, "Tell me the story of your life; make believe that you are writing your autobiography." All patients will understand that they are expected to give all the particulars of what they have lived through, together with their free associations, thoughts, memories, dreams, and so on (see Chapter Two).

Anna Robeson Burr (1909) describes three great archetypes of autobiography: the writings of Julius Caesar, St. Augustine, and Jerome Cardan. No one of these is strictly autobiographical in the modern vein, yet each presents a certain model that therapy patients also follow.

Caesar's famous comment *"Veni vidi vici"* ("I came; I saw; I conquered") sums up his presentation of himself. He is going to tell the world of his exploits. Augustine, on the other hand, studied himself for the glory of God. He began with the story of his sins, continued with the tale of his conversion, and concluded with an ode to the almighty ruler of the universe. His autobiography could be summed up: I sinned (especially sexually), I saw the light, and I glory in the eternal forgiveness of God. In fact, the confessions of Alcoholics Anonymous and similar groups follow in this path: I was wicked (drank too much), I converted, and I glory in the AA.

Jerome Cardan (1501–1576), although unknown to the general public, in his *Book of My Own Life* ([1575] 1930) had a far-reaching influence. Cardan was mainly concerned with describing himself. He wrote, "Speech shrill—if one may trust to the reproaches of those who profess to be my friends—and yet cannot be heard when I lecture. My gaze is fixed, as one who meditates, my color red and white, my face an oblong, though not large, my upper teeth larger than the lower" (Burr, 1909, p. 102). Yet toward the end he confesses his true passion: "Therefore it is no wonder that, thus compelled, I burned with the love of fame; rather is it a marvel; that notwithstanding these reasons this strong desire persists" (p. 114).

The Unconscious Self

What psychoanalysis had added to the traditional notion of self is the idea of the unconscious and the developmental points of view. No one is fully aware of all aspects of self. Those analysts who have been most concerned with psychosis have contributed heavily to the theory of the self, because in psychosis it is clear that patients are totally *un*aware of what they are doing. Yet this is also partially true of the average person: of some of our traits we are aware; of others we are not. Nor are neurotics in touch with their whole history (development), though more so than the psychotic.

The psychoanalytic process explores the person's image of him- or herself in the minutest detail. This involves tracing one's development as fully as possible, making the unconscious conscious, and reflecting on the many different ways in which the individual judges or misjudges oneself. For self-observation is never neutral: it always involves some evaluation of self as either good or bad. This is one of the factors that lead to so much resistance in therapy; even an innocuous comment such as, "You're two minutes late," on the part of the analyst can have momentous repercussions. It is because their words are so heavily invested with all kinds of meanings by the patient that analysts choose the path of saying less than directive therapists.

The conscious and unconscious aspects of being have also been formulated as the *true* self and the *false* self—the self that is presented to the world and the self that is concealed behind the mask. The word *personality* derives from the Latin *persona*, which means "mask." Eugene O'Neill wrote a play once in which the characters wore masks, showing themselves sometimes with the mask on and other times with the mask off (*The Great God Brown*). O'Neill was one of the first American writers to value the contributions of Freud; in his plays he gave eloquent expression to many basic psychoanalytic ideas.

The traditional self-image of the average American man can be described as macho, hypersexual, highly rational, much more important than women, a member of the greatest nation on earth, and psychiatrically "normal" (in his own eyes); he brooks no put-downs, restrains feelings, heads the family, plays a leading role in society, works to make money for early retirement (where he will not have to do anything except perhaps fish and hunt), avoids communication, and views creativity as "sissy" stuff. While this image is changing rapidly, and was never true of all American men, it still plays a dominant role in the thinking of the average male patient. In presenting himself to the analyst, like the three autobiographers mentioned above he is presenting an image of what he would *like* to be—what Sulli-

van calls "the personified person I." In analysis he has a chance
to compare this image with the reality of life; he has to "drop
the mask," as Eidelberg (1949) puts it in a book of case histories (*Take Off Your Mask*).

The various aspects of the self are not perceived clearly
by the man. Making the unconscious conscious is still the essence of the working-through process, which deals at one stage
or another with everything in the man's life. Even at the most
superficial level, men are often unaware of what they are doing
or of what is going on in them.

Almost two hundred years ago, the poet Robert Burns
expressed the same idea when he wrote, "O wad som Pow'r the
giftie gie us To see ourselves as others see us! It wad frae many a
blunder free us, And foolish notion" (from "To a Louse").

The historian Warren Sussman (1984) relates that at one
time he did some oral history, interviewing Americans who lived
in France between the two world wars. He soon discovered that
frequently they knew less about their lives than he did from
reading other sources. He realized that they could not tell him
what had happened to them. What they called their memories
were actually recollections of what had appeared in the papers
about American expatriates. Much of their reconstruction of
the past was definitely incorrect, as he could ascertain from
what he knew about them. As I have mentioned, one reason
why men cannot see themselves as clearly as others can is that
any self-description is at the same time a sign of approval or disapproval (superego pressure).

In 1899 an American writer, Orison Sweet Marden, published the book *Character: The Greatest Thing in the World.*
Embodying the American images of that time, it was one of the
most popular books of the day. He described a true Christian
gentleman as being pure, upright, intelligent, strong, and brave;
possessing a sense of duty and having benevolence, moral cour-
age, personal integrity, and "the highest kinship of soul." It is,
of course, hardly possible to live up to these exalted demands;
consequently, every man distorts the record of what went on
in his life.

Development of the Self-Image

In the developmental process, the growth of the self-image can be traced in the minutest detail. Current research has concentrated heavily on this topic; we know now that formation of the self-image begins early in the period often called "unrememberable and unforgettable" (the first eighteen months) and continues to change throughout life. Even as he approaches death, the man is concerned with what people will say about him after he is gone.

Sometimes the self-image is the result of a broad variety of factors in the family; sometimes it results almost directly from competition with the father. In an achieving society such as ours (McClelland, 1961), where men are openly judged by the amount of money or prestige acquired, the average man feels like a failure, as I have noted. No matter how successful he is, there is always the fear that someone else has done better. Freud himself knew a similar fear. In his earlier years he was highly subservient to many of his teachers, particularly Breuer and Fliess. The history of psychoanalysis has been distorted because he gave too much credit to Breuer, too little to himself. As for Fliess, Freud was taken in by his bizarre theories to an unbelievable extent—believing, for example, the notion that our lives are all dominated by periods of twenty-three days (men) and twenty-eight days (women) (Fine, 1979b; Jones, 1953, 1955, 1957).

Even the most brilliant men, acclaimed as geniuses by their contemporaries, often feel like failures inside. Norbert Wiener, the famous mathematician, is a good example. Norbert was the son of a Harvard professor of Slavic languages who early recognized his son's genius and supervised his educational program from the first. The boy was reading Dante and Darwin at the age of seven, graduated from Tufts College at fourteen, and took his Ph.D. in philosophy at Harvard at eighteen. In 1919 he joined the Department of Mathematics at MIT, where he remained until his death in 1964.

In his frank autobiography, published in 1956 (Wiener,

1956), he describes the enormous influence that his father had on him: "As I gradually acquired a limited amount—a very limited amount—of independence from my father, I found that the dawning freedom of approaching manhood was largely a freedom to make mistakes and know failure. Yet even this joyful freedom was limited by my father's proneness to make sudden decisions affecting my whole future which bound me as much as if these decisions had been my own" (p. 21).

Wiener's father was also a brilliant and neurotic man. He had left Germany to engage in a nebulous scheme for founding a humanitarian vegetarian colony somewhere in Central America. Finally, by a roundabout route, he returned to linguistics. Without a higher degree he was appointed professor of Slavic languages at Harvard. But as his son describes him, he remained throughout life a disappointed and unhappy man. At one time he set himself the task of translating all of Tolstoy in two years, which led to a nervous breakdown.

Wiener himself is known to have had a number of breakdowns in his life, some of the details of which he lets filter through in his autobiography. He says (p. 118) that it was no pleasure for his wife to be involved with him, because he was a severe problem and his parents had glossed over all of his emotional difficulties.

Later he gives some particulars of his various analyses. Evidently he wanted to discuss creativity and literature with his analyst, who would rather talk about Wiener's personal problems. This he regarded as a demand to "submit." He left his first therapist with a deep feeling of having been misunderstood and misrepresented. He resorts to the conventional attack that "I never have valued contentment and even happiness as the prime objects of my life, and I began to fear that one of the aims of the conventional psychoanalyst was to remake his patient into a contented cow" (p. 214).

Clearly Wiener's father had set himself an impossible goal in life, which made him feel depressed and bitter, while Norbert had done the same thing. In spite of the fact that Norbert had done so much in life, he had not lived up to his father's deathbed demand that he become as great as Gauss (known as the "prince of mathematicians"). Other problems of a personal nature filter throughout his story. He is a good example of the theory that the self-image of a man depends on the unconscious ideals that he has set for himself, not on his real-life achievements. This ideal in turn goes back to the rivalry with father.

In the case of Sheldon, a twelve-year-old boy, the rivalry was quite open. He would take his father to an imaginary court for various crimes and misdemeanors, acting as both judge and jury. Naturally father would always be found guilty and have to submit to suitable punishment.

This intense rivalry isolated him from other boys and girls and accentuated Sheldon's rivalry with them. At one point he received a grade average of 97.223 percent but was terribly disconcerted to find that a girl in his class had attained a grade average .003 percent higher; he could not claim to be the brightest in his class.

Changing the Self-Image

While it is easy enough to locate the roots of the self-image in the family structure, in the social surround, and in the internal projections and introjections, it is far from easy to *change* this self-image, even with the most intense psychotherapy. The following case is cited to show how this process of change works. The various components of change will be delineated from one another; the activity of the patient and the activity of the analyst will be kept separate.

Establishment of the Relationship. Richard was a thirty-five-year-old man who came to analysis because he was constantly anxious, especially when he heard loud noises. One aspect of his fear of noises related to barking dogs; if he came near one he would become petrified. Because of this fear he had moved around frequently. (Later in the analysis he had his hearing tested, and it was hyperacute.) Through the years he had visited no fewer than eight neurologists, none of whom could find anything wrong with him. All treated him with medication, however. One rather naively asked him, "You're not suicidal, are you? If you are, I won't give you this medicine."

Finally he decided to seek out an analyst whom he knew by general reputation. When he began, he had no clear idea of what analysis entailed; he just wanted to get better.

As usual, he began by relating the essentials of his life history. The only son of an Italian immigrant, he had always done poorly in school, in spite of his high intelligence. He was never really very interested in studying and never really worked hard at it. However, after the war (World War II) his standing had improved noticeably: he had a good job with one of the *Fortune* 500 companies.

When he started analysis, father and mother were both still alive; he was an only child. But it was never very clear what his father did or had done to make a living. At one time he worked for an insurance company and was seemingly well off, but then in his forties he started a downhill road. When the treatment started, Richard described his father as a "finder": somehow he was supposed to find business deals, put them together, and make a commission. Only no business deals ever emerged. The parents lived on a very modest scale and never seemed to do anything with their lives.

In college Richard was afraid that he had made a girl pregnant (although she was not really pregnant), so he married her. A few months later the marriage was annulled. Richard was brought up a Roman Catholic and adhered to Catholicism's principles for a long time, so guilt was an essential part of his self-image.

Then came a second marriage, which was quite painful. His wife was pretty and alluring, but after marriage she became increasingly difficult. Even though he was already in his early thirties, he struggled with the idea of seeking a divorce because of his Catholic background. So he went to his mother and asked her for permission to get divorced. She allowed him to do so.

While he was married to his second wife, he began a sexual affair with a woman in his office, who pleased him in many ways. After his divorce they married and had three children. In all respects his third marriage seemed a happy one. What remained was his guilt and anxiety, which he was unable to overcome on his own.

The analysis began with a long analytic honeymoon and a strong positive transference. Father he described as a ne'er-do-well; mother, as a woman filled with senseless suspicion. She chased all Richard's friends away and would not allow him to go out with girls—which he did anyway, but surreptitiously. In the third session he reported a sudden new memory from childhood: waking up with his father's penis between his legs; there were no more details.

It often appears strange to persons not analytically trained that much could result when the analyst is relatively silent. Yet progress results over and over again. In the present case the analyst's silence allowed Richard to reveal all kinds of memories, while in contrast the neurologists' uniform prescription of medication had kept him tied to his childhood experiences. The analyst need do no more at this stage than wait for the transference to develop, and here it developed in a very positive manner.

In this early stage much came through about Richard's self-image. He was a successful businessman, yet he was dissatisfied with his achievement and constantly strove for more prestige and more money. He still felt guilt about his sexual "misdeeds" with his first and second wives. He loved his children but was rather distant from them. In essence, he was an upward-striving, competitive man whose major goal was to get ahead as far as he could. It was this self-image that eventually became the essence of the working-through process.

Hidden Fears and Memories. Richard's fear of dogs was traced back to sexual play with his dog while he was a child. At first he would play with the dog's penis. Later, when he reached puberty, he had the dog lick his penis. At that time he also had some homosexual play with other boys. He expressed the fear that analysis might reveal that he was a homosexual. In childhood he had been given the nickname of a girl, and he was already then afraid that he might become a homosexual. Thus another aspect of his self-image came to the fore: questions about his masculinity.

In spite of the fact that his present marriage was a happy one, his first dream in analysis brought out his suspicion of his wife: "I'm married to Sally; we have three children. I catch her with the family doctor; she's unfaithful to me. She says, 'It's because you've been out playing tennis.' " Thus there emerged another aspect of his self-image: the fear that his wife would find another man more attractive. The dream helped to clarify his fear of women.

The release of memories brought him considerable relief. One of his pet fantasies was that he would march up and down Broadway with a sign, like a sandwich man, advertising the services of the analyst.

First Resistances. After this extremely positive period, some resistances appeared. "I'm in the analyst's office; he demands money from me, because he has to pay his bills." Then again: "I'm in the analyst's office. There are several women there. The analyst dismisses me."

At this point he also revealed that while he had been a heavy drinker before analysis, once he started he had taken a vow that he would never have a drink during the analysis. He had bought a bottle of Scotch, which he was saving to share with the analyst when they had finished.

Other disturbing fantasies emerged. He suddenly acquired the fear that his wife was a lesbian, and recalled that his mother had accused her sister of being a lesbian. A relevant memory was that when he had started masturbating in puberty, he was afraid that he would be overheard by his mother. Then some anger toward women came out. In one dream: "There's a white angel hovering overhead. I shoot her in the nipple; blood comes out." In another dream one of his daughters was badly cut. Then he dreamed that he and the analyst were walking in the country. Thus the strong transference covered over hostilities to women.

The Working-Through Process. The analysis went along in this working-through process for a long time. The themes were repetitive and revealed more of his self-image: his wife's imaginary infidelity, hostility to his children (resentment of being a father), a wish to get closer to the analyst (whom he at one point identified as Dr. Freud), homosexuality, passivity, complaints about working too hard, feelings of being criticized, dissatisfaction with his place in life.

The Symptom Remains; More Resistance. In spite of the positive transference and the new insights acquired almost with each session, Richard's anxiety did not go away. This led to a new pattern of hostility—toward the analyst, toward his wife, and toward his children. Usually he was very sarcastic during the sessions, often making fun of the analyst and of analysis. He also brought more of his identification with the dog and more of the wish to be a child. In one joke he related, a man calls a theatrical agent to seek work. "Do I want to hire you?" the agent asks. "Okay, what do you do?" "I talk." "What's so unusual about that?" "I'm a dog."

This was followed by a direct homosexual dream, which included the wish of beating up his wife as well. Another facet of the self-image thus appeared here: underneath his business success, Richard still wanted to be a little boy who, like a dog, could run around with no obligations.

Around this time a major national magazine ran a piece attacking psychoanalysis by a psychologist, a professor in a midwestern university. (Similar attacks on psychoanalysis occur all the time.) The patient wrote the journal a letter in response, which was printed. He said, "Those who are better informed [than the psychology professor] know that psychoanalysis is the process of a patient probing his own mind for a greater self-understanding with the help of a trained psychoanalyst. . . . What modern psychoanalysis recommends is greater love of children and a distinctly firm discipline tempered with understanding."

One of Richard's real fears was that he would not be able to make a speech. Although he had no real occasion to make speeches, he was terrified. Typically, he tackled the fear: he took a course with Dale Carnegie on how to speak in public. He passed this course at the top of his class, but that experience did not have the slightest effect on his fear of speeches.

In this process of working through resistance, Richard tried to expand in a number of directions. He had many hobbies

—tennis, fishing, and the like. But he also wanted to establish a part-time business, and he now made many efforts in that direction. His wife was of considerable help. Clearly his self-image would not be given a good grade unless he set himself up in a more lucrative business, although his income was already high. He felt that he had not achieved enough, even though in the eyes of the world he had done a great deal. In fact, he was being promoted on the job at such a rate that it became burdensome; he simply did not want to work so hard. With such overinvolvement, it was suggested that a group could be helpful to him, although the major resistance and the major guilt feelings attached to his functioning had still not come out.

The Group Experience. In the group Richard related well. Shortly after he started he began to have an affair with one of the women in the group, an unhappily married woman some fifteen years his junior. The affair elicited a great deal of guilt. It also brought back his childhood identification with Jesus, which was so conscious that for a while he had wanted to become a priest.

Yet with all his successes, the anxieties persisted. He decided to consult Dr. Lawrence Kubie, a well-known analyst, then head of a hospital in Baltimore. Kubie felt that while Richard had made great progress, he had reached a plateau. His main recommendation, one that he had espoused in general in a number of papers, was that Richard should switch to another analyst, although he might try a retreat first.

Richard did not accept Kubie's recommendation. Instead, he decided to retire and go into a service profession. He felt that he had been running around in circles by starting one business after another when he would already have enough money to live on comfortably if he took the generous retirement package his company offered.

At this point he reported that many of the top executives in his company had taken similar routes. One became a priest; another, a counselor for alcoholics. For men in their fifties and sixties, the relentless grind of business was often unsatisfying.

Richard himself turned to social work. Even though he was already in his early sixties, he was accepted into a school.

When last contacted, he was active as a social worker and very happy in his new life. "I have had a large emotional experience and it has been extremely revelatory. . . . I feel that I have found a sense of values in life I never knew existed. I even begin to experience a feeling of peace instead of the restlessness of which I have always been possessed."

This case has been presented at some length to show how the self-image can be changed. In the beginning Richard was an anxious, hard-striving, successful businessman, full of anxieties and guilt feelings; underneath, he was very suspicious of women, sometimes to the point of paranoia, and troubled by activities in the past (such as his first two marriages) that still made him feel guilty. In spite of all his worldly success, he yearned for a quiet, noncompetitive life in which he could help people rather than beat them out all the time. His view of his life and his human relationships, as well as his view of himself, had all undergone dramatic changes by the end of therapy.

Vincent, a forty-two-year-old electrical engineer, came to therapy in a state of near-panic: he was afraid of losing his job and thought he might be going out of his mind.

Childhood he remembered as horrible. The younger of two siblings, he was only one year old when his father died. Mother had never remarried. The children were brought up on welfare supplemented by gifts from charitable agencies. An uncle who had a store was not good to them.

About ten years before coming to treatment, Vincent had had a breakdown, with consequent hospitalization. Although he was hospitalized for nine months, there was no after-care. The details of this hospitalization he would never reveal. After several months of therapy, he revealed that his sister had also been hospitalized a few years before.

All his life he had been a frightened, insecure boy, feeling inadequate in his work life and fearful of responsibility. This self-image was contradicted by much of his life history: he had a degree in engineering and was married, with two children. He was always reticent about his sex life—it was "private" and "good"; however, at one point he admitted being afraid to kiss his wife's vagina. Otherwise everything was handled by denials;

in particular he denied any connection between his sexual difficulties and his breakdown, as well as any connection between
childhood and the present.

He had been anxious all his life. In defense he had worked
out a routine for keeping busy, which no longer was effective.
Part of his anxiety was a terrible sense of isolation from the
other workers in his plant, which led him to say that as a boy
he had felt great solitude. When he went to parties as an adolescent, he would feel terribly out of place because he could not
match the humor of the other fellows. He had married young
and was still a rather solitary person, relying chiefly on his wife
for any kind of social contact.

Vincent accepted therapy at two sessions per week, con-
tinuing for two years. At the beginning he had been on sleep
medication, which he was able to discontinue after a short time.
In spite of his negative attitude to therapy, a transference improvement made itself felt very quickly.

In his self-awareness Vincent felt threatened by every
other human being except his wife. The therapy centered around
this feeling of threat. He produced no dreams and relatively little fantasy material. Mostly he wanted to talk his fears out, to
get some reassurance that he was all right. The transference,
though on the whole positive, remained ambivalent throughout.

In spite of the minimal material produced, he felt much
better, was able to work and feel less threatened. While he cannot be said to have grasped the basic interpretations offered, the
whole experience seems to have been of great benefit to him.

The reader may be surprised at the paucity of material
produced by this patient. Such surprise rests on a common mis-
conception of psychotherapy: that the therapist can force the
patient to produce material even if unconscious resistances are
great. On the contrary, *in psychotherapy it is the patient who
plays the major role.* With Vincent there was no dream material
and almost no childhood material, he refused to talk about sex
in any but the most general terms, and he was by and large only
too eager to escape from treatment. In spite of all this, he seems
to have lost much of his anxiety, functioning at a considerably
higher level at termination than when he started. Again we are

up against the problem of evaluating the outcome of therapy; in my opinion such an evaluation can be meaningful only if it is based on careful clinical investigation, which invalidates many of the statistical studies that are so widely quoted (Smith, Glass, and Miller, 1980).

Even though therapy is guided by the various components of the analytic ideal, in practice the therapist has to deal with what is important to the patient. Many times the traditional conflicts surrounding incest and the Oedipal situation are so prominent that they force themselves into the therapy. Such a case was the following.

The most prominent resistance in the analysis of Zachary was the fact that he came ten minutes late all the time. He worked as a repair person on a special machine, available on call from 6 P.M. to midnight. After work he would stay up half the night talking to friends. He very much wanted to become a teacher of literature, for which he was enrolled in graduate work, but so far it had been hard sledding.

The background of his late-coming was soon traced to a total feeling of discouragement about the possibility that analysis would help him. This in turn was a reflection of his childhood in Cuba. He was the son of an American army officer and a Cuban woman. Father had disappeared after he got mother pregnant; Zachary was told that his father had drowned.

As he described it, his mother must have been a prostitute; she would take Zachary with her to visit different men, staying with them all night while he slept in another room. He described her as very seductive, walking around half-dressed or sometimes completely nude. As a child he had formed the fantasy that someday he would go to America, where he perceived a much higher level of morality, to tell them what his mother had done. Mother had relatives in the United States. When Zachary was thirteen, he was sent to them to go to school, where he did quite well.

His present job required a great deal of skill. Sexually he was quite competent, but he was terrified at night. What came out in terms of self-awareness was that he slept with a knife under his pillow, ready to stab any man who attacked him. It was not plausible that he should be attacked; the fear related to his childhood. Clearly he had wanted to attack many of the men with whom his mother slept, and had been afraid that they would attack him.

His first dream was clearly connected with his Oedipal conflict: "I'm playing with trains on 125th Street or Grand Central. I push the trains into the tunnel, then pull back; otherwise I'll be killed. Suddenly my right arm is torn off. . . . Out on the platform I see the torn-up bodies of a lot of young men."

The push into the tunnel was a symbol for incest with the seductive mother; the punishment was castration (arm torn off). After Zachary's rage was brought to the surface, it was thoroughly analyzed in terms of his wish for mother and regrets about the abandonment by father. Eventually he made an excellent adjustment. I have noticed that many times people who have had near-incestuous experiences as children develop serious problems but have the capacity to come out of them into a fairly good social adjustment.

Societally Induced Changes in the Self-Image

Political revolutions have visible signposts: the storming of the Bastille in the French Revolution, the shots at Bunker Hill in the American Revolution, the attack on the Winter Palace in the Russian Revolution, and so on. Social revolutions cannot be pinned down so precisely. Yet there is no doubt that we have gone through almost a continuous social revolution since 1900, and are still in the throes of one. When social revolutions take place, the self-image, which is in considerable measure a reflection of the surrounding society, also changes. Our therapeutic efforts must take account of these changes if those efforts are to have any meaning for the people who come to us.

In 1957 Congress established a Joint Commission on Mental Illness and Health to evaluate "national resources of coping with the human and economic problems of mental illness" (Veroff, Douvan, and Kulka, 1981a, p. 3). The commission staff, recognizing at the outset "that no nationwide information was available on what the American people themselves think of their mental health" (1981a, p. 3), asked the Survey Research Center at the University of Michigan to design and conduct an interview survey with a sample of 2,500 "normal" adults in order to obtain such information. The results of this study have been reported many times; the best source is in the two volumes by Veroff, Douvan, and Kulka, *The Inner American* and *Mental Health in America* (1981a, 1981b). The first part of the study was done in 1957; the second, in 1976. Thus it offered an unequalled opportunity to compare Americans at two points in time.

In general, the major change that was revealed was a shift from external to internal values. In particular, the authors list as major findings:

1. There is increased concern about an uncertain future.
2. There has been a movement from social to personal integration of well-being.
3. There has been an increase in the psychological approach to understanding one's own behavior.
4. Above all, there has been an increased emphasis on interpersonal intimacy as opposed to social organization as a means of integration.

Yankelovich (1974) lists five similar changes in moral values: (1) changes in sexual morality; (2) changes relating to the authority of institutions, in the direction of "deauthorization"; (3) changes in relation to the church and organized religion as a source of guidance for moral behavior; (4) changes associated with traditional concepts of patriotism, automatic allegiance, and the idea of "my country right or wrong"; and (5), particularly noteworthy, changes from the emphasis on money and economic success to self-fulfillment.

Other authors have reached similar conclusions, though with varying emphases (Yankelovich, 1981; Canciano, 1987; Bellah and others, 1985; Blumstein and Schwartz, 1983; and many others). In all the reported societal changes, the role of the man has undergone a number of notable shifts. Mainly, there has been an increased emphasis on sharing, intimacy, love, affec-

tion, warmth, and other aspects of the analytic ideal, and a
turning away from violence, distance, conquest, and regulation
of social life by formal arrangements (for example, the widespread substitution of live-in relationships for formal marriages).

Although these lists do not use the term *analytic ideal,*
they come very close to its various components. There is first of
all the shift from violence to love as a primary value. It is important to note that in virtually all surveys about values, love ranks
first, with self-fulfillment a close second (Canciano, 1987). Even
though love is ranked as a primary value by almost all people,
its meaning is very unclear. Much of psychotherapy, as has been
seen, is concerned with the clarification of what love is. Yet
agreement is increasingly universal that violence, love's antithe-
sis, is to be abhorred, to be treated by psychotherapy. This is in
one sense the most important single shift going on.

Evidence of this shift can be seen in Joshua, a writer, who
went into a bakery to order some cakes. When the attendant
was slow in waiting on him, he angrily swept all the cakes on
the counter to the ground, breaking a number of them. Although
he had had other reasons for going to therapy, this incident
made up his mind for him.

The trend against violence is increasingly strong, at least
in the United States and other Western democracies. Aggression
and violence are now characteristic of the far right, by and large
a minority. In spite of many local conflicts, the world at large
has been free from the catastrophic interactions that reached a
height in World War II.

Traditionally, the man defended himself in terms of his
capacity to fight. To "show the yellow feather," either as an individual or as a nation, was utterly disgraceful. That is still the
case with some individuals and peoples; there are many countries in the world that obviously do not share the new ethic of
peaceful rather than violent measures. A tug of war ensues in
the democracies—the same kind of split of the ego that Freud
noted after World War I: in the democracies the peacetime ego
is taught to abhor violence; then war comes and a total shift
must take place in people's minds. Obviously we are still far
from a lasting universal peace. But the findings of this chapter

indicate that the man must seek a different definition of masculinity than has been used before.

Changes in sexual morality are by now fairly well accepted. It is generally agreed that women are entitled to sexual satisfaction as well as men and that sexual gratification is a personal value that each person, male or female, is free to pursue in his or her own way. Even the paradoxical defense of homosexuality by the three major mental health organizations derives more from this wish to be equal than from any careful study of the total psychology of the person who chooses a homosexual way of life. The man's self-image is quite different from what it was before, and much more insistence is placed on his being able to satisfy the woman.

A greater emphasis on inner values goes along with the shift from the social role to the self. "Who am I?" The famous question on so many lips can be answered only in terms of inner values, not in terms of external achievements.

The move away from religion and blind reliance on all authority has been going on since the French Revolution. In the United States it was undoubtedly accentuated by the Vietnam War, which seemed to run counter to all American principles of fairness, and by the scandalous criminalities of the Nixon administration. At the same time, among many others a quiet return to seeking in religion a sense of the meaning of life is also found. Perhaps the personality of the present pope has something to do with that search, but primarily it is the chaotic violence of the present century that has bred a renewed demand for order and stability in life.

As social codes, these new views are all admirable. What they leave out, however, is the unconscious forces that keep people tied to the values of the past. There is now available a novel method for making these new values realistic: psychotherapy. Hence the extraordinary growth of the therapy movement.

Psychotherapy and the Self

At this point it has become obvious that psychotherapy has a broader meaning than bringing psychotics or neurotics back into the mainstream of life. In the first place, many of the patients who come to us are already in the mainstream. The worried well function adequately in society, in contrast to the older neurotics and psychotics, who had to drop out of society to be cured. This was actually the conscious philosophy of the "asylum"; it was a place to which people could retreat from the world and nurse their wounded egos till they were ready to return. In the case of Richard, above, a man as prominent as Lawrence Kubie could still counsel a patient who was in the middle of the social whirl to retreat to find some quiet and work out his problems from a different vantage point. Retreat versus engagement has been one of the traditional disagreements among psychoanalysts. The tendency for a long time has been against hospitalization, and today it is actually extremely difficult to get patients into a mental hospital (unless they are flagrantly at odds with the norms of society).

De Tocqueville ([1836] 1969), in his famous book *Democracy in America*, wrote, "A new political science is needed for a world itself quite new" (p. 12). Bellah and others (1985) argue that social science should become public philosophy. The boundary between social science and philosophy is still open, Bellah states. In spite of the importance he attaches to psychotherapy, he fails to see that psychotherapy must be at the root of any new philosophy, whether based on social science or not.

Bellah does confirm that the language and some of the assumptions of the therapeutic attitude have penetrated quite deeply, at least into middle-class mainstream culture. He quotes a businessman who urged that marriage be grounded in religious truth; the man answered a question about what makes a relationship good by saying, "I'd say a big part of it is just being able to understand, sympathize and empathize with each other's problems. Just to be able to talk to each other and share each other's problems, sort of counsel each other a little bit. Just helping each other deal with the world" (1985, p. 102). And a woman, asked why she went into therapy, replied, "You need to get to know people; well-connected persons live longer, healthier lives" (1985, p. 135).

Americans believe in love as the basis for enduring relationships, even if they are less than sure of what love is. A 1970 survey found that 96 percent of all Americans held to the ideal of two people sharing a life and a home together. When the same question was asked in 1980, the same percentage agreed. Yet when a national sample was asked in 1978 whether most couples getting married today expect to stay married for the rest of their lives, 60 percent said no (Bellah and others, 1985, p. 90). For in addition to love there is self-fulfillment, and the two are frequently in conflict, especially in this day of women's liberation, when so many women reject their traditional roles as sweetheart and caretaker.

There is also disagreement among both psychoanalysts and philosophers over the essence and importance of love. In my book *The Meaning of Love in Human Experience* (1985), I urged that love is the basis of the analytic philosophy of life. Many reviewers disagreed, arguing that I was trying to force a given philosophy on the patient and claiming that that is not the business of analysts, who should limit themselves to bringing out the best in the person they are treating, wherever that may lead. If my thesis is correct, and I believe it is, then psychoanalysis becomes the principal element in the philosophical reorientation of society that is so sorely needed. One critic who at first disagreed with my thesis on more careful reflection came to agree with me (Robertson, forthcoming).

As far as the philosophers are concerned, most today still remain quite removed from human concerns. Socrates saw love as the love of the everlasting possession of the good, thus ruling out the normal definition of love as the love of one human being for another. Nor are the philosophers of today much different; very few have anything to say about love. McGill (1967) is an exception. He writes, "The fact that this conception [of happiness] is logically connected with medical therapy or with objective tests and controlled studies gives it a significance lacking in earlier theories" (p. 322).

If psychoanalysis, and psychotherapy in general, are really the basis of philosophy, in spite of the denials from both sides, then the emphasis on medicine seen in McGill's statement is misplaced, as it is in our society at large. With our materialistic conception of the world, medicine has been accorded too much of a role in the therapeutic process. Of the 300,000 or so therapists in the United States today, only a relatively small percentage are physicians. Freud himself was the great proponent of nonmedical analysis, writing in 1929, "The opposition to lay analysis was 'the last mask of the resistance to psychoanalysis, and the most dangerous of all' " (Jones, 1953–1957, p. 298). By now this question has been brought into the law courts in the legal suit brought by the Division of Psychoanalysis against the American Psychoanalytic Association and the International Psychoanalytical Association.

The genesis of this lawsuit may be briefly outlined. In 1938 the American Psychoanalytic Association forbade the training of lay analysts in their official institutes, unlike all other countries in the world and in direct defiance of Freud. In spite of this, many persons were trained "unofficially." After the formation in 1979 of the Division of Psychoanalysis in the American Psychological Association, this ban was challenged in the courts on the grounds that it violated antitrust laws. The suit is still in progress (1988). One significant result has already occurred: the bylaws of the International Psychoanalytical Association (IPA) have been amended to permit psychoanalytic institutes in the United States unaffiliated with the American Psychoanalytic Association to apply directly to the IPA for membership.

Let us come back to the topic of this chapter: the self-image. If therapy is a psychological procedure for bringing people closer to the analytic ideal, then distance from that ideal should be the main criterion for sending men to therapy. Unfortunately, it is not. The field is still dominated by the psychiatric profession, which works in terms of "diagnoses" that are changed every ten years or so and seeks to expand its power inordinately (Robards, 1980). And other societal forces are also at work. Warner has recently gathered evidence that schizophrenia is really a political phenomenon (Warner, 1985): he demonstrates how political, economic, and labor market forces shape social responses to the mentally ill, mold the psychiatric treatment philosophy, and even influence the onset and course of one of the most common forms of major mental illness. What he says of psychosis is even more true of neurosis. One text-book of psychiatry (Freedman and Redlich, 1966) does not use the term *neuroses* but refers to "psychosocial disorders."

The net consequence of these considerations is that men must come to define themselves in a different way, which will make the therapeutic process more meaningful and closer to the heart of its philosophy. The self-image is highly dependent upon the cultural atmosphere and is, therefore, not merely an individual problem.

Jerry and Susan have been going together for nine years. They have a free sex life and enjoy one another as well as other partners. Both wish to marry, yet something holds them back. They are dissatisfied, so they consult a psychotherapist to find out why they do not marry. If they could see psychotherapy as a philosophical undertaking to bring them closer to the analytic ideal, they would be much more eager to enter therapy. The therapy stopped after one consultation.

In traditional thinking, a man evaluates himself by the amount of money he has, or by the amount of success he has achieved. As this thinking changes in response to the more pertinent values discussed in this chapter, the man's self-evaluation will necessarily change.

Enoch, a fifty-five-year-old uncle of a young woman in analysis, is a typical product of the thinking of the older generation. He worked as an auditor for the IRS, specializing in criminal cases. He took undue delight in catching the "bastards." But Enoch lived with his sister and had neither women friends nor other social relationships. He was an isolated man, caught up in the boy's psychology of cops and robbers, where the only goal that counted was to "catch the crook." Admittedly, we need police officers who do their job properly, but to do so at the expense of every other pleasure in life is pathological.

In the light of the analytic ideal, the need for psychotherapy must be approached in a different way. It is not a question of curing symptoms; it is a question of examining the man's whole life-style. Many men on the present scene have come to recognize this, and they have entered psychotherapy accordingly. But many have not. It is essential for both therapist and patient to realize that neurotic difficulties can be expressed in many different ways and to be guided in their evaluation by the concepts of the analytic ideal.

10 | Work: Curse or Blessing?

THE PRESENT-DAY IDEA THAT WORK CAN MAKE PEOPLE HAPPY is a novel one in human history. Aristotle did not think so, nor did the Christians for many centuries look upon work as anything but an interference with God. In fact, in Christian mythology work is punishment for humanity's sins. And Buddhists actually institutionalized begging and poverty, arguing—like Buddha himself, who left a well-appointed situation to wander around the country looking for Nirvana—that the goods of this world are worthless. Slavery was dominant in all cultures until the nineteenth century, and the image of the "gentleman" (Evans, 1949) who lived on the work of others but did not labor himself became the dominant ideal.

In part this goes back to the Greeks, whose system of slavery also turned them against work. Both Plato and Aristotle saw those who did not work as superior. The good life was the contemplative life for them, not the active one. Plato based his argument on the notion that God had created people of three kinds: the best, the second-best, and those who did manual work. Aristotle in turn held that men who worked for their living should not be admitted to citizenship. Far from being theoretical, these ideas influenced human conduct when they were first propounded, and they still do. For example, in the early history of the United States, the arguments raged between the party of Hamilton, who favored government by an elite, and that of Jefferson, who pleaded for government by the people. It was only after several decades of American history that non–property holders were admitted to vote and hold office.

Evolution of the Work Ethic

In line with these views, before modern times it was generally held by classical economists that people work only because they are forced to. The most significant departure from this classical theory was Max Weber's concept of the Protestant ethic, which has such a compelling quality that it has become part of the language of virtually every cultured person today (Weber, [1904] 1958; Fine, 1983). His central thesis was that the modern capitalist is dominated by this special ethos (called the *Protestant* ethic because it is far stronger in Protestant countries than Catholic or non-Christian ones), which emphasizes the virtues of industry, thrift, sobriety, work, and the accumulation of wealth—all of these having religious sanction. The greatest good, as seen by the Protestant ethic, is the earning of more and more money combined with the strict avoidance of all spontaneous enjoyment of life. John D. Rockefeller, founder of the greatest fortune seen up to his day in the United States and a member of the Baptist Church (to which from an early age he regularly contributed), is a good example of the work ethic, although in his old age he did turn to depleting his fortune by supporting worthy causes.

A subsidiary confirmation of Weber's position is the work by McClelland on the achievement motive (1961). McClelland emphasizes that what is basic to capitalism as well as to any other society that grows rapidly is a certain psychological frame of mind that stresses achievement, responsibility, enterprise, and growth. His thesis is that it is not profit per se that makes the businessperson tick, but a strong desire for achievement in doing a good job. He has published a number of empirical studies that support this rather surprising thesis in a number of ways, currently and historically. Galbraith (1973) also identifies motives beyond that of profit: he sees four major motives that lead modern Americans to work—pecuniary compensation, compulsion, identification, and adaptation.

Since World War II a lively discussion has ensued about work satisfaction and work happiness, together with their corollaries in the good life. This problem of work satisfaction is the one that will concern us most in this chapter.

Source of Work Dissatisfaction

For most men today work is either a curse or a blessing. The dictionary confirms the double meaning of the word. On the one hand, synonyms for work are labor, toil, exertion, effort, travail, moil, drudgery, industry, grind, slavery. Other synonyms give a favorable connotation: job, occupation, calling, employment, profession, vocation, métier, industry, business, trade.

The most comprehensive study of work satisfaction is found in the research of Frederick Herzberg (Herzberg, Mausner, and Snyderman, 1959; Herzberg, 1966). On the basis of questionnaires submitted to 200 engineers and accountants, Herzberg found that five factors, which he calls "motivators," stand out as strong determinants of job satisfaction: achievement, recognition, the work itself, responsibility, and advancement. The major factors that stand out as "dissatisfiers" are company policy and administration, supervision, salary, interpersonal relations, and working conditions. It is the motivators that lead to work satisfaction as well as mental health.

As the hold of the Protestant ethic and religion lessen, the demand that work should be gratifying has brought about some searching reevaluations. The most comprehensive examination of the American work experience is found in the report of a special task force to the Secretary of Health, Education, and Welfare, published in book form with the title *Work in America* (1973).

Although a superficial Gallup poll (cited in *Work in America*) question asking, "Are you satisfied with your work?" evokes positive responses 80 to 90 percent of the time, the more sophisticated approach of *Work in America* immediately reveals the deep dissatisfactions that affect the American worker. These dissatisfactions can be grouped as follows: (1) blue-collar blues, (2) worker immobility, (3) white-collar woes, (4)

challenge by young workers of the work ethic, (5) frustrations
facing minority workers, (6) inequities facing women at work,
(7) financial problems of older workers nearing retirement, and
(8) work and health. The main features of the task force's report can be outlined here.

1.   *Blue-collar blues.* Work problems spill over from the factory
     into other activities of life; one frustrated assembly-line
     worker will displace his job-generated aggression on fam-
     ily, neighbors, and strangers, while a fellow worker comes
     home so fatigued from her day's work that all she can do is
     collapse and watch TV.
          An earlier study of work alienation among 1,156
     (cited in *Work in America,* 1973, p. 31) employed men re-
     vealed that the best independent predictors of work aliena-
     tion are a work situation and hierarchical organization that
     provide little discretion in pace and schedule, a career that
     has been blocked and chaotic, and a stage in the life cycle
     that puts the squeeze on the worker (large numbers of de-
     pendent children and low amounts of savings). All of these
     predictors are common among blue-collar workers.
2.   *Worker immobility.* Many blue-collar workers do not be-
     lieve that there is a great deal of opportunity to move up
     the ladder of success, and the lack of alternatives produces
     frustration. Further, manual work has increasingly become
     denigrated by the upper middle class.
3.   *White-collar woes.* There is increasing evidence of manage-
     rial discontent. One out of three middle managers indicates
     some willingness to join a union, while a large percentage
     seek a job change in middle life.
4.   *Challenge by young workers of the work ethic.* A consis-
     tent attack on the work ethic is found to be particularly
     strong among young people. Yankelovich (1971) found that
     in 1968, 69 percent of young people expressed the belief
     that hard work would always pay off, while by 1971 this
     had fallen to 39 percent. Young managers in the 1970s re-
     flected the passionate concern of youth for individuality,
     openness, humanism, and change, and they were determined
     to be heard.

5. *Frustrations facing minority workers.* Minority workers and their families are serious casualties of the work system in our society. One out of three minority workers is unemployed, is irregularly employed, or has given up looking for a job. Another third of minority workers do have full-time, year-round jobs, but these are mainly laboring jobs and jobs in the service trades, which often pay less than a living wage.

6. *Inequities facing women at work.* In addition to the fact that half of all women between the ages of eighteen and sixty-four are presently in the labor force, Department of Labor studies have shown that nine out of ten women will work outside the home at some time in their lives (*Work in America,* 1973, p. 50). Because of the widespread dissatisfaction with the kinds of jobs that women have traditionally held, women can be expected to speak out ever more forcefully on the quality of working life. In this search for equality, women have emphasized over and over the need for better economic rewards, yet have come out with what Sylvia Hewlett (1986) calls a "lesser life"; she even calls the whole women's liberation movement a "myth."

7. *Financial problems of workers nearing retirement.* In 1900 two-thirds of American men who were sixty-five years old and older were still working. By 1971 the figure had dropped to one-fourth, with a smaller proportion on a year-round, full-time basis. The problem that has arisen out of that shift is the inadequacy of pension plans.

    Since the task force's report was written, many have noted a different attitude toward retirement. In many places the mandatory retirement age has been extended to seventy; in others all mandatory retirement has been eliminated, as long as the worker is physically and mentally able to do the job (*Work in America,* 1973).

8. *Work and health.* A surprisingly positive correlation exists between work satisfaction and physical and mental health. In one fifteen-year study of aging (Palmare, 1969), the strongest predictor of longevity was work satisfaction.

    Since the time of that study, and as an ongoing enterprise, the connection between work and health has been intensively studied. Sweden is perhaps the country that has made the greatest inroads, thinking most deeply about the problem (Gardell and Johansson, 1981). It could be argued that gradually the analytic ideal is taking the place of the Protestant ethic. In fact, Robert Kahn (1981), director of the Institute for Social Research in Michigan, has made this point explicitly: "Criteria of social and psychological well-being are less well established. There is some convergence, nevertheless, around the Freudian definition of well-being as the ability to work, love and play, around the idea of freedom from distressing symptoms (gastric discomfort, inability to sleep, etc.), around veridicality of perception, and around positive affect towards self and towards life" (p. 19).

Those studying the psychology of work have moved on to consider work in the broad frame of the life cycle. There is even a journal—*Social Indicators*—that covers questions related to the measurement of the quality of life, thus spanning both work and leisure-time activities.

In one study (Diener, Horwitz, and Emmons, 1985), the happiness of the very wealthy (100 persons from the *Forbes* list of wealthiest Americans) was examined, with 100 persons selected from telephone directories as controls. When the major sources of happiness mentioned by the two groups were coded for Maslow's needs, it was found that the wealthy group more often mentioned self-esteem and self-actualization and less frequently mentioned physiological and security needs, which were filled.

A majority of people hold a belief consonant with this finding, that money can help provide happiness but that there are other factors that are more important. Of these other factors, the one most valued by all groups was love (see Chapter Nine). Thus there is ample reason to believe that the Protestant ethic is giving way to the analytic ideal as the greatest cultural good.

It goes virtually without saying that the work problem is much more acute among men than among women. At the simplest level, the man who does not work is still faced with the penalties of jail (if he is married) for nonsupport of his wife and children, a penalty that is applied more often than most people think. At another level, the amount of money that a man earns becomes an integral part of his self-image—much more so than with women. Finally, men are brought up to work and support others, while women are brought up with an emphasis on affection and interpersonal interaction (Gilligan, 1982).

However, whichever way one turns, the problem of the manual or unskilled worker remains almost insoluble in terms of work satisfaction. Yanowich (1977) has drawn together data from Soviet sources showing the wide differentials in satisfaction that exist in the Soviet Union between the lowest and highest classes. Allardt (1981) notes that in all cultures the lower classes remain ungratified. He writes (p. 107), "It seems . . . correct to say that today in the so-called welfare societies there exists a kind of discontent which cannot be explained by the convention of the ever-changing aspiration levels. Rather it is a question of a historical situation in which a certain kind of optimism and belief in continued growth has changed into certain forms of pessimism and skepticism as regards both the possibilities and the benefits of growth. . . . In all advanced industrial societies there has been a growth of new forms of protest directed against the speedy development of new technologies such as nuclear power plants, or against new forms of economic concentration, as in the opposition to the EEC [European Economic Community] and multi-national corporations, or against the very foundations of the state as in certain terrorist actions."

Other studies have confirmed this point of view: the worker at the lowest rung of the ladder is the hardest to motivate. Most interesting in this connection is a report by Herzberg from the Soviet Union, to which he was invited in 1934 to help the Soviets straighten out their work lives (Herzberg, 1966). He writes (p. 167), "In the case of the unskilled manual laborer, the widening of his mental horizon and the increase of his education does not improve, but rather, worsens his attitude to work and it impels him to quit his job. In this case the appeal to the social value of labor hardly helps, since other work is more useful to society due to its greater productivity. It is not by accident that the manual labor group was found in our research to be the least stable."

Many psychotherapists are imbued with the laudatory ideal of helping the lower classes out of their miserable economic lot. Over and over I have had students say to me, "You treat the affluent middle and upper classes; we want to help those at the bottom." Unfortunately, as I have noted, all the evidence suggests that even with the greatest optimism, psychotherapy for the lower classes is at best a dubious proposition, though it does occasionally work. It is necessary for the therapist to know the limits of what he can do. For the economically disadvantaged, the solution seems to lie in changing economic conditions.

One way of looking at the problem is this. Halliday (1948) showed by his work in Great Britain during an economic depression that a lack of hope for advancement led to physical illness and a total outlook of discouragement among the working classes. Hope is an essential component of psychotherapy, and when the hope offered is illusory, and the patient realizes that, the remedy of psychotherapy is of little value.

The Soviet Union guarantees full employment for all its citizens yet still finds that the manual worker is poorly motivated. The Soviet system of declaring workers who do not want to work "parasites" is, of course, unacceptable to our way of life. Holland is perhaps the first modern country that has officially recognized, or has been *willing* to recognize, that the modern industrial state cannot provide satisfactory work for all its citizens; the government is willing to subsidize that portion of the population that cannot look toward advancement. Perhaps this sets a dangerous precedent, similar to the bread and circuses of the Romans. I cannot offer a clear solution, but therapists should be aware of the problem as they undertake to help their economically depressed patients.

The Psychoeconomic Disorders

Fortunately, the number of those who can hope for better economic conditions through their work is considerable in the capitalist countries. Yet the psychological problems connected with work remain intense. Since the 1970s, when the Vietnam War ended, a large number of companies have directed their attention to the mental health needs of their workers. They have set up EAPs (employee assistance programs) on a large scale, offering limited free psychotherapy to the frustrated or troubled worker. Usually these EAPs offer brief therapy and treat at a superficial level, but it may well be that in the course of time they will go deeper. Other measures have also been adopted to help the worker: flex-time, participation in management, close attention to psychological needs (for example, by avoiding unnecessarily monotonous and tiring work), and the like. However, in spite of everything, a certain group of workers remain whose psychological problems come out on the job. These men suffer from what I call "psychoeconomic disorders," by analogy with psychosomatic disorders, in which the psychological disorder comes out in the form of somatic illness. In the psychoeconomic disorders the psychological problem comes out through inability to deal with the economic circumstances of one's life. Again this disability is seen more in men, who have an urgent need to work, than in women, many of whom can assume a more passive role in society if they choose to do so.

Six of these psychoeconomic disorders can be distinguished: (1) work inability, (2) work incapacity, (3) work instability, (4) work dissatisfaction, (5) underachievement, and (6) paradoxical overachievement. These will be discussed in more detail below, with reference to typical patterns seen in various patients.

Work Inability. The total inability to work is more characteristic of the schizophrenic than of any other group. Sometimes the work problem is the first symptom to really bring out the severity of the illness.

Konrad, a thirty-year-old, had been hospitalized twice for violent attacks on his father but was helped each time and went back to work. He got a job in the post office for which the qualifications were minimal: he had to file letters at the direction of a supervisor, who walked around on a platform above him.

Even though he got along in the post office for a while, his symptoms were quite serious and eventually made his work situation intolerable. He heard voices calling him names, he could not go with girls because of his fears of rejection, and he could not socialize, even with his family, without becoming dangerously angry. His fears of the street were so strong that he was permitted to spend some time in the therapist's office after each session was over.

Then one day he thought he heard the supervisor calling out his hallucinations to all the crew working on the floor. Protests, of course, against this alleged behavior did no good. He was forced to leave the job, which left him little alternative but a halfway house connected with the hospital where he had stayed.

One of Konrad's sources of satisfaction was to go to the dance halls, where girls walked around half-nude, and stare at their breasts. In the halfway house that he attended, there was a girl with big breasts similar to those he could see in the dance halls. After much hesitation he approached her, and they went to her apartment and had sex. After this he broke down again and had to be rehospitalized.

It is not uncommon for a young man with Konrad's psychological make-up to have an enormous guilt reaction when he does succeed in having sex with a "good" girl, who in the unconscious represents mother. That was the case here. After another period of hospitalization Konrad was released, but the future seemed bleak.

Work Incapacity. In this disorder, which is also quite common, patients find themselves unable to handle the work that is assigned to them even though it is fully in line with their level of competence. Various dynamic mechanisms may be at play here: a negativistic reaction to authority, excessive daydreaming, personal rivalries or hostilities with other members of the staff, and so on. This disorder may occur even when the management or person in charge thinks the employee is doing just fine; many mistakes can simply be covered up.

A man who worked as a correspondent for one of the larger magazines was assigned the job of answering letters from readers. For some reason the notion of writing letters to them terrified him to such an extent that he did not write a letter for two years. Finally his employer caught on to him and fired him.

Sean, a thirty-year-old research scientist, came to analysis because he was so blue about life that he could not concentrate on his job. He was married, with no children. He had to work at a highly independent level, which made him very uncertain about what he was supposed to be doing. He was the youngest of four children. At the time he came for treatment, the parents, both in their sixties, were negotiating for a divorce but still lived together in the house in which the children had been brought up. The pending divorce left him feeling very let down by his parents.

Sean had many childhood memories: at one time he ate feces when he was a little boy; even though there were four children, he was generally left to his own resources; he had had some homosexual experiences as an adolescent.

He served in World War II, where he was placed in the Marines because he was so tall. There they called him "she" (a play on his name), which left him feeling terrible. Sexual experience was rare until he got to wartime Japan, where he had a lot of sex with prostitutes.

In the second session he came out with one of the reasons for his work difficulties: he would sit around daydreaming about sex. He brought the therapist a drawing of a penis he had made that morning instead of plugging away at his work. This presentation was followed by numerous sexual associations: he wanted to screw a girl in his office, had dreams about seeing two lesbians having sex, and had many associations to the penis and testicles of the analyst. Through all this, depression remained the main emotion.

The sexual associations continued to form the main content of the material: his sister once put her breasts in his mouth; he always went out on only one date and then quit seeing the woman; he wanted to see the therapist aroused or excited; he fantasized that he could see the therapist's wife urinating like a man; he wanted to know if the therapist went out with other women.

In one dream he saw the therapist as a minister holding him back. Much of his life he had felt bored, held back, he said. Depression had run his entire life. Once as a child, during a summer vacation, he had spent a lot of time alone, just looking out of the window. Now his entire fantasy life was dominated by the thought of sex with women. He approached one woman in his office directly, but she turned out to be married and pregnant. The fantasies could be traced back to a beginning around age nine, when Sean had daydreamed about Joan and Betty, two girls in his class. During this same childhood period he would go to his room and make believe that he was protected by surrounding cannons to keep all intruders out.

After some years of his constant fantasizing, in which his work was almost entirely neglected and he barely squeaked by, he developed heart palpitations. A doctor he consulted suggested analysis and gave him a referral. In the meantime he had been bombarding his current analyst with the question, How long does this go on? His brother had had an experience at another analytic institute that frightened him: after some years of treatment the analyst had suggested that he go to a hospital. Sean was afraid that his therapist would do the same.

The referral whom he consulted was also asked how long the process would take. When the doctor said four or five years, Sean quit analysis on the spot.

In this case the patient could just as well be considered to have intense sexual conflicts and love conflicts. This again shows that the various components of the analytic ideal are interrelated; which one is emphasized depends on the patient's material and on his receptivity.

Work Instability. Another incarnation of a psychoeconomic problem is the man who constantly goes from job to job, unable to settle on any one post. Usually these men also go from girl to girl without being able to decide which one is best for them. Sometimes, as in the following case, there is also a great reliance on drugs.

Tad was a thirty-three-year-old proofreader whose presenting complaint was that he was unable to relate to women on a long-term basis. He was the older of two brothers and came from a small town in the Midwest. Before very long the central battle with father came to the fore. Father had been an employee of one of the *Fortune* 500 companies, very regular in his habits but inspiring little excitement or zest for life in his two sons. The patient emphasized particularly his father's regularity: to work at nine o'clock in the morning, back home at six in the evening, rarely any vacations, rarely any communication. Mother was a housewife, also very passive, sticking to her daily routine.

At an early age Tad came to New York to seek more excitement in life. But without any special skills, he could qualify only as a proofreader. In this job his rebelliousness came out very quickly, and he would move on from one publisher to another. Because he worked for so little, they did not delve into his background.

Tad's father had died at an early age, unexpectedly. Mother had also died young. The boys were left what was for them a sizable amount of money, but they were not permitted to touch it until they were forty. The bank in his home town was the trustee and made all decisions about the money.

Against this arrangement Tad rebelled very strongly. He should have the money immediately, he claimed; he should not have to wait for years. Actually, he had, even before his parents' death, led a very disordered life—relying heavily on drugs, going from one woman to another, being angry at the world. He had even experimented with living in a commune with six other people, two of whom were living together and open about everything, including sex. Once they had sex right in front of him, and he became extremely jealous.

His first dream brought out strong homosexual feelings about father. "I'm with the Kennedys. John lies down in bed, Robert gets on top of him." Later that night he dreamed: "I'm with my father. I start to cry and put my arms around him."

The dynamics became pretty clear soon after analysis started; in his well-regulated home environment, there had been just too little enjoyment. His father had had his routine; his mother, her routine. The boys had been left out. The younger brother had stayed on in the house when the parents died. He now related to no one, seemed to be schizophrenic. Tad took the other route: anything for a fling. He had been going along in this way for years when he first entered therapy.

After the early stages of analysis, the transference became

strongly negative; Tad identified the analyst's routine with that
of his father. His hostility to the father, who was identified as
the analyst, was insurmountable, even though under the surface
the longing for love from father was so powerful. Eventually he
left to go to a female analyst. (See Chapter Four for a discussion of the question of the sex of the analyst.)

    Work Dissatisfaction. Work dissatisfaction is so pervasive
that it would be superfluous to cite any examples. Virtually
anyone who is looking for therapy or is in therapy is dissatisfied
with work, and as a rule for reasons that have little or nothing
to do with the work. And yet there *are* many objective reasons
for being annoyed by superiors, working conditions, pointless
demands, and the like—all of which go on all the time in the
world. More than 100 years ago Veblen, the iconoclastic econ-
omist, wrote a take-off on the alleged efficiency of business.
His sarcastic book, *The Theory of Business Enterprise* (1919), is
still read and still true. When American industry was dominant,
in the years after World War II, its defects were overlooked. For
example, it was not until Ralph Nader wrote his famous book
Unsafe at Any Speed that the inadequacies and the dangers of
the American car were brought to light, yet they were always
there—a source of worker frustration.

    Still, the objective reasons for dissatisfaction must be
sorted out from the subjective. (To do this, a whole new profession has arisen—that of industrial psychology, also called industrial sociology or other, similar names.) Sometimes the selection
process is at fault in employee dissatisfaction; it fails to identify
people who would be dissatisfied with any working conditions (an
example is Tad, who was in full rebellion against all of society).

    In the famous Hawthorne experiment (Roethlisberger
and Dickson, 1939), it was discovered that people need attention. Industry has paid attention, changing in many ways to
provide such advantages as flex-time, vacations for new parents,
workers promoted to the board of managers, and so on. Yet
with all of these measures, there remains a strong element of
dissatisfaction at all levels of the work ladder. Many scholars
feel that the boundary line between economics and psychology
has been drawn too sharply (Hogarth and Reder, 1987; Simon,

1982). Work, as was noted earlier, can be both a blessing and a curse, and many people are unable to decide which it is.

As far as the practicing therapist is concerned, he or she can reasonably assume that there is always *some* reason for the dissatisfaction expressed. Organizations have been much studied, and few are as rational as one might hope. At the same time, individuals tend to express their own inner problems through a criticism of their organization. Accordingly, inner and outer factors must both be weighed. It can be assumed by any therapist who is going beyond the superficial, however, that some feeling of disappointment with his life's achievements will be found in every man in therapy. I prefer to handle these problems in terms of the analytic ideal—what the person has accomplished compared with the ideal set up by his superego.

Underachievement. Many men approach psychotherapy with a complaint of underachievement: they *should* have done so much better; they *could* be doing so much better. In fact, without such a feeling in some aspect of life, the person would not be coming to therapy. Sometimes it is justified; sometimes it is not. Much, of course, depends on the field in which the man is functioning.

Alex, a thirty-five-year-old professor of science, decided after a brief therapeutic experience that he was in the wrong field and should become a therapist. Accordingly, he moved to New York, where he continued his therapy in a more intensive way.

It turned out that Alex was gifted in many different areas: science (his professional field), art, music, even singing. The initial awareness of all these talents in the first therapy aroused in him the feeling that he was an underachiever. He felt that only by becoming a therapist could he reach his true self.

Accordingly, he enrolled in an analytic institute, where he remained for several years. In order to make a living while in training, he took a job as a teacher in a private school—a job well below his previous position.

Some time into the analysis, he had some revealing dreams. One was: "There's a sunlit park. I'm guarding a prisoner. Suddenly he escapes, and I start shooting at him, but missing. Then a girl appears. I shoot at her, but also miss. Later I curse myself for not having sent out a general alarm for the prisoner." This dream brought out a great deal of hidden aggression, which was very relevant to his change of career. Somewhat later he had a dream: "I go up in the air in an inflated balloon." And then: "I'm a pupil in a school, serving shredded lettuce on a plate." Here the hidden grandiosity comes to the fore (the inflated balloon), together with the wish to demean himself (a pupil in a school, serving shredded lettuce).

In the course of time, he found himself really unsuited for a therapeutic career and went back to his former field. But the liberation provided by the therapy had a surprisingly good effect: he became immensely creative in his work, achieving an international reputation.

In this case the feeling of underachievement derived from having such an excess of abilities. In gifted persons this is often the case: they *can* really do so much, yet they have to settle on one thing. In his studies of gifted children, Terman (1928) found that at ages eight and nine the children were good at everything, from art to science; then in puberty they had to make a definite choice. The knowledge that one has unused abilities often results in a feeling of underachievement, which is largely a reflection of a poor self-image, as was the case with Alex.

A comment is in order about changing careers from some other fields to doing therapy. Many people, like Alex here, enter analysis at least partly in order to facilitate a change in career; many others reach such a career decision only as a result of a long period of self-reflection, such as occurs during therapy. Sometimes this wish to change is positive, sometimes not. The therapist must be able to help patients disentangle the various motives that lead them to want to become an analyst.

As I noted earlier, it is not only not uncommon, it is virtually the rule that anyone who enters analysis for the resolution of personal problems will at some time or other want to become an analyst. One such case (Abraham, in Chapter Two) was noted before. Here the question of academic preparation enters into the decision. Therapists who regard a medical degree as essential will discourage the patient; those who regard it as nonessential will be encouraging. Firestein, in his book *Termination in Psychoanalysis* (1978), describes eight patients, none of them physicians. Of these eight, five expressed the wish during analysis to become an analyst themselves. In accordance with his medical training, Firestein discouraged them.

On the other hand, as a follower of Freud, I have always been in favor of nonmedical analysis, whether one has a medical degree or not. If patients of mine (especially those in an older age bracket) find themselves wanting to become analysts, I usually recommend that they go to a school of social work. The master's degree in social work is now well established in New York and other states; social workers are eligible to receive insurance, for example—an important consideration for many patients. Furthermore, the whole therapeutic experience, in my opinion, works out better for those with a nonmedical orientation than for those with a medical one; the latter tend to fall back on prescribing drugs in times of crisis.

This whole question of preparation (which is discussed in more detail in Chapter Two) is in a state of considerable flux. In ten years there may be a direct route to a degree in psychotherapy that is not present today, given that all authorities in the field decry the immense expenditure of time and effort now required to become a licensed therapist.

Another very successful scientist decided, as a result of his own analysis, to become a therapist. He entered a school of social work at a fairly late age, because his wish to get closer to people had been brought out so strongly in therapy. Upon applying for admission to our training institute (the New York Center for Psychoanalytic Training), he submitted the following statement, reprinted here with his permission:

> In 1964, during my psychoanalysis, I realized that I wanted to change my career from the field of science to a profession which was basically people oriented. I had entered analysis because I had become increasingly dissatisfied with my life. As my analysis progressed, I became aware that a large part of

my dissatisfaction was that I was working in a field dealing with inanimate objects which could be used for destructive purposes. I realized that I wanted to change from the field of science to one that dealt primarily with people and was constructive. I wished to help people in need or distress. My own analytic experience led me to believe that I had the empathy, sensitivity, awareness and maturity to move towards this goal by becoming a psychotherapist....

As I gained more experience with the spectrum of problems facing people in distress or need, I became aware of the limitations of intrapsychic processes. I began to feel that consideration of the whole constellation of human experience as encompassed by social workers who deal with external, as well as internal, human problems makes for more effective interventions with individuals, families and other societal groups.

My personality is such that I enjoy being involved with people. I feel great empathy and sympathy toward people and I feel moved to help people in distress or need. My philosophy can best be summed up by "I am my brother's keeper." I feel that I will find social work a very important and rewarding part of my life. After much searching I have come to understand how important it is to help people. At first, I thought I could achieve this through scientific accomplishments, but this was not satisfying because of the nature of the field and its distance from people. In my search, I next went on to the field of psychotherapy, which I found far more fulfilling, yet still missing a necessary direction. This led me to the field of social work which I feel provides the training and opportunity to help the total person, which will be the most rewarding.

Overachievement. Men tend to push themselves so hard in our society that they sometimes become overachievers. As with underachievers, the therapist's job is to help to bring them back to the one or two fields in which they show the most promise. This disorder is not at all unusual, because achievement is often the result of superego pressure: the boy comes home with a mark of 99.9 percent and the mother or father says, "Why didn't you get 100?" I have even seen situations where, when the boy came home with 100, the father said, "Why didn't you get 102?"

A good example of an overachiever is the mathematician Norbert Wiener (Chapter Nine), whose father, on his deathbed, made him promise that he would be as great as Gauss. Wiener achieved much in mathematics (though not as much as Gauss), but he expanded to other fields as well. For example, he was the one who coined the term *cybernetics* and did much of the original work in that field. Yet Wiener was never satisfied with himself, suffering from recurrent depressions all through his life. The man who has too little ability and the man who has too much are both serious therapeutic problems.

11 | Inexpressive Man

IN HIS THIRTEENTH-CENTURY CHRONICLE, SALIMBENE RE-
ports on a linguistic experiment of Frederick II. Duke Frederick
wanted to find out what manner of speech children would have
when they grew up if they spoke to no one before they themselves acquired speech. So he bade foster mothers and nurses to
suckle, bathe, and wash the children, but in no way to speak
with them, for he wanted to learn whether they would speak
the Hebrew language, which is the oldest, or Greek or Latin or
Arabic, or perhaps the language of their parents. But he labored
in vain, because all of the children died. They could not live
without communication.

What Is Communication?

Language, in Sapir's (1921) definition, is a purely human
method of communicating ideas, emotions, and desires by
means of a system of voluntarily produced symbols. While Sapir
emphasized that language is specifically human, more recent
material casts doubt on that assumption.

Communication, because of the understanding offered by
psychology, has become what Ruesch (1972) calls the "social
matrix of psychiatry." Schizophrenia is obviously a disorder of
communication. Even to the layperson, the major characteristic
of schizophrenics is that they are "unintelligible." In fact, they
come to the attention of their social circle or mental health professionals only when their utterances and/or actions reach the
point of unintelligibility, even though more careful examination

would have revealed serious sources of difficulty much sooner. On principle, however, the seemingly "crazy" utterances of the schizophrenic can be decoded and understood.

Freud's explanation of the dream (1900: SE IV-V) is one of the great milestones in the decoding of communication. For Freud showed that, in principle, all dreams are intelligible. Basically, they express a disguised form of wish-fulfillment; thus they embody both the basic id impulses of the individual and the ways in which these impulses are transformed. With this new understanding, the dream became and remains a major cornerstone of psychoanalysis. It marks a wide gap between psychoanalytic therapy and all other forms of therapy (for example, behavior therapy), which usually pay no attention to dreams at all. Inherently, however, there is no reason why other approaches to therapy should not use dreams, and in such hybrid approaches as hypnotherapy dreams are used.

Many neurotic symptoms—such as hysterical conversions of all kinds, obsessional maneuvers, and the like—are symbolic ways of communicating with other people. The very first patient in psychoanalytic history, Anna O. (Freud and Breuer, 1895: SE II), who invented the term "the talking cure," had a specific linguistic problem: for a while she could speak only English instead of her native German.

The process of psychotherapy focuses in the most intimate detail on the ways in which two people communicate with one another, both verbally and nonverbally. Actually, it could be said that interpretation in psychoanalysis represents the attempt to put into adult words what the patient is trying to communicate in other ways, either by actions or by linguistic utterances from an earlier stage of development.

There has been a strong and growing realization that the entire process of alienation, neurosis, and psychosis represents a failure in communication. As has been noted, women nowadays often come into analysis with the complaints about their partners: no sex, no communication. Men are trained to communicate less than women; they are taught to be "strong and silent."

The extraordinary power displayed by propaganda in the

totalitarian countries emphasizes that communication can vary widely from the traditional meanings of the words used. George Orwell, in his mordant *1984*, satirizes this as "newthink," which can prove beyond the shadow of a doubt that black is white.

Research in recent years has uncovered a wide variety of communication patterns in the animal world. The whole environment is organized into one ecosystem, the disturbance of any part of which may and often does affect the whole; communication among animals serves the biological purpose of maintaining this ecosystem.

Many instances of communication can be drawn from the animal world: the waggle dance of bees (Frisch, 1965), the songs of birds (Thorpe, 1972), contact calls of zebras (Moss, 1982), the dominance-submission patterns of so many animal species (Houpt and Wolski, 1982), the capacity, only recently demonstrated, of chimpanzees to learn sign language (Terrace, 1979), the vocalizations of monkeys in the wild (Cunningham, 1985), and numerous others. If communication is so widespread in the animal kingdom, its fundamental importance in human life is all the greater because of our further development of language.

For the young infant, crying is the primary mode of expressing and communicating basic needs and events; it is a social behavior that has powerful effects on the parent-infant relationship, and it elicits strong emotions in parents (Lester and Boukydis, 1985). The development of mature language from infant crying has been traced in the minutest detail (Edgcumbe, 1981). Thought and language have been analyzed in the greatest of depth in the adult schizophrenic as well. There the characteristics most often mentioned are "word salad," double meanings, lack of causal connections, disorganization, and overinclusion (Arieti, 1974).

Problems of Communication

Manipulative Communication. At the more neurotic level, a primary distinction must be drawn between manipulative and expressive communication. Expressive communication conveys a normal wish; manipulative communication is designed, either consciously or unconsciously, to manipulate another person to do something. A certain amount of manipulative communication is quite consciously dishonest, even cynical, as in propaganda. But a good deal of it is unconsciously determined. Rose Spiegel (1959) suggests a fivefold classification of manipulative communication: grossly destructive communication, authoritarian communication, disjunctive communication, pseudocommunication, and noncommunication.

The Lie. An important but neglected area of communication is the lie. Lying may be a symptom of a deeper disturbance, as in the pathological liar, or it may be a sign of a healthy ego, as in the liar who is aware that the communication of the truth may be more painful than telling a "little white lie." Ludwig (1965) rightly comments that most of his material on the subject had to be taken from literary rather than clinical sources. Because psychoanalysts place such a premium on telling the truth, little interest has been expressed in the patient who lies.

Kernberg (1984) is one of the few psychoanalysts to devote attention to the problem of the patient who lies. He writes that "with major and chronic dishonesty in the transference, a defensive dehumanization of all object relations has taken place, so that there is no longer a danger of love being destroyed by hatred or of hatred evoking devastating retaliation" (p. 300). Then he mentions a man who claimed that he had been charged for a session that they had agreed to cancel. At first Kernberg agreed, uncertain of the situation. But when the same situation was repeated a few months later, Kernberg felt that he was unlikely to have made such a mistake twice. Confronted by a denial, the patient reacted with intense rage, vehemently accusing the analyst of lying. When an analogous situation occurred yet again a few months later, the patient's assertion that the analyst was lying about his bill had to be faced directly. It was worked out satisfactorily, which, Kernberg felt, marked the beginning of the resumption of psychoanalytic work.

A paranoid medical student asked for a reterral at a low fee to a therapist, which fortunately could be arranged. After a few sessions he left analysis, accusing the therapist of everything under the sun, including lying about her fee. He called the director and demanded that disciplinary action be taken against her. When told that it was he who had problems, and that if he did not like her he could simply shift to another therapist, he refused, saying that his primary goal now was to "get her out of the clinic." He was so vehement that the director hung up on him.

About a year later the patient called again, demanding a copy of his file; otherwise, he said, he would have his lawyer sue. Because seeing the file was his legal prerogative, the request was granted, provided he would put the request in writing—always a problem for paranoids. This verbal demand was the last that was heard from him.

In general, if patients lie too much in the analysis, it destroys the prospects of therapeutic success. The lying can be analyzed only if patients will bring some reason to bear on the situation; if they use lies to vent spleen, or to gratify some extraneous wish, the case becomes hopeless.

Bob, a patient in our Center for Creative Living, had made up a story that he was the descendant of Spanish nobility. His last name was one that could have been pronounced in either a Spanish or an Irish manner. He kept up this fiction for quite a while. Then one day the therapist happened to meet a parish priest who asked about the patient, saying that he had heard that Bob had gone to therapy. The priest also revealed Bob as an ordinary, poor Irish boy. With this his mask fell and he quit treatment.

Silence. Psychotherapy always involves an increase in the communicative capabilities of the patient. The dream alone, which is rarely disclosed to anybody in ordinary life, affords a powerful expansion of awareness.

While communication problems come up in every analysis, in the following case they were central to the process. Dennis, a seven-year-old boy, came to psychotherapy because of an acute phobic reaction to movies showing accidents. One time he vomited; another he ran out of the room shouting, "No, no!" The parents had no special interests or hobbies; their lives centered around the children, especially the boy, who was brilliant.

In spite of his brilliance, however, speech development had been slow. He had begun to speak in words at about eighteen months, in sentences at about twenty-one months; and from an early age he had demonstrated a speech problem. He had been sent to a speech therapy center, where therapists diagnosed him as a boy with "oral inaccuracies." When he first came to psychotherapeutic treatment, his speech was only barely intelligible. His voice was very thick and guttural.

For the first eight months of his therapy, he said little, except to express occasional grandiose fantasies; and when he did communicate, he was often unintelligible. At the very first session, he gave an indication of how he was going to behave with the therapist. Without even looking at him, he dashed off into the playroom, where he quickly grasped what was available. Moving some dolls around, he said to himself, "The little boy sets out to save the world, from either the hurricane or a hydrogen bomb. He succeeds. And that is how a seven-year-old boy by his scientific and mechanical genius saved the world." After about eight months, however, a dramatic shift occurred. One day when he came in he said, "I want to talk to you. I can't sleep lately."

From that point on there was a steady growth in his capacity to communicate. Much of this was in symbolic form, which he could share with the therapist, who understood his symbolism. He even had a dream of a millionaire who gave him the atomic bomb. Thus all along he was flirting with the idea of world destruction, which at a deeper level meant his father, who was the particular object of his anger. His progress can actually be divided into periods of communication that finally ended in directly talking to the therapist about his problems (Fine, 1979a).

Not all analytic or therapeutic cases lend themselves to an easy summation. Nor does this one, though it does lend itself to an intelligible division into various stages on the road to adult communication. Noteworthy here is the fact that Dennis could make such dramatic progress in spite of his parents' obtuseness in psychological matters. They provided a holding environment in which he could grow with the help of a therapist. In turn, he and his younger sister provided a goal in life for the parents; once they were out of the house, the mother in particular went to pieces.

Another striking feature of this case is that after a while Dennis seemed to arrive at the feeling that he and the therapist could communicate on a nonverbal level, in that the therapist could readily grasp all his fantasies, games, and dreams as well as all his other communications. Yet the attempt to put these into ordinary English almost always made him become silent. It was as though he wanted to keep the therapist as his secret companion, held to him by a secret language, not just another person in the real world.

In the adult therapeutic situation, silence, while rare, can occur. A symposium on the topic was held by the American Psychoanalytic Association in 1958 and reported on in 1961. Zeligs (1961), a participant in that symposium, lists the following meanings of silence: (1) revenge (against mother), (2) teasing, (3) defense against fear of attack, (4) defense against fear of death, (5) respiratory fantasies, (6) repression of thought, (7) defense against fear of being seen, (8) defense against the potential going away of the analyst, (9) defense against feelings of inadequacy, (10) a form of autohypnotic evasion, (11) defense against feelings of unreality, (12) destruction of reality. These meanings of silence related to one of his patients, but one or all could be found in any patient who is extremely silent. One patient of mine, for example, was afraid to lie on the couch, because it meant that the analyst had gone away; his own father had committed suicide.

Loomie (1961), another symposium participant, tells of a thirty-year-old childless attorney who usually paused for a considerable period between sentences. The patient's avocation was writing, and he was composing his remarks during these pauses. He used silence constantly, although in small doses, to bolster a network of defenses.

This man was the only child born to a late marriage of religiously devout parents. His father had combined a successful professional career with some public recognition in elected office. The patient's mother, who had always wanted to be a nun, explained her loveless marriage as due to the combined pressure of her suitor and her own widowed mother.

He grew up with a feeling that he had committed a crime in being born, for his mother hypochondriacally guarded herself from the supposed consequences of childbirth injuries; she perceived herself as having been hurt during his birth. Even as a youngster, when his parents slept in separate rooms, he interpreted their separation as a reflection of his mother's fear of sex. But after his father's death, when the patient was seven, mother began sleeping with the patient, a practice that was continued for five years. This led him to suppress and repress all emotion, including the wish to masturbate.

One persistent symptom was the feeling of unreality he experienced toward his marriage and the blocking of his emotional response to his wife. The block related to the childhood feeling that his father had never mattered to him. Yet he reported little or no subjective sadness, grief, or frustrated anger. At one point he began to cry a lot during the sessions. The prevailing transference reactions were, on the one hand, a grateful dependence on treatment and, on the other, a fierce competitiveness. Silence served the function of blocking off reactions to both his wife and the analyst. The frequent brief silences, which used up perhaps one-third of each session, played a role in the denial of feeling.

In this case the lack of communication was traced directly to the blocking of a variety of feelings. This is the basic mechanism that leads so many men to become noncommunicators, whether in therapy or in real life. The capacity to cry during the sessions, for which he felt so grateful to the analyst, undoubtedly had great therapeutic meaning for him.

The case of Glen, an unemployed, thirty-year-old alcoholic homosexual, shows certain similarities to the previous one. Glen was the son of a mathematics professor who had always beaten him down; he could never do anything right in school and was constantly presented at home with math problems that were too hard for him and made him feel like a total failure.

Glen had been in analysis with a woman who had become pregnant. She switched him to a male analyst when the baby

was born. He was glad to see someone else, though he never expressed feelings about it directly.

To pay for the analysis, Glen took a job as an editor in a
publishing house. In this second analysis he began to fall asleep
while he was on the couch. All efforts to rouse him failed. The
analyst tried sitting him up, but even sitting up he slept through
most of the analytic hour.

For this uncommunicative behavior Glen's only explanation was that he drank too much, though he did keep his job
without interruption. He had a vivid memory from the previous
analysis of one session when he was very loquacious. The analyst had given him some interpretation that annoyed him, and
although he did not remember the interpretation, he did remember being extremely hurt at being stopped in the middle of
his narration.

In the second analysis he began to report a few dreams,
mostly about women. Later he had a number of vivid dreams
that frightened him. In one he was with two girls in a wooded
area. A boy peed in the water, and he looked up to see what the
girls wanted to do about the odor. Then he dreamed that he
went to see Dick and Peggy, two friends of his. Dick went out,
and he embraced Peggy.

To the wooded area he associated Panama, where he had
served when in the army. The other soldiers had all gone to the
open houses of prostitution there, but he had refrained: Peggy
was a woman who had changed radically after marriage, for the
worse. The dreams brought out his wish for a woman and his
fear that he would "stink" (odor of pee) or be rejected by Peggy.

Later he had a direct dream about his father: "My father
and I are riding in a cab. He puts his hand on my knee. Then he
turns into my brother. . . . I have the tickets." To the tickets he
associated a sense of control. When he was a boy he had collected tickets from baseball games and movies that he attended.
The homosexual wish for father is clear here.

After this period when he reported dreaming, the patient
became more and more sleepy. When the analyst suggested that
the analysis be terminated because of his sleeping, Glen protested
strongly, listing a long string of accomplishments in the analysis:

he had stabilized himself on the job, was not cruising as much, had even given up homosexuality for a while, was sleeping better, and was feeling better about himself—all accomplishments that he had never revealed before.

In one sense, all therapy involves a systematic unveiling of the communications of the patient, making the unconscious conscious. But while this may be easy enough for the analyst to see, the real effort comes in convincing patients of the nature of their communication.

Private Language. Body language is common enough among all people. With schizophrenics such language is apt to wander off into many arcane meanings, which is one of the factors that make it so hard to understand and treat them. Every schizophrenic has a private world of symbols that others cannot understand. Konrad, described in Chapter Ten, had a whole collection of meanings associated with movements or gestures. A black man rubs his face to show that he is a man. The sound "ff" stands for fag, while "ss" stands for sissy (sucking off the girl, a fag sound.) (He was highly concerned with proving that he was not a homosexual.) A cough is a manly way of being critical. A woman always looks in a sneering way, while a real man crosses his legs. Awkward movements mean anger. Walk up to a cop and he slips out with his left foot. So it went, on and on. This man obviously lived in a world of signs and symbols that could not be shared completely with anybody.

Self-Communication. The question comes up as to whether patients should be encouraged to keep notes about themselves— to communicate with themselves, as it were, in a kind of analytic diary. Some have even proposed this diary-keeping as a form of therapy. The problem is that whatever the therapist suggests arouses a transference reaction. If the patient does respond and keep a diary, that record may replace the more pertinent material aroused during the hour. If the patient does not respond, writing down little or nothing (the more usual case), that may arouse a feeling of guilt because he or she has not pleased the therapist. However, the diary is something that comes quite naturally to many Americans, so it is best to leave it up to patients what they do or think about the therapy in their spare time. One patient used to spend an hour three or four times a week, apart from the analysis, lying on the couch and free-associating with no one present. He felt that it helped him, but to prescribe such a procedure in general would raise the transference problems just noted.

Communicating Through Writing

There are roughly fifty million men in America who have expressed the wish to become a writer. Not surprisingly, then, of men who go into therapy, a large number express that wish. It is therefore of some interest to examine how some writers—who apparently have no difficulty expressing themselves and can even publish their writings—can communicate so well, and what this writing means to them.

From time immemorial the writer has been believed to have some divine gift (the psychology of the creative artist in general will be discussed more fully in Chapter Twelve); writers themselves, especially those who have been successful, have held on to that belief. As with so many other self-images, however, psychology has tended to shatter this belief as an illusion. Writers may or may not have enormous gifts, but they cannot do much more than put their own experiences into artistic form. Freud began the analysis of literature with his paper on Jensen's *Gradiva* (Freud, 1907: SE IX); Jensen was a popular writer of that day (he died in 1911), since forgotten. Freud's investigation of Jensen's personality, insofar as it could be done, showed that almost all his writings centered around the theme of an intimate association between brother and sister, while in his own life Jensen saw a sister in the woman he loved.

Since then the psychoanalysis of writers and other artists has grown into an enormous enterprise. Even the writing of "nonwriters" is revealing: in the Thematic Apperception Test, the task of writing has been transformed into a psychological ("projective") test; the subject is shown a series of pictures and asked to make up stories about them. From these stories many inferences can be drawn about the subject's personality structure. Thus it has come to be taken for granted that the writer uses writing as a form of self-expression, and that writings, if properly examined, will tell us a great deal about the inner life of the person. Two examples may be taken from writers in the twentieth century—men who might have gone into therapy to get over their problems but chose not to do so. (For fuller details, see Fine, 1987b).

F. Scott Fitzgerald (1896–1940) is regarded as the voice of the jazz age, the 1920s. At twenty-three he was already a best-selling author. He married Zelda Sayre; at their wedding they snacked on champagne and spinach, went cartwheeling down the halls, and dived into the fountain at the Plaza Hotel in New York until they were asked to leave.

Writing, drinking, and carousing, Scott and Zelda went through the twenties. Then Zelda had her first breakdown in 1930; eventually she was to die in a mental hospital. Scott himself was a severe alcoholic and continued to drink until his death. After his early successes his reputation began to slip; after a while, instead of writing fiction, he had to take a job as a Hollywood script writer.

Although faced with his wife's psychosis and his own obviously neurotic life-style, he never seems to have considered therapy seriously, although it was readily enough available in his time.

Psychologically, his most interesting novel is his fourth, *Tender Is the Night*, published in 1934. The novel is the story of a woman, hospitalized in a Swiss psychiatric sanitorium, whose psychiatrist falls in love with her. She is wealthy enough to take him back to the United States, where she sets him up in practice in a small town. Here he goes steadily downhill and neglects his practice; she finally leaves him.

The novel reveals a way of deflating the analyst (psychiatrist) by buying him off and destroying him. It is still a common fantasy among analysands today.

John Berryman (1914–1972) was one of a group of poets considered to have had marked influence on the course of poetry: Delmore Schwartz, Robert Lowell, Randall Jarrell, R. P. Blackmur, and others. All of them were seriously disturbed psychologically, except perhaps Blackmur; Jarrell and Berryman com-

mitted suicide (although Jarrell's suicide is questionable), while
Lowell was psychotic, hospitalized part of his life. The life of
Berryman has been described by his ex-wife, Eileen Simpson
(1982), in her book *Poets in Their Youth.*

Berryman was the son of John Allan Smith, a bank examiner who began to speculate in Florida real estate. After losing a
good deal of money, he killed himself. John was then twelve,
and the suicide had a deep impact on him. His mother remarried, and John took the new husband's name; forever after he reproached himself for not retaining the name Smith (although he
could easily have changed back at any time).

To his wife John seemed desperately in need of love; if
she did not declare unconditional love for him, he would lose
his mind. He was a severe insomniac; he and Delmore Schwartz
(later to become a complete paranoiac) called Cambridge "Insomnia Valley." Schwartz once said to Simpson, "Poet's wives
have rotten lives" (Simpson, 1982, p. 31).

From the beginning John was driven to seek fame. When
he met Eileen he was out of a job, broke, and dubious of his
prospects. Fearful of rejection, he held back from committing his
work to print. When he finally did so, it was with a combination
of arrogance and terror.

Soon alcoholism set in. Yet even when admitted to the
hospital in a state of acute exhaustion or alcoholism, he would
rather be writing about his state of mind than trying to correct
it. He felt both grandiose and a failure. In one poem he tried to
express that duality (p. 399):

> He wondered: Do I love? all this applause
> young beauties sitting at my feet and all . . .
> One sole beauty only . . .
> she saw through things, she saw that he was lonely
> and waited while he did behind the wall
> and all.

Eventually Eileen left Berryman. He went on to two other
marriages and acquired fame, security, and even some fortune.
Then, without any apparent reason, he jumped from a bridge and

killed himself. Eileen became a psychotherapist, describing the illnesses of Berryman and his friends in a sympathetic way.

I do not wish to be misunderstood as saying that artists per se are neurotic, as some others have held. Quite the contrary: they are often gifted, intuitive, and able to penetrate the human disguise with insights that are denied to others. But unfortunately, at times they also suffer from a variety of neurotic problems. In writers these seem to be connected more with their grandiosity than with their writing. Meyer Levin (1953), a writer, once expressed this dilemma: the writer, he said, historically was believed to have the deepest of all insights into human nature; then Freud and the psychoanalysts came along claiming this privilege for themselves. No wonder the writer and other artists may feel slighted. But generalizations about the creative individual are notoriously open to question. As will be seen in more detail in Chapter Twelve, art can be a form of healthy self-expression in a mature individual, it can be a form of grandiose self-enhancement, or it can be a combination of the two.

It has been known for a long time (Freud, 1905: SE VII) that the reader of a work of art tends to identify with one or more of the characters. Thus murder, rape, rebellion, crazy behavior, and the like can be portrayed on the stage or in books; readers want to bring out their own urges toward these violent or crazy acts but are unable to do so because of the superego and because of societal pressures.

The other side of the coin must also be noted: artists release their feelings, but unconsciously they find that release dangerous. It is revealing that both Fitzgerald and Berryman were severe alcoholics, that Fitzgerald married a psychotic woman (with whose antics he identified), and that Berryman eventually committed suicide. The release of feelings in these two men was followed by a severe deterioration that runs parallel to what the average man feels—if he lets such things out, he will be punished in some unknown way by his harsh superego. Eileen Simpson quotes Wordsworth appropriately (1982, p. 3), "We poets in our youth begin in gladness; But thereof in the end comes despondency and madness."

Keeping Secrets

People have all kinds of secrets that they wish to conceal from the world. In therapy the attempt to get at these secrets creates many resistances; an extreme case is cited in Chapter Six: for a year and a half, the patient would not reveal his real name to the analyst, a "disguise" that concealed the wish to be raped by the analyst.

It is often dangerous for the analyst to try to probe into these secrets too vigorously. The superego will protect patients as long as they hide what they did or thought but will punish them severely if they let the secret out.

Barry, a twenty-eight-year-old college instructor, was faced with a severe dilemma after three months of analysis: he was overcome by a wish to get up and punch the analyst in the nose. "If I do it," he reasoned, "he will surely stop the analysis, while if I don't do it, I will be extremely uncomfortable." The anger he felt like releasing was the childhood anger he had felt toward a millionaire uncle who was always held up as a model by his mother (it was her brother), and whom he accordingly hated. The dilemma was revealed by the patient only years later.

An equally striking event occurred in the analysis of Clifford, who suffered from a conflict felt by many men. He worked on a newspaper and wanted to write the great American novel. When three chapters of the novel were finished, he began to send it around to various publishers, hoping for a substantial advance, but was consistently refused. He begged the analyst to read the novel critically and tell him why they were not accepting his work. (Similar requests are frequently made, not because analysts have any great critical skills but because they approach artistic material from a different point of view.) Clifford saw his analyst as a magician, so he was confident that he would pick up whatever was missing.

The analyst consistently refused to read the manuscript, which was the wisest course. The patient had described the first and third chapters but would not say anything about the second. Finally, in a moment of weakness, the analyst asked him to bring in the second chapter. In it Clifford described a homosexual scene similar to something in his childhood that had made him feel very ashamed of himself. When the analyst commented on the homosexual scene, the patient abruptly quit treatment.

Once the secret is out, the patient as a rule feels greatly relieved. Where before he may have put up the fiercest resistance, now the opposite occurs: he has great trust in the analyst, who has done nothing about the secret, and even begins to idealize him or her as the most forgiving of mortals. This is one factor that makes for a long period of time in therapy—patients feel they will never get the same understanding on the outside.

In another case—that of Emmett, a rather timid lawyer—the patient carried on a secret life with prostitutes and girls in massage parlors, a life that was hidden from everybody else. For a long time he hid it from the therapist as well. When it finally came out in analysis, he felt a great sense of relief.

The question may well be asked whether the man's self-strictures are stronger than the woman's, because obviously women have their secrets as well. The answer is that, in general, in our culture women grow up more repressed, especially in sexual matters, than men. Thus their sexual fantasies or wishes do not come to consciousness and hence require less superego control.

Here is a typical instance of secrets held at the conscious level. The Stillwell family looked like a model middle-class family. The father was a middle manager, the mother was a beautician, and the three children were in school. When the mother discovered that the father was seeing another woman, they made an appointment for family therapy. At first the mother was reluctant to go; later she became enthusiastic about it. In the beginning the father was also reluctant, especially when his wife discovered that he not only had another woman but also visited a place where he could spend the night—clearly a drug and prostitute hangout. The mother, however, also had her secret: she had an illegitimate child boarded out somewhere in the Midwest. There were also terrible fights going on in the house between the mother and a son. Almost every session brought some new revelation.

Some secrets are held at the unconscious level. A typical case is that of Mrs. Biddle, who discovered that on a buying trip to Paris, her husband had spent some time in a hotel room with two women; she discovered this by piecing together receipts from the hotel bill.

Like the Stillwells, on the outside the Biddles were a model couple. They had a successful store, at which they spent all their time; in fact, neither one ever seemed to be alone. They were well into their forties and had been married for many years. The husband denied the accusation, saying he had only hired a secretary to take some dictation. The wife might easily have forgotten about the whole thing—he was strictly faithful in other respects—except that unconsciously her own sexual desires were aroused by her fantasy of her husband alone in Paris with two women. Yet it was easier to imagine him with two women than herself responding to another man.

Although women are still more repressed sexually than men—and thus have more unconscious secrets—a change in mores comes out in a comparison of three books: the Kinsey report, written in 1948 (on men) and 1953 (on women), and the Blumstein-Schwartz report, written in 1983. In the earlier book women were unfaithful much less frequently than their husbands. In the later two books a desire for sexual variety comes to the fore in women as well; usually it is even justified as a natural desire. It is only the appearance of AIDS in 1981 that has made women "scared sexless" again; should AIDS be conquered, the move to fuller sexual equality will undoubtedly resume its march. Already most people openly express the philosophy of the sexual revolution: that sex should be enjoyed equally by both sexes, with as few barriers as possible. But there is many a slip between the cup and the lip. What is verbalized in theory is often the source of guilt in practice.

Language

There was a time when it was completely unladylike to utter such words as *fuck, shit,* and the like. The censorship of D. H. Lawrence's novel *Lady Chatterley's Lover,* in which the word *fuck* is tossed about so freely, is still within the memory of most people; while today almost anything seems to go.

However, we live not just in one contemporary culture but in ten different cultures, if not more. The traditional culture, in which women would not use any "dirty" words, is still the one that governs most people.

Nelson, a thirty-five-year-old businessman, was in a marital quarrel with his wife, for which he was seeing a woman therapist. In reality, Nelson was a rather inhibited man who would occasionally go to Harlem (a dangerous area in New York City) to pick up prostitutes, even though he had had his life threatened there several times. But Nelson had also been through the war, and it was fashionable for the returning GIs to use the word *fuck* as often as they could.

In therapy he could use the word *fuck* three times or more in every sentence. Instead of analyzing the discrepancy between his speech and his actions, the therapist reproached him for using such language in the presence of a lady. In reality, the problem was that Nelson's wife did not want to have children, while he did. To break through her resistance, he made a hole in her diaphragm with a pin, as a result of which she became pregnant. She came to love the child dearly, but she never knew why she had become pregnant at that particular time.

Although I have never seen a study of this kind, I imagine that a careful analysis of the language of men and women would reveal many subtle differences, both in the use of "dirty" language and in the kinds of material that come out in conversation. For example, men will often tell dirty stories or dirty jokes among themselves, while women rarely engage in such an exchange. And of course silence on the part of the man is also part of the macho self-image; he may turn to the TV and sports rather than engage in any kind of conversation.

Research on Marital Communication

In her book *Blue Collar Marriage* (1967), Mirra Komarovsky presents some illuminating data about the kinds of communication in which blue-collar couples engage. For example, asked whether she thought it was (in general) difficult for a husband to understand his wife, a twenty-eight-year-old woman with eight years of schooling said, "we tell each other things, but I don't know as how we talk about them. He'll tell me or I'll tell him something has happened, but there ain't nothing much to say" (p. 155). When, after a long series of questions on communication, the interviewer remarked that the wife appeared to talk more easily to her girlfriend and to her sister than to her husband, she exclaimed, "But they are girls!" (p. 150). A twenty-one-year-old wife with ten years of schooling remarked, "Men are different, they don't feel the same as us. That's the reason men are friends with men, and women have women friends" (p. 151).

Dr. Komarovsky attempted to tap the different images of marriage by asking for reactions to a story. The story was this: "A couple has been married for seven years. The wife says that her husband is a good provider and a good man, but still complains to her mother about her marriage. She says he comes home, reads the paper, watches TV, but doesn't talk to her. He says he 'doesn't like to gab just for the sake of talking.' But she says he is not companionable and has nothing to say to her. What do you think of this couple?" (pp. 114–115).

Komarovsky, apart from incidental references to personal experiences (for example, "My husband is just like that"), found three themes expressed in the responses to this story. The first theme reflects the view that the lack of husband-wife conversation in the story presents a genuine problem. Thirty-seven percent of respondents (ninety-nine men and women) took this position. In contrast with this attitude, another 37 percent of the group categorically denied that the wife in the story had any legitimate grievances. In that subgroup it was the wife who was criticized for her immaturity and selfishness, by women as well as by men. One woman, married for twenty-eight years, said, "Gee, can you tie that? He's generous, don't bother her, he just keeps out of the way, and she's fussing and wants him to sit there and entertain her" (p. 116). Eleven percent of the interviewees read into the story a particular situation that is a source of great concern to women: "Maybe the husband's got something on his mind; she should leave him alone" (p. 117).

Komarovsky also found that feelings about marital communication depended very strongly on the educational level of the respondents. The high school graduates tended to deplore the lack of conversation—this might be called the "companionable" or middle-class response. Those with less than high school education were apt to feel that there was no legitimate grievance.

In another aspect of her study, Komarovsky asked eighty-five men and eighty-five women to list the qualities of a good husband and a good wife. The level of education strongly affected the responses. Of the 361 qualities of a good mate listed by the less educated, only 15 percent referred to psychic congeniality, against 20 percent of such traits from a total of 202 qualities volunteered by high school graduates. The main finding in Komarovsky's study was that for some of these families, marriage is "not for friendship." It is not merely the meagerness of verbal communication that characterizes these marriages, but the absence of certain norms—especially the norm that the spouse should be one's closest confidant. (Compare her findings with Cuber and Harroff's study of upper-class marriages, cited in Chapter Three, which found that there is a strong trend toward marriages of convenience.)

While this study tends to be superficial, in that Komarovsky did not probe the deeper conflicts within these families, it does suggest that there are widely different preoccupations among men and women. All the material described so far in this book fits into the picture. Women are more concerned than men with love, much more frightened by adultery, and much more alarmed about adultery if they suspect their husbands. They move closer to the children, while the men move away and often feel isolated from their children.

But as usual, generalizations are very difficult. A couple's compatibility depends on so many different factors. Furthermore, the rather vague notion of intimacy, which has become so central to many modern people, lends itself to a variety of different interpretations. If there is a regression in the service of the spouse, for example (see Chapter Three), intimacy may and often does assume a rather infantile character. (One man who asked to be seen for therapy went nowhere without his wife—not even to his job.)

In the recent book by Shere Hite (1987) on marriage and love, Hite tends to blame the man for the loneliness and lack of companionship that many women complain about. Yet a study of men would probably yield the same feelings in men about women—that is, their trouble stems from their wives' excessive demands. (After all, the nagging wife has become a standard cliché.) When each side blames the other so much, the analyst would suspect that some paranoid complex is operative in either one or the other or both.

In seeking an answer to the dilemma of communication, the forces of repression and the unconscious must be given greater weight. Both men and women are cut off from large areas of their personality's functioning. When that happens, misunderstandings and quarrels are inevitable. This becomes another root cause for seeking a therapeutic revolution.

12 | Creative Man

FROM THE BEGINNING PSYCHOANALYSIS TOOK AN INTEREST IN creativity and the creative individual. The early attempts at understanding creativity came when id psychology reigned supreme (1900–1914). It was soon discovered that the material of writers, artists, and other creative individuals centered around the same basic impulses that motivate ordinary people: sexuality, aggression, and so on. The theory then arose that artists were able to display these impulses in a socially acceptable form and that artists transferred their narcissism from themselves to their work. Most simply, narcissism is self-involvement. This early theory was most explicitly set forth by Hanns Sachs, in his book *The Creative Unconscious* (1942). Creative artists (in the wide sense of the term, including scientists), then, are narcissistic individuals who are able to display impulses that are forbidden to the average person, because they present them in a distorted form, where the gratification is hidden. Because of their closeness to the primary process, creative artists are constantly hovering on the brink of a serious disturbance. The literature is full of biographies (originally called "pathographies") of famous artists who either broke down or were on the verge of doing so, beginning with Freud's own biography of Leonardo da Vinci (1910: SE XI).

Narcissism and the Artistic Process

Inherently, the narcissism of artists is a form of healthy narcissism, because it is transferred to their work rather than focused on themselves. They share their narcissistic experiences with an audience. A number of possibilities now arise:

1. Frequently this artistic process fails because artists are dealing with dangerous material. If the basic impulses come out too strongly, artists may become more interested in gratifying them than in doing their work (consider Gauguin, who suddenly left Paris and took off for Tahiti). In artists the gratification of the impulses without a brake carries in it all the dangers of psychosis, suicide, and self-destructive activity that it does in persons who are not artists. This is one reason why pathology is so frequent among artists: they are playing too close to the fire (consider van Gogh and his suicide).

2. When the artistic process succeeds, it may often do so by a regression in the service of the ego (Kris, 1952); the regression is permitted because the ego can make use of it. However, that regression may become too far-reaching, and the artist may not "come back" readily, or may not come back at all. Such regression is sometimes encouraged in analysis as well, although the possibility of a malignant use of the regression limits its therapeutic application.

    The frequency of psychosis among famous artists of all kinds is so common that it is sometimes taken as a matter of course. A top actor at one time requested that he be excused from a contract for a movie because he was mentally ill, and the studio held that this was not a valid excuse. Nijinsky, the top ballet dancer of his day, became psychotic and spent the rest of his life in a mental hospital. Among poets, John Berryman and his colleagues have already been noted (see Chapter Eleven).

3. In another kind of artist, there is a healthy acceptance of the basic impulses. This is the image of the Renaissance person—a hearty individual capable of enjoying life to the full. Rank (1932) sees this kind of person as normal, in contrast to the conforming average person and the will-crippled neurotic. (This concept can be used therapeutically: a patient with an oversupply of libido can be encouraged to move

into artistic expression. The development of occupational therapy for psychotics is another instance of the same principle.)

4. Quite often artists remain stuck in their narcissism. They have intimate contact with a small portion of reality, but outside of that sphere they are no different from the ordinary, inhibited person.

5. The artists' narcissism may become so severe that it takes the place of art. In that event artists no longer have the buffer of their artistic production; they become directly interested in displaying themselves. Such an increase in narcissism frequently leads to a greater or lesser degree of psychosis—or it may lead to an artistic idiosyncrasy copied by others.

    Among contemporary artists this identification of the artist with the art is often seen. Lucas Samaras provides one such instance. He often projects himself into his own paintings or photographs—sometimes clothed, sometimes in the nude. Reportedly, he has sometimes received visitors in the nude. All the motifs of his previous work reappear in the patterned cloth he stitches together into dazzling patchworks, "as if he were piecing the whole fabric of his past art into a grandiose and comedic crazy quilt" (R. Levin, 1979, p. 8). His identity is embedded in these hangings. One critic says of his work (R. Levin, 1979), "Narcissistic, radically eclectic, irreverent, his *Reconstructions* hang on the walls like glorious shrouds for an irretrievable past, ambivalent icons, security blankets for a postmodern future" (p. 7). It is interesting and relevant that Samaras, an immigrant, once wanted to study psychology and become a psychotherapist. Then his interest in other people receded and he turned back to himself.

6. Because of the opportunity for narcissistic gratification, many people are attracted to art as an avenue of release for their narcissism. They may have little or no talent for art, and little or no interest in it. They play artist in order to be bohemian; they are not bohemian because it is indispensable for their art.

The motto of such people is summed up in Edna St. Vincent Millay's sonnet (Stollworthy, 1974, p. 343):

> What lips my lips have kissed, and where, and why,
> I have forgotten . . .
> I cannot say what loves have come and gone;
> I only know that summer sang in me
> A little while, that in me sings no more.

While art may be used for neurotic purposes, it should not be supposed that art per se is neurotic. The true artist has a gift; as Freud once said, "The nature of the artistic function is inaccessible to us along psychoanalytic lines (1913: SE XI, p. 136). Phyllis Greenacre (1957) wrote, "I am myself largely convinced that genius is a 'gift of the Gods' " (p. 48).

But art is not all genius or divine inspiration; in fact, the confusion of artistic activity with inspiration is an error. If simple common sense is applied to creative individuals, it is immediately apparent that what characterizes them more than anything else is their capacity for work. The creative act is *work;* we speak of workmanship or craftsmanship in admiring terms. Similarly, the "creative block" represents an inability to work. This inability usually comes out as depression.

Michelangelo, in the Sistine Chapel, spent years lying on his back on an erected platform in order to execute his paintings. We marvel at the paintings but forget that he devoted every bit of his energy to the task, day and night, for four years. It is well known that many artists paint all their lives, that musicians practice six, eight, or ten hours a day for years. Such dedication is also typical of scientists, whose sublimations are the same as those of artists (Sharpe, 1935). The mathematician G. H. Hardy (1940) tells us in his autobiography, rather naively, that as far back as he could remember, he could beat the other boys in the class at mathematics; so all his life he did little besides mathematics. Anne Roe (1956), in her studies of scientists, repeatedly found that their major concern in life was work: relationships were kept at a minimal level and their major interest was in their scientific pursuits. Picasso, who turned out some

35,000 productions in the course of his long life, obviously could have had little time to do anything but work (Gedo, 1983). The sculptor Chaim Gross, in his introduction to Edrita Fried's (1958b) *Mental Health in the Creative Individual,* expresses some surprise at the psychoanalytic theory of creativity, stating that what he loved most in life was his artistic work, and that in fact what most of the artists he knew loved most was their work. And artists spend most of their time at it. Writers tell us that they devote a certain amount of time every day to writing, and many of them amass an extraordinary production in the course of their lives. August Strindberg, the Swedish playwright, found that when his works were collected, they ran to some fifty-five volumes, while Balzac notoriously worked all night and drove himself to an early death with his excesses. Bergler (1949) asks whether writers can ever really give up their calling, as they are so often asked to do; and he comes to the conclusion that they cannot. They are psychologically tuned to write, and the unconscious forces driving them in this direction are so strong that they cannot be overcome.

In fact, common sense dictates an observation about work in the creative individual that is the exact opposite of that in the noncreative individual. We are surprised when creative individuals suddenly give up their creative outlet, when they do nothing or turn to some other kind of activity. This creative block is found occasionally in every creative activity and poses a problem. On the other hand, if a businessperson or teacher or some other kind of person who ordinarily engages in some noncreative activity gives up work and lives life leisurely, or is incapacitated or retired, that usually engenders no wonder. Thus the naive reaction to creative individuals emphasizes the fact that they can work and that they can *enjoy* their work, in contradistinction to the average noncreative person.

Creativity and the Creative Block

Two forms of creativity can be distinguished: inner and outer. In inner creativity, seen most clearly in the growth of the child (Gardner, 1982), what counts is the growth process in the individual. The child sees something new, though it is old hat to everybody around him or her. In this form of creativity, expression is the major need. It is an aspect of the child's inner development, often lost as the child gets older.

In outer creativity the artistic product says something new to the outside world. This is the creativity of the professional artist or the expert in the field (who produces a "creative" idea). Often the gifted artist, after some initial successes, is able to develop a technique that is especially impressive to the outside world but that requires no new inspiration or ideas from him. Experts may see that the artist has stagnated, but the public continues to welcome his works. Such stagnation occurs in many creative artists in all fields.

Creativity is an essential ingredient in human existence. Genius, as Freud observed, is poorly understood; it is a special gift that so far has defied further scrutiny. The gift is more or less innate; the personality structure and the social environment determine how it will be developed or transformed. Social and familial conditions obviously play a prominent role; and some cultures—for example, Italy of the Renaissance, or Athens of the fifth century B.C.—are creativogenic, while others crush the creativity of the individual, demanding complete allegiance and subordination to the social order.

Creativity comes to the attention of the analyst in one or more of four ways: (1) the creative block, (2) the creative outlet for the average individual, (3) the understanding and analysis of the creative artist in any field, and (4) the growth of inner creativity through the process of psychoanalysis. Because creative block is the most important therapeutically, it will be considered in greater depth below.

Because the creative act is so close to the impulse life, it rarely flows smoothly. Almost all creative artists at times feel a block; they cannot go on with their creative activity, or they feel "uninspired." A typical case with an almost magical outcome is the following.

Irwin, a forty-year-old singer in a Broadway show, suddenly became panicky and could not sing his part any more. In consultation what came out was that he was an overt homosexual living with a twenty-year-old man in a most unhappy relationship that he was reluctant to explore. His mother, sixty-seven, had just come to town and, among other things, she took him around to help her buy brassieres.

The part that he was singing was that of a cantor officiating at a wedding. He had shared the part with another man, who had just been dismissed because he was so alcoholic that he could not come to work regularly. Thus Irwin had the part all to himself.

This enforced push to masculinity was too much for him to handle. When all the material was put together and pointed out to him by the analyst, he recovered so quickly that he was able to get back to the show the same night. As a precaution he sang only half of the part his first night back, reserving the full part for the second night.

Although he was urged to enter a full analysis to explore his unhappy love life, he refused.

As this case shows, phobic reactions such as stage fright often lend themselves to a quick resolution. Most likely this is why therapists of all persuasions have had the most success with phobia therapy. Here are two more instances.

The conductor Bruno Walter relates in his autobiography that in 1904 he suddenly developed a severe pain in his right shoulder (the conducting arm), which prevented him from conducting. He consulted Freud, who told him first to go to Italy for three weeks of vacation. When Walter objected, Freud persisted. Finally he did what the doctor had told him to do. When he came back, the pain was still there. Freud then told him to conduct and it would go away. Again he was reluctant to take the advice but again, obedient to authority, he did as he was told. The pain did disappear, so that he was able to conduct again (Pollock, 1975).

It is surprising to find Freud using suggestive therapy at this late date, when he was experimenting with the perfection of his analytic tool. But we do not know all the circumstances from Freud, only from Walter, who obviously wanted to get rid of the pain rather than probe into his psyche.

Emil, a thirty-year-old violinist, consulted a therapist for help because he had the constant obsession that a big guillotine would come down and chop off his penis. The fear was so great that he was unable to perform.

He was now being seen at a university clinic by a young therapist, a graduate student in training; he had been in analysis five times a week for a year in another town. Because of postwar conditions, the clinic was placed in a ramshackle old house. The toilet was next to the therapy room, so Emil could hear what went on there. In five sessions he spoke almost continuously about his life; the therapist said little, except to point out that he had an inordinate fear of the audience, thinking that they would not like his playing.

Even though the therapist offered virtually no interpretation, the patient's anxiety cleared up in about a month of once-a-week sessions. When asked why he felt so much better, he said, "I could hear the girls piss."

The patient's explanation of his improvement here should be taken seriously. His sexual problems involved the usual idealization of women, so that when he heard the women students go to the toilet, it took them off the pedestal on which he had placed them. The main interpretation given, that he was too concerned with the audience, relieved him enough that he could concentrate on his playing rather than on audience reaction.

Nurturing Creativity

In looking at the creative individual, the first question that arises is, Where does the extraordinary gift come from? Freud could not answer this question; nor can we today, with far more knowledge at our disposal. Somehow the ability seems inborn. But one thing is clear: whatever the gift, it appears early and is nurtured through a lifetime. Of this there can be no doubt. It has been documented innumerable times in the biographies of famous artists, writers, and other creative individuals. Picasso, the son of an artist, painted from an early age—as soon as he could hold a pencil or brush (Gedo, 1983). Van Gogh, whose active career lasted only ten years, had earlier filled his letters to his brother with innumerable sketches and drawings. In music

Mozart is the shining example (Schonberg, 1963): at the age of three, he was picking out notes at the harpsichord—not aimlessly, as most babies would, but carefully selecting thirds and other consonances. This amused him for hours at a time. At four he was studying little minuets. At five he was composing them. His ear was so accurate that it was bothered by quartertones and so delicate that the close-up sound of a trumpet made him faint dead away. Mozart's genius eclipsed that of his gifted father, whose book on teaching the violin is still used today. Other musicians show similar histories. Arthur Rubinstein (1973), for example, displayed his talent at the piano so early that he was sent to Berlin to study with great teachers when he was only six. In his autobiography he makes this revealing comment: "I have never kept a diary. . . . But it is my good fortune to be endowed with an uncanny memory which allows me to trace my whole long life almost day by day" (p. vi). This remarkable memory existed in him for music and for his life. Psychologically, we would say that his healthy narcissism comes to the fore here.

Mary Gedo (1983) draws striking parallels between the lives of Picasso and van Gogh, even though they seem so different on the surface. Picasso's creative life was characterized by a series of disruptions whenever his human milieu failed to live up to his stringent requirements. The most celebrated of these so-called dry spells followed the birth of his daughter, Maya, in 1935, when Picasso was equally estranged from his wife and from the mother of the newborn child, his mistress Marie-Thérèse Walter. A number of briefer episodes of the same kind occurred throughout the artist's career. Picasso always needed the reassurance of some beloved person—first his father, then his numerous mistresses and wives as well as friends—to do his best work. During numerous episodes in Picasso's life, he was on the brink of psychosis and rescued himself by finding a new woman and a new milieu in which to operate.

Van Gogh was much more isolated, but he still needed the stimulation of his brother, Theo, to be able to produce his astounding paintings. Thus besides the gift, the artist must have a teacher or mentor and he must work at his craft incessantly.

When the mentor is absent, or the work does not flow freely, a deep depression sets in.

Another example of the nurturing of creativity is found in Lawrence, who was twenty-six when he first came to treatment. He sought therapy because he felt too depressed to paint. He lived in a poor section of town, insisting on supporting himself by selling his paintings, which then brought about $200 or $300—enough to tide him over for a month or so. When he was out of money altogether, he would take a job moving paintings for galleries and museums around town, a job that called for some expertise in art.

He agreed that he would come twice a week for therapy, paying for one session with cash and the other with a painting. Later this was to arouse considerable resentment in him.

Lawrence's background was unusual. He was an identical twin, inseparable from his twin for the first four years of his life. He could communicate with his twin in their own private language until they were three and a half; his ordinary command of words did not come on until he was almost four.

Oddly enough, although he had been born in the apartment house in which the analyst lived and had lived there until he was eight, he could not remember the apartment. Father, who had been in the advertising business, was so enchanted with his twin sons that he wrote a book about them, with his own illustrations, which was published. Lawrence had warm feelings about father.

As far back as he could remember, he had been interested in painting. But he could not paint real-life objects. Once in high school a teacher had urged him to paint the real world, to which he had replied, "I want to look more into the inner world than into the outer."

He went to a progressive college where he could do pretty much as he pleased; so he painted, studying little of the academic material. He knew some girls there. In fact, though he always felt very lonely, there seem to have been many contacts with women all through his life.

After college he went to Europe to study, staying mostly in France. While there he had a severe depressive episode, for a while spending time in the south of France with a French prostitute. Consciously and unconsciously, he felt he was imitating van Gogh; he even had suicidal thoughts like van Gogh and tried to paint in startling colors, as van Gogh did in some of his work.

Initially he said that he did not know whether he could trust the therapist, so he interviewed him, placing importance on every detail that he learned about the therapist's life.

In his depressive periods he painted a circle, with no content, over and over. Gradually, as he began to mellow under the influence of the therapy, the circle began to fill up. This was to continue all through his career: clearly the circle had tremendous meaning for him. Eventually he found a woman, joined the Buddhist church (which gave him a great deal of serenity), and moved to Europe. There he lived on an island, isolated from most of the world, painted, raised his family, and was quite contented with his lot in life. In his work he was quite successful; he was able to have various one-person shows, and some of his paintings were bought by museums.

Lawrence's artistic capacity is traced readily enough to his father and the constant drawing he did as a child. Yet even though he was an identical twin, his brother went into another artform. His was a healthy narcissism (Fine and Fine, 1977) that focused exclusively on his artwork.

The symbol of the circle that he drew over and over again had many meanings. It was his world, his life, also his mother's breast. The depression and creative block that brought him to treatment represented a depressive regression to the breast; had it gone further, he might, like his idol van Gogh, have committed suicide. (What might have happened to van Gogh had he had a chance to be psychoanalyzed?)

Lawrence's positive reaction to the analysis can be explained by the gratification of the need to express himself in almost any form. As far back as high school, he had consciously formulated the idea that he wanted to explore his inner world, not his outer, and finally he seized the chance to do so. The analyst also served as a mentor, who provided him with a holding environment to curb his unruly impulses.

Male Versus Female Creativity

Why, among the creative geniuses in history, have there been so many more men than women? This question has frequently been raised, especially since the advent of the women's liberation movement. Some have seen this disproportion as an expression of the subjection of women, but that interpretation does not seem to hold up. The analytic theory has been that the artistic product represents for the artist—especially the male—a child. Because a woman can have her child naturally, she does not have to do so through an artificial artistic medium (Greenacre, 1960). Even when the woman does not have children, so much of her energy, bodily and spiritual, is taken up with the question of her child-bearing capacities that she cannot give other matters her undivided attention.

There are other factors involved as well. Women have more of a drive to socialize, which also means less of a need to abstract themselves, or to move into strong narcissism. Their libido tends to turn to other people more easily than to their own achievements. One could therefore expect great singers or great actresses, but not great physicists or great mathematicians.

The effect of the environment, however, should not be underestimated. The case of a first-class female chess master has recently come to world attention. Susan Polgar's father, a Hungarian—a psychologist by training—is committed to the thesis that women can do anything that men can do if they just try hard enough. He has three daughters, of whom Susan is the oldest. He directed them to train in mathematics. Susan soon found this rather difficult and turned to chess, where she displayed an astounding virtuosity, winning top prizes while she was still in her teens. She did not want to go to school; she wanted to study chess on her own. After some battles with the school authorities, she received permission to continue at home, under her father's tutelage. In a short time she climbed pretty high on the chess ladder—so high, in fact, that she refused to play in women's tournaments. It is the first time a young woman (she is now nineteen but started when she was fourteen or fifteen) has consistently been able to make her way with men in that field. At the same time it is reported that she still remains "female," making herself pretty, dating, and so on.

The Creative Artist in Therapy

Many creative people come to analysis for the resolution of their inner problems. Some succeed; some do not. As is so often the case, the realities are beyond the control of the analyst, and the realities for the gifted are often grim. Van Gogh's paintings have recently brought prices in the neighborhood of *$50 million,* but van Gogh almost starved to death, requiring financial support from his brother just to manage to live. In other respects the pathology of others may play a role too; for example, one actor was offered a part in a show on condition that he have sex with all the men in the show. This was especially galling for him because analysis had helped him to dispel his lifelong fear of homosexuality.

Like Norbert Wiener (discussed in Chapter Nine), many creative people on the current scene express the fear that analysis will rob them of their talents or, in Wiener's phrase, turn them into "contented cows." This fear is wholly unjustified. Actually, creative individuals such as Lawrence (above) often make excellent analytic subjects, because they have so much access to their inner world of fantasies, which the "normal" person tends to block off.

Edrita Fried has edited a book, *Artistic Productivity and Mental Health* (1958a), that reports the results of a research project at the Postgraduate Center for Mental Health in New York. The project involved the analysis of a number of artists. Details from the case of one, a painter, are included here.

Jonathan Norton, a painter, sought treatment because the multiple work blocks from which he suffered had virtually choked off all ability to paint. In his other areas of activity— teaching and administering; the daily life of his family and himself—he seemingly functioned well, even when he entered treatment. (He is a good example of someone with an adjustment neurosis.) However, a peek behind the facade of "normality" revealed that he had daily quarrels with his wife and had woven his intensely competitive and hostile feelings into a somewhat paranoid system that he projected upon colleagues to the point where they cut him off.

In appearance, manner, social relations, and self-image, he regarded himself as a father-figure to whom people would bring their problems. He had been an excellent art teacher for years. His classes were well attended; teaching was his major source of income.

Several factors in the life history were quite significant. At the time he started treatment, he was in his early forties. He had been introduced to painting by his cousin, twelve years older, who had then been living in the parental home. The cousin had later given up painting to become a successful advertising man.

At fourteen Jonathan had stolen one of his cousin's paintings and, presenting it as his own, had won a citywide contest. He remembered with embarrassment and humiliation the ridicule of his cousin and others when he said that he would be a famous artist someday. In spite of his later successes, he held on to the notion that his cousin, not he, should have been the artist. He lived in vague dread that his cousin would return to painting and outdistance him. This fear was constantly re-enacted with fellow artists, with guilt projected as betrayal and injustice.

Jonathan attended art school. Upon graduation he looked forward to a year abroad, to be financed by his cousin. When the cousin changed his mind, Jonathan had a somatic breakdown, although previously he had always been in excellent health. He had an emergency appendectomy, a hernia operation, a minor infection of the testicles, and his first hay fever attack. Later he developed asthma and diabetes, both of which cleared up in the course of psychotherapy.

Dreams were analyzed throughout treatment. At first Jonathan confirmed, in dreams, his feelings of injustice and betrayal. Gradually he saw how he used this defense, as well as others, to guard against real feelings of fear, hostility, and envy. He then began to use dreams in two ways: to clarify his conflicts and to withdraw from them by denying and detaching himself from his dreams. He recognized that this detachment occurred whenever new awareness became threatening. Periods of nondreaming were usually periods of even greater resistance, during which the therapist became a new transference figure preliminary to working through the next stage of therapy conflict. There were many dreams of inadequacy about his body and his genitals. In one his penis was awkward, and he splattered the wall with urine. In another a friend criticized the small size of his penis, as he in reality had criticized Jonathan's paintings.

Relieved of inner conflict, Jonathan began to feel healthy and energetic. Fatigue and all other somatic complaints were infrequent. Asthma waned. His sugar level, for the first time in years, was normal; he went off insulin, went on a strict diet, and lost thirty pounds. He now felt equal to his cousin. He said he felt as if at last he had attained his manhood.

Creatively, he was able to make new beginnings, with new forms, new styles. Emphasis had shifted from the compulsion always to begin again, with no feeling of continuity, to the joy and hope of new beginnings and their continuity. He found new strength in the reality of gratifying, positive situations that now seemed to be everywhere. In his love life there was also great change for the better.

Striking changes in his professional work also resulted from treatment. When he started therapy he had sold very few paintings. He was ashamed to sell them on a social basis, and the galleries were less and less eager to represent him because his work had shown no development. In addition, his suspicious manner alienated many gallery owners. In therapy he said that he sold himself whenever he sold a painting, and he felt that he did nothing worth selling. At one time, he held two one-person shows, and though he told everyone he was doing badly, the fact indicated quite the opposite. At the end of treatment, he was looking forward to his third one-person show, predicting that it would be a great success, which it was. His case shows how creative artists so readily fit into the analytic process.

Narcissism, Creativity, and Depression

I have already mentioned that artists transfer their narcissism from themselves to their work, and that there are dangers

inherent in this process. One of them is depression. The artist
thinks, "If you reject my work, you reject me, so I may as well
not live." The narcissism tends to be taken to extremes; many
artists never feel that they get enough recognition.

A number of years ago, I had the interesting experience
of standing next to Salvador Dali at an exhibition of surrealist
works, which naturally featured some of his. He had made a little sculpture entitled *Nude with Drawers:* the nude figure of a
woman, with drawers inserted at the levels of the vagina, the
breasts, and the mouth. Dali spent virtually the entire evening
playing with this figurine, pulling the drawers in and out. Nothing else at the show seemed to be of any interest to him. In spite
of his unquestioned genius, Dali seems to have fallen short of
greatness. No doubt one reason is that his narcissism became
too strong. Eventually he became much more interested in himself than in any of his productions, limiting himself for a time
to one painting per year. For a while he was close to psychosis,
if not actually psychotic.

Many artists, dissatisfied with the reception given their
work, fall into depressions. Lawrence presented one such picture, as did Jonathan Norton (both above). So too does Lincoln,
who after a promising start as a painter seemed to be able to go
nowhere. The best that he had ever done was to sell one painting to a client in Philadelphia, who paid him $2,500 for it.
Every once in a while Lincoln would go down to Philadelphia to
take a look at his painting and to relive his past success. To support himself he took a job working in silk screens.

Unfortunately, when he came to treatment he had a hack-
ing cough, which he had neglected. The therapist insisted that
he have a medical checkup, which he did. The diagnosis was
tuberculosis, and he was shipped off to a sanitarium. But the illness was so far progressed that he died within a year. Had he
attended to the disease sooner, he might still be alive. Narcissism had literally cost him his life: he fantasized so much about
painting that he had ignored his health.

As can easily be seen, narcissism is a variable quantity.
Some people are proud of their achievements but keep this
pride within bounds; others become so grandiose that they lose

all perspective of what they have done. This latter is true of many of the patients and well-known artists mentioned throughout the book. If artists' narcissism is excessive, success can literally "go to their head."

A further difficulty arises because the narcissism is directed at the production, not at the artist. And what artists want is praise of themselves; for narcissists the production can have a secondary value. It is in such men and women that we see the deepest depressions and extremes of self-condemnation. Nothing is ever good enough for them because the ultimate goal —infantile grandiosity—always eludes them.

Two attitudes may be distinguished among artists: the artistic and the esthetic. In the artistic the emphasis is on the positive creation by the *individual;* in the esthetic it is upon what *others* have done. In those with the artistic attitude, unhealthy narcissism substitutes art for life. Esthetic individuals are frequently severe critics of everything that is contemporary to them. They live in a world of "greatness," of "genius," of "immortal works" (as in Adler's "hundred greatest books"), which humbles the living who are working in the field. No sculptor can be as great as Michelangelo; no writer, as great as Shakespeare; no analyst, as great as Freud; and so on. With such an attitude, little of value is allowed to come through, and the person's creativity becomes stifled.

For such people art is more important than social suffering, so that if it is pointed out, for example, that August Strindberg was a most unhappy man with near-psychotic episodes several times in his life, that suffering is seen as insignificant in the light of all that he produced. As estheticians we may admire Strindberg and his insights, but as therapists we have to treat such an attitude as part of the neurotic picture.

One patient who wanted to be a poet would often express the feeling that his own personal suffering was entirely inconsequential. He felt a block in creating poetry, which had led him to therapy, and removing that block was all that counted. He was not interested in a better sex life or in better social relationships. He was familiar with the works of many great poets and focused on them in his spare time. Even in producing poetry, however, he was extremely narcissistic, because while, on the one hand, he felt that he had the capacity to be a great poet, on the other hand, he could not show his work to any critic. Eventually he abandoned treatment, because it could not make him a great poet. While seemingly extreme, this case is not so unusual. Grandiosity and grandiose achievements precede everything else in importance for some patients, and the notion that great people can be extremely unhappy in their personal life makes no impression on them. Psychoanalysis has been criticized for its emphasis on mental health. Yet we can recognize a man's genius and still be objective about the misery he experienced in his life.

Franz Kafka is a good example of the interweaving of personal misery and artistic genius (Brod, 1963). Kafka was born in Prague in 1883, the son of a businessman. His father opposed his wish to be a writer, and Kafka had to write privately, publishing very little during his lifetime. His great works came to light only after he died in 1924.

Because of his great insights into the problems of loneliness, suffering, and internal distress, Kafka was brought to light during World War II. In his novel *The Castle,* Kafka provides a beautiful description of how many modern people react to the world; it features a lonely man who would like to be a member of human society but does not know how, a man who turns everybody against him, a stranger. Kafka's biographer, Max Brod (who was also his best friend and who brought his works out after Kafka's death), comments that this is the special feeling of a Jew who would like to take root in foreign surroundings, who tries with all his might to get nearer to the strangers, to become one of them entirely, but who, because of his terrible inner fears, does not succeed in thus assimilating himself.

Kafka's biography shows that this was his own personal dilemma. He graduated from law school and took a job with the government that left him free after one o'clock in the afternoon. But because his father did not approve of his writing, he spent much of his life arguing with him (in his works) rather than getting his books printed. An important document in his psychic life was the *Letter to His Father.* He begins, "Dearest

Father, you once asked me why I maintain I am afraid of you. As usual, I didn't know how to answer you, partly because of this very fear I have of you, and partly because the explanation of this fear involves so many details that when I am talking I can't keep half of them together" (Brod, 1963, p. 16). About his relationship with his mother we are not well informed; she seems to have been a retiring housewife. But we do know that Kafka never could relate lovingly to a woman until the last year of his life. The fear and anxiety that he describes reveal the typical Oedipal conflict—closeness to mother, fear of father, inability to produce because father will not permit it. It happened that his personal conflict fitted very well the terrible anomie, isolation, and fear of our age, but it was still his personal isolation that he was describing, not the general state of the world.

Many artists on the scene today are enamored of the bohemian kind of life, in which they rebel against the conventional mores without substituting any real values of their own. As Rank (1932) points out, they wish to "play bohemian." Unfortunately, many persons in the arts fit into this category. They may have talent—perhaps even genius—but their rebellion and wish to suffer are so great that they ruin their lives. The comedian Lenny Bruce was such a person: to defy society he took to drugs. To the drug generation he represented the defiance of authority, yet that defiance was an expression of his deep insecurities. It was not surprising that Bruce, who was in legal trouble because of his excessive use of foul language (which would readily have been accepted ten years later) and drugs, finally committed suicide.

The social rewards that people often get for their narcissism—publicity, notoriety—are of considerable importance. Most artists in any field are poorly compensated financially; the few who make millions are the exception. The average writer earns about $4,000 per year; the few literary stars who get million-dollar advances for their books are few and far between. The discrepancy in social rewards that give a basketball player a million dollars each year while a research scientist who creates inventions that revolutionize the state of the world gets peanuts is indicative of the state of our society. (When Einstein published his epoch-making paper on the special theory of relativity in 1905, for example, he was an obscure clerk in the Swiss patent office.)

As a result of social rewards, the same kinds of narcissism that operate in artists operate in other people as well. Consider the scandal surrounding Nixon and Watergate: the fact that so many prominent men, up to and including the president, could engage in criminal or semicriminal activity to gain their own ends and consolidate their power is alarming for the state of the country. John Dean (1976), one of the "president's men," describes his state of mind as blind ambition; in therapeutic language we would say that he had a narcissistic search for power. On the flyleaf of his book, he records a conversation with a Mafia man in jail in 1974. The other man says, "Let me ask you something, if you don't mind. You look a little wet behind the ears to be the President's lawyer. How'd you get there so young? Your old man put in the fix?" Dean's response: "No. I just kissed a lot of ass, Vinny, a lot of it."

Narcissism and the Hero

A particularly dangerous aspect of narcissism grows out of society's tendency to glorify prominent people as heroes (Hook, 1943). The search for grandiosity is found at all levels of society, and from time immemorial some would literally murder to be seen as great or powerful. This is one element in the psychology of artistic individuals; they come to value recognition rather than merit. Sometimes, if others identify with them, they achieve recognition beyond their abilities; we find some of the most worthless writers or painters glorified in one generation only to be forgotten in the next. Average people, if they cannot become great themselves, will often idealize some other person, often a charismatic figure, join in a group that surrounds the charismatic figure, and pursue their own search for glory through the hero they have chosen. Even in psychoanalysis this psychology plays a significant role, in that theoreticians have at times been glorified who made no real contributions other than to participate in an "anti-Freudian crusade" (Fine, 1983, 1984). Wilhelm Reich is a good example. His theories of the orgone, bione, and so on are too absurd to be taken seriously, yet they *have* been taken seriously and praised to the skies by some of his followers. If an artist such as Nijinsky becomes psychotic, we can be sympathetic; but if an analyst such as Reich becomes psychotic (and he did: he was completely psychotic at the time he insisted that the orgone box cured cancer), we can only deplore the lack of social judgment that turned such a man into a hero.

Creativity and Madness

The idea that a positive correlation exists between genius (or at least intellectual ability) and mental illness is an old one that recurs from time to time. An Italian psychiatrist, Lombroso (1864), originally put the thesis in pseudoscientific form (*Genius and Insanity*), and he has often been quoted. For several decades Lombroso's works enjoyed a great popularity in America and Europe. With the advent of scientific psychology, however, these views were exploded as popular myths—although there have been, as I have mentioned, many geniuses who were also psychotic. Lange-Eichbaum (1921) mentions a large group of geniuses who became psychotic only after they had completed their great work. Today we know that a novel intellectual or artistic discovery can in fact have such strong repercussions in the individual that he or she may become psychotic. But this is better understood as the depressive or narcissistic reaction to the insufficiency of acclaim or reward that is received by the genius than an inherent component of the genius itself.

For the record, however, it should be stated that many eminent individuals have been disordered in mind and have made their contributions in spite of their emotional disturbances. Isaac Newton suffered from a psychosis that appeared as withdrawal from close contact with other human beings and the grandiose idea that, after he had discovered God's plan for running the universe on physical lines, he had to devote much of the rest of his life to trying to uncover what God's plan was in creating the history that humanity had endured. It should also be realized that a person may be exceedingly gifted in one area and incompetent, or totally disordered, in other areas. Many of the patients whom I have discussed in these pages had various emotional problems yet could still function and make their contributions. The human being is not all of one piece; the ego may be strong in one area and weak in another.

Positive Aspects of Creativity

There is a strong tendency to criticize a new idea, whether in art or science, as being "crazy." This has been the fate of new ideas in psychoanalysis and psychology for a long time. Yet sooner or later that criticism is often seen as due to envy or misunderstanding.

Otto Rank (1932), one of Freud's earliest collaborators, who later broke with him to form his own school, made his most significant contribution in the area of creativity (*Art and the Artist*). Rank saw the average person as bowing to the will of the majority, the neurotic person as crushed by the majority; the superior person was really the artist, whose creativity could transform the world. At the conclusion of his book, he wrote (pp. 430–431), "For the artistic individual has lived in art creation instead of actually letting his work live or die on its own account, and has never surrendered himself to life. In place of his own self the artist puts his objectified ego into his work, but though he does not save his subjective mortal ego from death, he yet withdraws himself from real life. And the creative type who can renounce this protection by art and can devote his whole creative force to life and the formation of life will be the first representative of the new human type, and in return for this renunciation will enjoy, in personality-creation and expression, a greater happiness."

Rank's position has not been followed by other analysts. We now see the creative individual as admirable, as someone to be imitated, but not as someone to make into a new kind of hero. That is really the fantasy of the artist who becomes too grandiose. Inner creativity has been offered as the growth of the child and the growth of the individual in psychotherapy. That is enough: creativity should be used, not glorified.

13 | Epilogue

THIS BOOK CENTERS AROUND A NUMBER OF DIFFERENT THEMES related to the topic of troubled men. That so many men in our society are troubled comes as a surprise to many, especially those who do not wish to delve more deeply into the psychology of contemporary humans. It is essential not to blink away the widespread character of disturbance, however. The number of psychotherapeutic professionals, with and without degrees, has already grown to 300,000, as I noted earlier; and one in three Americans, according to one estimate, consults those professionals. If such a large percentage of the population seeks psychotherapy, there must be good reason for it.

How to classify these troubled men and present the dynamics and treatment of their disorders is a thorny problem. I have chosen to do so on the basis of the analytic ideal—the image of the good life held out by psychoanalysis and psychoanalytic psychotherapy. This analytic ideal is an extension of Freud's dictum that the healthy man is the one who can love and work. Of these abilities, love is fundamental. Psychoanalysis is a philosophy of love, the most profound ever invented.

The analytic ideal serves many uses. First of all, it provides an approach to treatment that is lacking in other systems, yet it is the approach adopted in practice by a large number of practitioners. If a man above a certain age is not married, for example, he needs psychotherapy, not a marriage broker. There must be inner reasons that have held him back from marriage.

This implies that psychoanalysis and psychotherapy in general represent a philosophical system that is gradually gaining in understanding and popularity. Such a philosophy is replacing the older ethico-religious bases of living with a newer, less guilt-provoking system that makes very good sense to those who accept its basic premises and understand what the psychoanalysts are trying to say. The analysts, and more broadly the psychotherapists, become the secular philosophers of our times.

Within the treatment process itself, the analytic ideal points out the directions in which the patient can move most effectively. Most therapists on the scene today deny that they are imparting a set of values to the patient. I do not believe that that is the case. Perhaps my view is partly due to having started my academic career as a student of philosophy. Largely, however, it has come about because of my practical experience with patients and therapists. Values can be taught in various ways. The most effective is to have patients examine values, accept what they like, and discard what they do not like. At some time in the course of therapy, the values become explicit. Sometimes this leads to a lively argument; most of the time it does not.

In all studies of values, love is far ahead in the race, for love is indeed our primary value. In the course of therapy, the various neurotic meanings of love are discarded, and replaced by more realistic goals. Everybody is looking for love, yet few people are able to find it because of the numerous misconceptions that are found in our society.

The actual move to love involves a growth process and an overcoming of the hatred that is so common. In the time of the Crusades, when Christians went out to murder Moslems (and many Jews) in the course of their marauding, Geoffrey Plantagenet said, "Do you not know that it is our inheritance from remote times that no one loves another, but that always, brother against brother, and son against father, we try our utmost to injure one another?" How can love be taught in such a climate of hatred? Psychotherapy teaches us that it is possible, in spite of everything, to create more loving people. Some go only a certain distance; some make it the center of their existence. But all therapists would agree, I think, that unless there is some increase in the capacity to love, the therapy has failed of its main goal, though it may resolve some minor symptom.

The analytic ideal also provides a better formulation of

psychoanalytic theory than those currently in use. Most psych
analytic theorists are more concerned with the operations of t
mind than with the goals toward which psychotherapy could
and should progress. The tripartite structure (id-ego-superego)
is useful, but it does not place love squarely in the center of
things. Kohut (1971, 1977) hardly mentions love in his books,
though in theory he would probably accept its centrality. And
the analytic ideal stresses the philosophical character of psychotherapy: that it is not just a question of getting over some
minor handicap but a larger scheme for reconstructing the life
of the individual in a more meaningful and more gratifying way.
Too many therapists focus too much on the rituals of therapy—
what to say or do if the patient does this or that—and pay too
little attention to its ultimate goals.

What promise does psychotherapy hold out to produce
such extensive changes in people? The promise of past achievement. For, in spite of all the obstacles placed in its path, psychotherapy has already touched the lives of thousands, perhaps
millions, of people in a positive way. Statistical studies are notoriously unreliable in this area, for how shall we measure love?
Yet the analytic ideal, when properly elucidated, is something
anyone can grasp and most people *do* grasp.

The division of psychotherapy into 365 different schools
obscures the philosophy that guides it as well as the results it
obtains. Every school seems bent on denying the validity of all
other schools. I do not take such a negativistic position, although I have my own views on what is more effective and less
effective in any given situation—views that are in essential agreement with the mainstream Freudian psychoanalytic movement.

The analytic ideal also provides guidelines for education.
In these pages, for example, I have tried to explain the differences between the maladjustment disorders (the traditional psychoses and borderline states) and the adjustment disorders (those
troubling the average individual in our society). Our goal should
be to make mental hygiene based on this ideal as integral a part
of all education as physical hygiene is for the body.

Finally, the analytic ideal lays the basis for the therapeutic revolution that has been going on for perhaps 100 years. The

presenting problem of each patient becomes a different one if the ideal is kept in mind. The real question is not whether people need therapy but whether they are in a position to benefit from it. So far as we can see, *everybody* needs therapy, even though a formal therapeutic procedure can be provided for only a relatively small number—even with the 300,000 therapists now working. It is the worried well who are most amenable to the kind of therapeutic revolution that comes out of the analytic ideal. It should not be thought that the problems presented by these worried well are trivial or inconsequential in nature. If not treated, they can easily lead to suicide, murder, divorce, learning blocks, and all the other evils with which psychology today is contending.

Therapy and education along the line of the analytic ideal hold out the hope of a better future for humanity. That is the true promise of psychotherapy. Ideally, it will lead to a New Man, a New Woman, and a New World.

REFERENCES

Abraham, K. "Ejaculatio Praecox." In K. Abraham, *Selected Papers on Psychoanalysis.* New York: Basic Books, 1955a. (Paper originally published 1917.)

Abraham, K. "The History of an Impostor." In K. Abraham, *Selected Papers on Psychoanalysis.* New York: Basic Books, 1955b. (Paper originally published 1925.)

Abrams, S. "The Psychoanalytic Normalities." *Journal of the American Psychoanalytic Association,* 1979, *27,* 821–835.

Ackerman, N. W. *The Psychodynamics of Family Life.* New York: Basic Books, 1958.

Adams, P. L., Milner, J. R., and Schrepf, N. A. *Fatherless Children.* New York: Wiley, 1984.

Alexander, F., and Selesnick, S. *The History of Psychiatry.* New York: Harper & Row, 1966.

Allardt, E. " An Attempt at a Discussion About the Quality of Life and Morality in Industrial Society." In B. Gardell and G. Johansson (eds.), *Working Life: A Social Science Contribution to Work Reform.* New York: Wiley, 1981.

American Psychiatric Association. *Diagnostic and Statistical Manual of Mental Disorders. DSMI.* Washington, D.C.: American Psychiatric Association, 1952.

American Psychiatric Association. *Diagnostic and Statistical Manual of Mental Disorders. DSMII.* (2nd ed.) Washington, D.C.: American Psychiatric Association, 1968.

American Psychiatric Association. *Diagnostic and Statistical*

Manual of Mental Disorders. DSMIII. (3rd ed.) Washington, D.C.: American Psychiatric Association, 1980.

American Psychiatric Association. *Diagnostic and Statistical Manual of Mental Disorders. DSMIIIR.* (3rd ed., rev.) Washington, D.C.: American Psychiatric Association, 1987.

Anthony, E. J., and Koupernik, C. (eds.). *The Child in the Family.* New York: Wiley, 1970.

Anzieu, D. *Freud's Self-Analysis.* New York: International Universities Press, 1986.

Arieti, S. *Interpretation of Schizophrenia.* New York: Basic Books, 1974.

Aristotle. "Politics"; *Rhetoric.* In W. D. Ross (ed., trans.), *Works.* Oxford: Clarendon Press, 1952.

Astrachan, A. *How Men Feel.* New York: Doubleday, 1986.

Barry, H., Bacon, M. W., and Child, I. L. "A Cross-Cultural Study of Some Sex Differences in Socialization." *Journal of Abnormal and Social Psychology,* 1957, *55,* 327–332.

Bartell, G. *Group Sex.* New York: New American Library, 1971.

Barlett, D., and Steele, J. *Empire: The Life, Legend, and Madness of Howard Hughes.* New York: Norton, 1979.

Bell, A. P., and Weinberg, M. S. *Homosexualities.* New York: Simon & Schuster, 1978.

Bellah, R., and others. *Habits of the Heart.* Berkeley: University of California Press, 1985.

Bellak, L. "Free Association." *International Journal of Psychoanalysis,* 1961, *43,* 9–20.

Bellak, L., Gediman, H., and Hurvich, M. *Ego Functions in Neurotics, Schizophrenics, and Normals.* New York: Wiley, 1973.

Bellak, L., and Goldsmith, L. (eds.). *The Broad Scope of Ego Function Assessment.* New York: Wiley, 1984.

Benson, L. *Fatherhood: A Sociological Perspective.* New York: Random House, 1968.

Berengarten, S. "A Pioneer Workshop in Student Selection." *Bulletin of the New York School of Social Work,* 1951, *44,* 3–12.

Beres, D. "Ego Deviation and the Concept of Schizophrenia." *Psychoanalytic Quarterly,* 1956, *25,* 460–462.

Bergler, E. *The Basic Neurosis.* Orlando, Fla.: Grune & Stratton, 1949.

Berliner, B. "The Role of Object Relations in Moral Masochism." *Psychoanalytic Quarterly,* 1958, *27,* 38–56.

Berman, P. W., and Pedersen, F. A. *Men's Transitions to Parenthood.* Hillsdale, N.J.: Erlbaum, 1987.

Bieber, I., and others. *Homosexuality.* New York: Basic Books, 1962.

Bleuler, M. *The Schizophrenic Disorders.* New Haven: Yale University Press, 1978.

Blumstein, P., and Schwartz, P. *American Couples.* New York: Morrow, 1983.

Bowlby, J. *Attachment and Loss.* 3 vols. New York: Basic Books, 1969, 1973, 1980.

Brazelton, T. B., and Als, H. "Four Early Stages in the Development of Mother-Infant Interaction." *Psychoanalytic Study of the Child,* 1979, *34,* 349–370.

Brod, M. *Franz Kafka.* New York: Schocken Books, 1963.

Brodsky, A., and Hare-Mustin, R. (eds.). *Women and Psychotherapy.* New York: Guilford Press, 1980.

Burnham, D. L., Gladstone, A. I., and Gibson, W. *Schizophrenia and the Need-Fear Dilemma.* New York: International Universities Press, 1969.

Burr, A. R. *The Autobiography.* Boston: Houghton Mifflin, 1909.

Calef, V., and Weinshel, E. M. "The New Psychoanalysis and Psychoanalytic Revisionism." *Psychoanalytic Quarterly,* 1979, *48,* 470–491.

Canciano, F. M. *Love in America.* New York: Cambridge University Press, 1987.

Cannon, W. *Bodily Changes in Pain, Hunger, Fear, and Rage.* Boston: Branford, 1929.

Caplow, T., and others. *Middletown Families.* Minneapolis: University of Minnesota Press, 1982.

Cardan, J. *Book of My Life.* (Originally published 1965.)

Casanova, J. *The Memoirs of Jacques Casanova de Seingalt.* New York: A. and C. Boni, 1932. (Originally published 1788.)

Cath, S. H., Gurwitt, A. R., and Ross, J. M. (eds.). *Father and Child.* Boston: Little, Brown, 1982.

Chafetz, M. E., Hertzman, M., and Berenson, D. "Alcoholism: A Positive View." In S. Arieti (ed.), *American Handbook of Psychiatry,* Vol. 3. New York: Basic Books, 1974.

Chein, I., and others. *The Road to H.* New York: Basic Books, 1964.

Chiland, C., and others. *Long-Term Treatments of Psychotic States.* New York: Human Sciences Press, 1979.

Cuber, J., and Harroff, P. *The Significant Americans.* East Norwalk, Conn.: Appleton-Century-Crofts, 1965.

Cunningham, S. "Research Finds Monkeys Convey Information in Calls." *APA Monitor,* 1985, *16* (18), 38.

Daniels, G. F. "A Case of Alcoholism." *Psychoanalytic Quarterly,* 1933, *2,* 123-130.

Darwin, C. *The Origin of Species.* New York: New American Library, 1958. (Originally published 1859.)

Dean, J. *Blind Ambition.* New York: Simon & Schuster, 1976.

De Mause, L. *The History of Childhood.* New York: Psychohistory Press, 1974.

de Tocqueville, A. *Democracy in America.* New York: Doubleday, 1969. (Originally published 1836.)

Deutsch, F. "Analytic Posturology." *Psychoanalytic Quarterly,* 1952, *20,* 196-210.

Deutsch, H. *The Psychology of Women.* 2 vols. Orlando, Fla.: Grune & Stratton, 1944.

Diener, E., Horwitz, J., and Emmons, R. A. "Happiness of the Very Wealthy." *Social Indicators Research,* 1985, *16,* 263-274.

Dohrenwend, B. P., and others. *Mental Illness in the United States.* New York: Praeger, 1980.

Dowling, C. *The Cinderella Complex.* New York: Summit Books, 1981.

Edgcumbe, R. "Toward a Developmental Line for the Acquisition of Language." *Psychoanalytic Study of the Child,* 1981, *36,* 71-104.

Ehrenreich, B. *The Hearts of Men.* New York: Doubleday, 1983.

Ehrenreich, B., and English, D. *For Her Own Good.* New York: Doubleday, 1978.

Eidelberg, L. *Take Off Your Mask.* New York: International Universities Press, 1949.

Ekman, P. (ed.). *Emotion in the Human Face.* New York: Cambridge University Press, 1972.

Ellis, G.F.R. "The Dimensions of Poverty." *Social Indicators Research,* 1984, *15,* 229–253.

Erikson, E. *Childhood and Society.* New York: Norton, 1950.

Evans, N. J. "The Passing of the Gentleman." *Psychoanalytic Quarterly,* 1949, *17,* 19–43.

Fenichel, O. *Problems of Psychoanalytic Technique.* New York: Psychoanalytic Quarterly, 1941.

Fenichel, O. *The Psychoanalytic Theory of Neurosis.* New York: Norton, 1945.

Fine, R. "The Search for Love." In A. Burton and Associates, *Twelve Therapists: How They Live and Actualize Themselves.* San Francisco: Jossey-Bass, 1972.

Fine, R. "Comments on Evelyn Hooker: The Psychology of Male Homosexuals." *International Journal of Psychoanalytic Psychology,* 1973, *11,* 471–475.

Fine, R. *Psychoanalytic Psychology.* New York: Aronson, 1975.

Fine, R. *The Intimate Hour.* New York: Avery Press, 1979a.

Fine, R. *A History of Psychoanalysis.* New York: Columbia University Press, 1979b.

Fine, R. *The Psychoanalytic Vision.* New York: Free Press, 1981.

Fine, R. *The Healing of the Mind.* New York: Free Press, 1982.

Fine, R. *The Logic of Psychology.* Washington, D.C.: University Press of America, 1983.

Fine, R. "The Anti-Freudian Crusade." *Journal of Psychoanalytic Anthropology,* 1984, *5,* 435–444.

Fine, R. *The Meaning of Love in Human Existence.* New York: Wiley, 1985.

Fine, R. *Narcissism, the Self, and Society.* New York: Columbia University Press, 1986.

Fine, R. *The Forgotten Man.* New York: Haworth Press, 1987a.

Fine, R. "The Psychoanalytic Theory of Homosexuality." In L.

Diamant (ed.), *Male and Female Homosexuality.* Washington, D.C.: Hemisphere, 1987b.

Fine, R., and Fine, B. "The Mathematician as a Healthy Narcissist." In M. C. Nelson (ed.), *The Narcissistic Condition.* New York: Human Sciences Press, 1977.

Firestein, S. K. *Termination in Psychoanalysis.* New York: International Universities Press, 1978.

Fischer, D. K., and Srole, L. (eds.). *Mental Health in the Metropolis.* New York: New York University Press, 1978.

Fitzgerald, F. S. *Tender Is the Night.* New York: Scribner's, 1960. (Originally published 1934.)

Flugel, J. C. *The Psychoanalytic Study of the Family.* London: Hogarth Press, 1921.

Fobes, L. J., and King, J. E. (eds.). *Primate Behavior.* New York: Academic Press, 1982.

Fortes, M. "Custom and Conscience in Anthropological Perspective." *International Review of Psychoanalysis,* 1977, *4,* 127–154.

Fraiberg, S. (ed.). *Clinical Studies in Infant Mental Health.* New York: Basic Books, 1980.

Frayser, S. G. *Varieties of Sexual Experience.* New Haven, Conn.: HRAF Press, 1985.

Freedman, D. X., and Redlich, C. *The Theory and Practice of Psychiatry.* New York: Basic Books, 1966.

Freeman, L. *Fight Against Fears.* New York: Lancer Books, 1951.

Freud, A. *The Psychological Treatment of Children.* London: Imago, 1946.

Freud, A. *Normality and Pathology in Childhood.* New York: International Universities Press, 1965.

Freud, S. *The Standard Edition of the Complete Psychological Works of Sigmund Freud.* 24 vols. (J. Strachey, ed.) London: Hogarth Press and Institute for Psychoanalysis, 1953–1974.

Freud, S., and Pfister, O. *Correspondence.* New York: Basic Books, 1963. (Originally published 1928.)

Fried, E. (ed.). *Artistic Productivity and Mental Health.* Springfield, Ill.: Thomas, 1958a.

Fried, E. (ed.). *Mental Health in the Creative Individual.* Springfield, Ill.: Thomas, 1958b.

Frings, H., and Frings, M. *Animal Communication.* Norman, Okla.: University of Oklahoma Press, 1977.

Frosch, J. *The Psychotic Process.* New York: International Universities Press, 1983.

Fuerstein, L. A. "A Case of Exhibitionism: Self-Hatred Beneath a Mask." *Current Issues in Psychoanalytic Practice,* 1984, *1,* 69–82.

Gabriel, T. "Why Wed?" *New York Times* magazine, Oct. 15, 1987.

Galbraith, J. *The New Industrial State.* Boston: Houghton Mifflin, 1973.

Galdston, R. "The Longest Pleasure: A Psychoanalytic Study of Hatred." *International Journal of Psychoanalysis,* 1987, *68,* 371–378.

Galenson, E., and Roiphe, H. *Infantile Origins of Sexual Identity.* New York: International Universities Press, 1981.

Gardell, B., and Johansson, G. (eds.). *Working Life: A Social Science Contribution to Work Reform.* New York: Wiley, 1981.

Gardner, H. *Art, Mind, and Brain.* New York: Basic Books, 1982.

Gedo, M. *Picasso: Art as Autobiography.* Chicago: University of Chicago Press, 1983.

Geertz, C. *The Interpretation of Cultures.* New York: Basic Books, 1973.

Gelles, R. J. *The Violent Home.* Beverly Hills, Calif.: Sage, 1972.

Gelman, D. "Marketing Shrinks." *Newsweek,* Dec. 14, 1987, pp. 70–72.

Gilligan, C. *In a Different Voice.* Cambridge, Mass.: Harvard University Press, 1982.

Gitelson, M. "On the Identity Crisis in American Psychoanalysis." *Journal of the American Psychoanalytic Association,* 1954, *12,* 451–476.

Glover, E. *The Technique of Psychoanalysis.* New York: International Universities Press, 1955.

Glover, E. "On Metapsychology or Metaphysics: A Psychoanalytic Essay." *Psychoanalytic Quarterly,* 1966, *35,* 173–190.

Goldberger, M., and Evans, D. "On Transference Manifestations in Male Patients with Female Analysts." *International Journal of Psychoanalysis,* 1985, *66,* 295–309.

Goldensohn, S. S. "Psychoanalytic Economics in the Coming Generation." *Journal of the American Academy of Psychoanalysis*, 1986, *15*, 433–458.

Goldensohn, S. S., and Fink, R. "Mental Health Services for Medicaid Enrollees in a Prepaid Group Practice Plan." *American Journal of Psychiatry*, 1979, *136*, 160–164.

Gomberg, E. S., and Franks, V. (eds.). *Gender and Disordered Behavior*. New York: Brunner/Mazel, 1979.

Gonsiorek, J. C. (ed.). *Homosexuality*. Beverly Hills, Calif.: Sage, 1982.

Gordon, M. (ed.). *The American Family in Social-Historical Perspective*. New York: St. Martin's Press, 1978.

Gove, W. R. "Sex Differences in the Epidemiology of Mental Disorders: Evidence and Explanations." In E. S. Gomberg and V. Franks (eds.), *Gender and Disordered Behavior*. New York: Brunner/Mazel, 1979.

Green, R. J., and Framo, J. L. *Family Therapy*. New York: International Universities Press, 1981.

Greenacre, P. "The Childhood of the Artist." *Psychoanalytic Study of the Child*, 1957, *12*, 47–72.

Greenacre, P. "Woman as Artist." *Psychoanalytic Quarterly*, 1960, *29*, 208–227.

Greenacre, P. *Emotional Growth*. 2 vols. New York: International Universities Press, 1971.

Greenson, R. R. *The Technique and Practice of Psychoanalysis*. New York: International Universities Press, 1967.

Greenson, R. R. "The 'Real' Relationship Between the Patient and the Psychoanalyst." In M. Kanzer (ed.), *The Unconscious Today*. New York: International Universities Press, 1971.

Greenson, R. R., and Wexler, M. "The Nontransference Relationship in the Psychoanalytic Situation." *International Journal of Psychoanalysis*, 1969, *59*, 27–39.

Grotjahn, M. *Psychoanalysis and the Family Neurosis*. New York: Norton, 1960.

Gunderson, J., Carpenter, W., and Strauss, B. "Borderline and Schizophrenic Patients: A Comparative Study." *American Journal of Psychiatry*, 1977, *1132*, 1257–1264.

Halliday, J. *Psychosomatic Society.* New York: Norton, 1948.

Hanson, S. M. H., and Bozett, F. W. *Dimensions of Fatherhood.* Beverly Hills, Calif.: Sage, 1985.

Hardy, G. H. *A Mathematician's Apology.* New York: Cambridge University Press, 1940.

Hartmann, H. "The Concept of Health." *International Journal of Psychoanalysis,* 1939, *20,* 308–321.

Hartmann, H. *Essays in Ego Psychology.* New York: International Universities Press, 1964.

Hartmann, H., Kris, E., and Loewenstein, R. M. "Comments on the Formation of Psychic Structure." *Psychoanalytic Study of the Child,* 1946, *2,* 11–38.

Hatterer, L. J. *Changing Homosexuality in the Male.* New York: Dell, 1971.

Hatton, C. L., Valente, S. M., and Rink, A. *Suicide: Assessment and Intervention.* East Norwalk, Conn.: Appleton-Century-Crofts, 1977.

Hendin, H. *Suicide and Scandinavia.* Orlando, Fla.: Grune & Stratton, 1964.

Henry, W. H., Sims, J. H., and Spray, S. L. *The Fifth Profession: Becoming a Psychotherapist.* San Francisco: Jossey-Bass, 1971.

Henry, W. H., Sims, J. H., and Spray, S. L. *Public and Private Lives of Psychotherapists.* San Francisco: Jossey-Bass, 1973.

Herzberg, F. *Work and the Nature of Man.* New York: World, 1966.

Herzberg, F., Mausner, B., and Snyderman, B. B. *The Motivation to Work.* New York: Wiley, 1959.

Herzog, J. M. "On Father Hunger." In S. H. Cath, A. R. Gurwitt, and J. M. Ross (eds.), *Father and Child.* Boston: Little, Brown, 1982.

Hewlett, S. *A Lesser Life.* New York: Morrow, 1986.

Hinchliffe, M. K., Hooper, D., and Roberts, F. J. *The Melancholy Marriage.* New York: Wiley, 1978.

Hinde, R. A. (ed.). *Non-Verbal Communication.* New York: Cambridge University Press, 1972.

Hite, S. *Marriage and Love.* New York: Knopf, 1987.

Hogan, A. P. *Transitions and Social Change: The Early Lives of American Men.* Orlando, Fla.: Academic Press, 1981.

Hogarth, R. M., and Reder, M. W. *Rational Choice.* Chicago: University of Chicago Press, 1987.

Hollingshead, A. B., and Redlich, F. C. *Social Class and Mental Illness.* New York: Wiley, 1958.

Holt, R. R., and Luborsky, L. *Personality Patterns of Psychiatrists.* New York: Basic Books, 1958.

Holt, R. R., and others. *LSD: Personality and Experience.* New York: Wiley, 1972.

"Homosexual Life Styles and AIDS." *New York Times,* July 23, 1985.

Hook, S. *The Hero in History.* Boston: Beacon Press, 1943.

Horney, K. "The Problem of the Monogamous Ideal." *International Journal of Psychoanalysis,* 1928, *9,* 318–331.

Hornick, E. J. "Psychiatric Residents in the Ghetto." *Book Forum,* 1974, *1,* 222–231.

Hosken, F. P. *The Hosken Report: Genital and Sexual Mutilation of Females.* Lexington, Mass.: Women's International Network News, 1979.

Houpt, K. A., and Wolski, T. R. *Domestic Animal Behavior for Veterinarians and Animal Scientists.* Ames: Iowa State University Press, 1982.

Hoyt, F. *The Kamikazes.* New York: Arbor House, 1983.

Hrdy, S. B. *The Langurs of Abu: Female and Male Strategies of Reproduction.* Cambridge, Mass.: Harvard University Press, 1977.

Hrdy, S. B. *The Woman That Never Evolved.* Cambridge, Mass.: Harvard University Press, 1981.

Hrdy, S. B., and Hausfater, G. (eds.). *Infanticide: Comparative and Evolutionary Perspectives.* New York: Aldine, 1984.

Hunt, M. *The Natural History of Love.* New York: Knopf, 1959.

Hunt, M. "Choosing a Therapist." *New York Times,* Sept. 27, 1987, Section VII, p. 8.

James, W. *The Principles of Psychology.* New York: Dover, 1950. (Originally published 1890.)

Jarvis, E. *Report on Insanity and Idiocy in Massachusetts by the Commission on Lunacy.* Cambridge, Mass.: Harvard University Press, 1971. (Originally published 1855.)

Jellinek, E. M. *The Disease Concept of Alcoholism.* Highland Park, N.J.: Hillhouse Press, 1960.

Jencks, C., and others. *Who Gets Ahead?* New York: Basic Books, 1979.

Jones, E. "Psychoanalysis and Psychiatry." In E. Jones, *Collected Papers on Psychoanalysis.* (5th ed.) London: Bailliere, Tindall, and Cox, 1948.

Jones, E. "The God Complex." Reprinted in E. Jones (ed.), *Essays in Applied Psychoanalysis,* Vol. 2. London: Hogarth Press, 1951.

Jones, E. *The Life and Work of Sigmund Freud.* 3 vols. New York: Basic Books, 1953, 1955, 1957.

Jones, E. E., Kerig, P. K., and Krupnik, J. L. "Some Gender Differences in Brief Psychotherapy." *Psychotherapy,* 1987, *24,* 336–352.

Jung, C. *Psychological Types.* Boston: Routledge & Kegan Paul, 1923.

Kahn, R. "Work and Health." In B. Gardell and G. Johansson (eds.), *Working Life: A Social Science Contribution to Work Reform.* New York: Wiley, 1981.

Kallen, H. (ed.). "The Philosophy of William James Drawn from His Own Works." *Encyclopaedia Britannica.*

Kaplan, H. *The Evaluation of Sexual Disorders.* New York: Brunner/Mazel, 1983.

Kardiner, A. *The Psychological Frontiers of Society.* New York: Columbia University Press, 1939.

Kardiner, A. *The Individual and His Society.* New York: Columbia University Press, 1945.

Karon, B. P., and Vandenbos, G. R. *Psychotherapy of Schizophrenia: The Treatment of Choice.* New York: Aronson, 1981.

Kelly, E. L., and Fiske, D. W. *The Prediction of Performance in Clinical Psychology.* Ann Arbor: University of Michigan Press, 1951.

Kernberg, O. F. *Severe Personality Disorders.* New Haven, Conn.: Yale University Press, 1984.

Kinsey, A. C., Pomeroy, W. B., and Martin, C. F. *Sexual Disorders in the Human Male.* Philadelphia: Saunders, 1948.

320

References

Kinsey, A. C., Pomeroy, W. B., Martin, C. F., and Gebhard, P. *Sexual Disorders in the Human Female.* Philadelphia: Saunders, 1953.

Klein, M. *The Psychoanalysis of Children.* London: Hogarth Press, 1932.

Klein, M., Heiman, P., and Money-Kyrle, R. E. (eds.). *New Directions in Psychoanalysis.* New York: Basic Books, 1955.

Kleinman, A. *Patients and Healers in the Context of Culture.* Berkeley: University of California Press, 1980.

Kleinman, A., and Good, B. *Culture and Depression.* Berkeley: University of California Press, 1985.

Klerman, G. "Diagnosis of Psychiatric Disorders in Epidemiological Field Studies." *Archives of General Psychiatry,* 1985, *31,* 723-724.

Kohut, H. *The Analysis of the Self.* New York: International Universities Press, 1971.

Kohut, H. *The Restoration of the Self.* New York: International Universities Press, 1977.

Kolb, L. C., and Brodie, H. U. H. *Modern Clinical Psychiatry.* (10th ed.) Philadelphia: Saunders, 1982.

Komarovsky, M. *Blue Collar Marriage.* New York: Random House, 1967.

Kris, E. *Psychoanalytic Explorations in Art.* New York: International Universities Press, 1952.

Kulish, N. M. "The Effect of the Sex of the Analyst on Transference." *Bulletin of the Menninger Clinic,* 1984, *48,* 95-110.

Lamb, M. (ed.). *The Role of the Father in Child Development.* New York: Wiley, 1981.

Lamb, M. (ed.). *The Father's Role: Applied Perspectives.* New York: Wiley, 1986.

Lange-Eichbaum, S. *The Problem of Genius.* New York: Macmillan, 1921.

Laplanche, J., and Pontalis, J. B. *The Language of Psychoanalysis.* New York: Norton, 1973.

Lasswell, H. D. *Psychopathology and Politics.* New York: Viking Penguin, 1930.

Laufer, M., and Laufer, M. E. *Adolescence and Developmental Breakdown.* New Haven, Conn.: Yale University Press, 1984.

Lerner, R. A., and Salt, R. E. *Men in Families.* Beverly Hills, Calif.: Sage, 1986.

Lester, B. M., and Boukydis, C. F. Z. *Infant Crying.* New York: Plenum, 1985.

Lester, E. "The Female Analyst and the Eroticized Transference." *International Journal of Psychoanalysis,* 1985, *65,* 285–293.

Levin, H. "War Between the Shrinks." *New York Magazine,* May 21, 1979, pp. 82–84.

Levin, M. "A New Fear in Writers." *NPAP,* 1953, *2,* 34–38.

Levin, R. (ed.). *Samaras.* New York: Pace Gallery, 1979.

Levine, S. V. "The Urban Commune." Quoted in B. Zablocki, *Alienation and Charisma.* New York: Free Press, 1980.

Levinson, A. J., and others. *The Seasons of a Man's Life.* New York: Ballantine Books, 1978.

Lewis, C., and O'Brien, M. (eds.). *Reassessing Fatherhood.* Beverly Hills, Calif.: Sage, 1987.

Lewis, F. "Iran-Iraq War." *New York Times,* Apr. 16, 1984.

Lewis, O. *La Vida.* New York: Random House, 1966.

Lewis, O. *Anthropological Essays.* New York: Random House, 1970.

Lidz, T., Fleck, S., and Cornelison, A. *Schizophrenia and the Family.* New York: International Universities Press, 1965.

Locke, S. *Foundations of Psychoneuroimmunology.* New York: Aldine, 1985.

Loomie, L. S. "Some Ego Considerations in the Silent Patient." *Journal of the American Psychoanalytic Association,* 1961, *42,* 56–78.

Ludwig, A. *The Importance of Lying.* Springfield, Ill.: Thomas, 1965.

McClelland, D. *The Achieving Society.* New York: Van Nostrand Reinhold, 1961.

Maccoby, E. E., and Jacklin, C. N. *The Psychology of Sex Differences.* Stanford, Calif.: Stanford University Press, 1974.

McDermott, M. (ed.). *The Writings of William James.* Chicago: University of Chicago Press, 1978.

McDougall, J. *Theaters of the Mind.* New York: Basic Books, 1985.

McGill, V. J. *The Idea of Happiness.* New York: Praeger, 1967.

Maetze, G. *Psychoanalyse in Berlin.* Meisenheim am Glan: Verlag Anton Hain, 1970.

Malinowski, B. *Sex and Repression in Savage Society.* San Diego, Calif.: Harcourt Brace Jovanovich, 1927.

Malleus Maleficarum. London: John Rodker, 1928. (Originally published 1484.)

Marden, O. S. *Character: The Greatest Thing in the World.* N.p., 1899.

Marsella, A., and White, G. M. *Cultural Conceptions of Mental Health and Therapy.* Boston: Reidel, 1982.

Masters, W., and Johnson, V. E. *Human Sexual Response.* Boston: Little, Brown, 1966.

Masters, W., and Johnson, V. E. *Homosexuality in Perspective.* Boston: Little, Brown, 1979.

Mayr, E. *The Growth of Biological Thought.* Cambridge, Mass.: Harvard University Press, 1982.

Mead, M. *Sex and Temperament in Three Primitive Societies.* New York: New American Library, 1935.

Mead, M. *Male and Female.* New York: Morrow, 1949.

Menninger, K. *A Psychiatrist's World.* New York: Viking Penguin, 1959.

Menninger, K. *The Vital Balance.* New York: Viking Penguin, 1963.

Mercano, S., and others. "Official Report to the Latin-American Congress on Psychoanalysis: Dominant Trends in Latin American Thought." *Current Issues in Psychoanalytic Practice,* 1987, *4,* 19–26.

Minuchin, S., and others. *Families of the Slums.* New York: Basic Books, 1967.

Money, J., and Ehrhardt, A. A. *Man and Woman, Boy and Girl.* Baltimore, Md.: Johns Hopkins University Press, 1971.

Moore, B. E., and Fine, B. D. (eds.). *A Glossary of Psychoanalytic Terms and Concepts.* New York: American Psychoanalytic Association, 1968.

Morgan, T. *Maugham: A Biography.* New York: Simon & Schuster, 1982.

Moss, C. *Portraits in the Wild.* Chicago: University of Chicago Press, 1982.

Moynihan, D., and Glazer, N. (eds.). *Ethnicity: Theory and Experience.* Cambridge, Mass.: Harvard University Press, 1975.

Murdock, G. *Social Structure.* New York: Free Press, 1949.

Norwood, R. *Women Who Love Too Much.* New York: Pocket Books, 1985.

Nydes, J. "The Paranoid-Masochistic Character." *Psychoanalytic Review,* 1963, *40,* 215–251.

Offer, D. *The Adolescent: A Psychological Self-Portrait.* New York: Basic Books, 1981.

Orlinsky, D., and Howard, K. "The Effects of Sex of Therapist on the Therapeutic Experiences of Women." *Psychotherapy,* 1976, *16,* 82–88.

Orlinsky, D., and Howard, M. "Gender and Psychotherapeutic Outcome." In A. Brodsky and R. Hare-Mustin (eds.), *Women and Psychotherapy.* New York: Guilford Press, 1980.

Paffenbarger, R. S., King, H., and Wing, A. L. "Chronic Disease in Former College Students." *American Journal of Public Health,* 1969, *59,* 900–907.

Paige, K. E., and Paige, J. M. *The Politics of Reproductive Ritual.* Berkeley: University of California Press, 1981.

Palmare, E. "Predicting Longevity." *Gerontology,* Winter 1969.

"Parental Leave." *New York Times,* June 18, 1987.

Pietropinto, A., and Simenauer, J. *Beyond the Male Myth.* New York: New York Times Books, 1977.

Plutchik, R., and Kellerman, H. (eds.). *Emotions: Theory, Research, and Experience.* 2 vols. Orlando, Fla.: Academic Press, 1980.

Pollock, G. H. "On Freud's Psychotherapy of Bruno Walter." *Annual of Psychoanalysis,* 1975, *3,* 187–296.

Prince, M. *Psychotherapy and Multiple Personality.* Cambridge, Mass.: Harvard University Press, 1975.

Provence, S. *Infants and Parents.* New York: International Universities Press, 1983.

Provence, S., Naylor, A., and Patterson, J. *The Challenge of Daycare.* New Haven, Conn.: Yale University Press, 1977.

Rado, S. "The Psychic Effects of Intoxication." *International Journal of Psychoanalysis*, 1928, *9*, 301–317.

Rangell, L. "The Self in Psychoanalytic Theory." *Journal of the American Psychoanalytic Association*, 1982, *30*, 863–891.

Rank, O. *Art and the Artist*. New York: Tudor, 1932.

Ravich, D. *The Troubled Crusade*. New York: Basic Books, 1983.

Razin, A. M., and Associates. *Helping Cardiac Patients: Biobehavioral and Psychotherapeutic Approaches*. San Francisco: Jossey-Bass, 1985.

Redican, W. M., and Taub, D. M. "Male Parental Care in Monkeys and Apes." In M. Lamb (ed.), *The Role of the Father in Child Development*. New York: Wiley, 1981.

Redlich, F. C., and Freedman, D. X. *The Theory and Practice of Psychiatry*. New York: Basic Books, 1966.

Reich, W. "Zwei Narzissistische Typen" [Two narcissistic types]. *Internationale Zeitschrift fuer Psychoanalyse*, 1922, *8*, 456–462.

Reich, W. *The Function of the Orgasm*. New York: Orgone Institute Press, 1927.

Reich, W. *Character Analysis*. New York: Orgone Institute Press, 1945. (Originally published 1933.)

Reik, T. *Masochism in Modern Man*. New York: Farrar, Straus & Giroux, 1941.

Reite, M., and Caine, M. G. (eds.). *Child Abuse: The Nonhuman Primate Data*. New York: Alan R. Liss, 1983.

Rennie, T., and others. *Mental Health in the Metropolis*. New York: McGraw-Hill, 1962.

Ribble, M. *The Rights of Infants*. New York: Columbia University Press, 1943.

Richfield, J. "An Analysis of the Concept of Insight." *Psychoanalytic Quarterly*, 1954, *23*, 390–408.

Ridley, M. "Paternal Care." *Animal Behavior*, 1978, *26*, 902–932.

Robards, J. *The Powers of Psychiatry*. Boston: Houghton Mifflin, 1980.

Robertson, J. "Reply to Fine on Book of Love." *International Review of Psychoanalysis*, forthcoming.

Rodrigue, E. "The Analysis of a Mute Three-Year-Old Schizophrenic." In M. Klein, P. Heiman, and R. E. Money-Kyrle (eds.), *New Directions in Psychoanalysis.* New York: Basic Books, 1955.

Roe, A. *The Making of a Scientist.* New York: Dodd, Mead, 1953.

Roe, A. *The Psychology of Occupations.* New York: Wiley, 1956.

Roethlisberger, F. J., and Dickson, W. J. *Management and the Worker.* Cambridge, Mass.: Harvard University Press, 1939.

Roheim, G. "Psychoanalysis of Primitive Cultural Types." *International Journal of Psychoanalysis,* 1932, *13,* 1–224.

Rohner, R. P. *They Love Me, Love Me Not.* New Haven, Conn.: HRAF Press, 1975.

Rosen, J. *Direct Analysis.* Orlando, Fla.: Grune & Stratton, 1953.

Rosen, J. *Direct Psychoanalytic Psychiatry.* Orlando, Fla.: Grune & Stratton, 1962.

Rosen, V. H. "On Mathematical Illumination and the Mathematical Thought Processes." *Psychoanalytic Study of the Child,* 1953, *8,* 127–154.

Rosenthal, R. R. *Experimenter Effects in Behavioral Research.* New York: Wiley, 1976.

Ross, J. "Fathering: A Review of Some Psychoanalytic Contributions on Paternity." *International Journal of Psychoanalysis,* 1979, *60,* 312–328.

Ross, N. "Domination-Submission Patterns in the Patriarchal Family Structure." In S. H. Cath, A. R. Gurwitt, and J. M. Ross (eds.), *Father and Child.* Boston: Little, Brown, 1982.

Rubinstein, A. *My Young Years.* New York: Popular Library, 1973.

Ruesch, J. *Disturbed Communication.* New York: Norton, 1972.

Ruesch, J., and Bateson, G. *Communication and the Social Matrix of Psychiatry.* New York: Norton, 1951.

Sachs, H. *The Creative Unconscious.* Cambridge, Mass.: Sci-Art, 1942.

Sandler, J., and Joffe, W. "Towards a Basic Psychoanalytical

Model." *International Journal of Psychoanalysis,* 1969, *50,* 79–90.

Sandler, J., Kennedy, H., and Tyson, R. L. *The Technique of Child Analysis: Discussions with Anna Freud.* Cambridge, Mass.: Harvard University Press, 1980.

Sapir, E. *Language.* San Diego, Calif.: Harcourt Brace Jovanovich, 1921.

Schafer, R. "The Clinical Analysis of Affects." *Journal of the American Psychoanalytic Association,* 1964, *12,* 275–299.

Schonberg, H. *The Great Pianists.* New York: Simon & Schuster, 1963.

Schrenck-Notzing, H. A. *Therapeutic Suggestion in Psychopathia Sexualis.* Philadelphia: N.p., 1895.

Shakow, D., and others. "Recommended Graduate Training Program in Clinical Psychology." *American Psychologist,* 1947, *2,* 539–558.

Sharpe, E. "Similar and Divergent Unconscious Determinants Underlying the Sublimations of Pure Art and Pure Science." *International Journal of Psychoanalysis,* 1935, *16,* 186–202.

Shneidman, E. S. *Definition of Suicide.* New York: Wiley, 1985.

Shweder, R. A., and Bourne, E. S. "Does the Concept of the Person Vary Cross-Culturally?" In A. J. Marsella and G. M. White, *Cultural Conceptions of Mental Health and Therapy.* Boston: Reidel, 1984.

Simon, H. *Models of Bounded Rationality.* Cambridge, Mass.: MIT Press, 1982.

Simpson, E. *Poets in Their Youth.* New York: Random House, 1982.

Slovenko, R. *Psychiatry and Law.* Boston: Little, Brown, 1973.

Smith, M. L., Glass, G. V., and Miller, T. I. *The Benefits of Psychotherapy.* Baltimore, Md.: Johns Hopkins University Press, 1980.

Socarides, C. "The Sexual Unreason." *Book Forum,* 1974, *1,* 172–185.

Socarides, C. "Abdicating Fathers, Homosexual Sons." In S. H. Cath, A. R. Gurwitt, and J. M. Ross (eds.), *Father and Child.* Boston: Little, Brown, 1982.

Solomon, K., and Levy, N. B. *Men in Transition.* New York: Plenum, 1982.

Spence, D. *Narrative Truth and Historical Truth*. New York: International Universities Press, 1986.

Spiegel, R. "Specific Problems of Communication." In S. Arieti (ed.), *American Handbook of Psychiatry*. New York: Basic Books, 1959.

Spitz, R. "Authority and Masturbation." *Psychoanalytic Quarterly*, 1952, *21*, 490–527.

Spitz, R. *The First Year of Life*. New York: International Universities Press, 1965.

Stein, H. *The Psychoanthropology of American Culture*. New York: Psychohistory Press, 1986.

Stevenson, I., and Wolpe, J. "Recovery from Sexual Deviations Through Overcoming Nonsexual Neurotic Responses." *American Journal of Psychiatry*, 1960, *117*, 737–742.

Stieper, D. R., and Wiener, D. N. *Dimensions of Psychotherapy*. Chicago: Aldine, 1965.

Stoller, R. J. *Sex and Gender*. New York: Science House, 1968.

Stollworthy, J. (ed.). *A Book of Love Poetry*. New York: Oxford University Press, 1974.

Stone, L. *The Psychoanalytic Situation*. New York: International Universities Press, 1961.

Strean, H. "The Patient Who Would Not Tell His Name." *Psychoanalytic Quarterly*, 1984, *53*, 410–420.

Strean, H. *Resolving Resistances in Psychotherapy*. New York: Wiley, 1985.

Sussman, W. I. *Culture as History*. New York: Pantheon, 1984.

Tartakoff, H. "The Normal Personality in Our Culture and the Nobel Complex." In R. M. Loewenstein, L. M. Newman, M. Schur, and A. J. Solnit (eds.), *Psychoanalysis: A General Psychology*. New York: International Universities Press, 1966.

Terman, L. M. *Genetic Studies of Genius*. Stanford, Calif.: Stanford University Press, 1928.

Terrace, H. S. *Nim*. New York: Washington Square Press, 1979.

Thorpe, W. H. "Vocal Communication in Birds." In R. A. Hinde (ed.), *Non-Verbal Communication*. New York: Cambridge University Press, 1972.

Tissot, R. "Long-Term Drug Therapy in Psychoses." In C. Chiland (ed.), *Long-Term Treatments of Psychotic States*. New York: Human Sciences Press, 1977.

Tomkins, S. S. *Affect, Imagery, Consciousness.* 3 vols. New York: Springer, 1961, 1963, 1979.

Torras de Bea, E. "A Contribution to the Papers on Transference by Eva Lester and Marianne Goldberger and Dorothy Evans." *International Journal of Psychoanalysis,* 1987, *68,* 63–67.

Tuchman, B. W. *The Proud Tower.* New York: Macmillan, 1966.

U.S. Secretary of Health, Education, and Welfare. *Alcohol and Health.* New York: Scribner's, 1970.

Vaillant, G. E. *Adaptation to Life (The Grant Study).* Boston: Little, Brown, 1977.

Veblen, T. *The Theory of Business Enterprise.* New York: Scribner's, 1919.

Veith, I. *Hysteria: The History of a Disease.* Chicago: University of Chicago Press, 1965.

Veroff, J., Douvan, E., and Kulka, R. A. *The Inner American.* New York: Basic Books, 1981a.

Veroff, J., Douvan, E., and Kulka, R. A. *Mental Health in America.* New York: Basic Books, 1981b.

von Frisch, K. *Tanzsprache und Orientierung der Bienen* [Dance language and orientation of bees]. New York: Springer-Verlag, 1965.

Wakerman, E. *Father Loss.* New York: Doubleday, 1984.

Wallace, A. F. C. *Culture and Personality.* New York: Random House, 1970.

Wallerstein, R. "Perspectives on Psychoanalytic Training Around the World." *International Journal of Psychoanalysis,* 1978, *59,* 477–503.

Wallerstein, R. "The Bipolar Self: Discussion of Alternative Perspectives." *Journal of the American Psychoanalytic Association,* 1981, *61,* 377–394.

Wallerstein, R. *Forty-Two Lives in Treatment.* New York: Guilford Press, 1986.

Warner, R. *Recovery from Schizophrenia.* Boston: Routledge & Kegan Paul, 1985.

Weber, M. *The Protestant Ethic and the Spirit of Capitalism.* New York: Scribner's, 1958. (Originally published 1904.)

Weiss, J. "Cezanne's Technique and Scopophilia." *Psychoanalytic Quarterly*, 1953, *22*, 413–418.

Weiss, J. M. A. "Suicide." In S. Arieti (ed.), *American Handbook of Psychiatry*, Vol. 3. New York: Basic Books, 1974.

Welldon, J. E. C. *Rhetoric of Aristotle*. Philadelphia: R. West, 1866.

Whiting, B. B., and Whiting, J. W. M. *Children of Six Cultures: A Psychocultural Analysis*. Cambridge, Mass.: Harvard University Press, 1975.

Wickler, W. *The Sexual Code*. New York: Doubleday, 1972.

Wiedeman, G. H. "Survey of Psychoanalytic Literature on Overt Male Homosexuality." *Journal of the American Psychoanalytic Association*, 1962, *10*, 386–409.

Wiedeman, G. H. "Homosexuality: A Survey." *Journal of the American Psychoanalytic Association*, 1974, *22*, 651–696.

Wiener, N. *I Am a Mathematician: The Later Life of a Prodigy*. Cambridge, Mass.: MIT Press, 1956.

Wilson, E. O. *Sociobiology: The New Synthesis*. Cambridge, Mass.: Harvard University Press, 1975.

Winnicott, D. *Holding and Interpretation*. London: Hogarth Press, 1986.

Work in America. (Report of a special task force to the secretary of HEW.) Washington, D.C.: U.S. Government Printing Office, 1973.

Yankelovich, D. *The New Morality: A Profile of American Youth in the Seventies*. New York: Random House, 1971.

Yankelovich, D. *New Rules*. New York: Random House, 1981.

Yanowich, M. *Social and Economic Inequality in the Soviet Union*. White Plains, N.Y.: Sharpe, 1977.

Zablocki, B. *Alienation and Charisma*. New York: Free Press, 1980.

Zeligs, M. A. "The Psychology of Silence: Its Role in Transference, Countertransference, and the Psychoanalytic Process." *Journal of the American Psychoanalytic Association*, 1961, *9*, 7–43.

Zetzel, E. R. "Current Concepts of Transference." *International Journal of Psychoanalysis*, 1956, *37*, 369–376.

PATIENT INDEX

A

A., Mr., 161
Abe, 43
Abraham, 38-39, 258
Adele, 76-77
Al, 81
Alex, 257-258
Allan, 101-102
Anna O., 263
Arnold, 66

B

Barney, 38
Barry, 180-181, 182, 276
Ben, 98
Biddle, Mrs., 278
Bill, 189-191
Bob, 266
Bryant, 102-104

C

C. T., 143-144
Carl, 196-198
Carlos, 104-105
Charles, 71
Clifford, 276-277

D

Daniel, 107
David, 73-74
Dennis, 266-268
Derek, 154
Donald, 60-61
Douglas, 199-200

E

Edward, 108-109
Ellen, 86-87
Emil, 289-290
Emmett, 277
Enoch, 241
Eric, 74
Everett, 200-202

F

Ferdinand, 125-126
Frances, 64-65
Francis, 202-203
Fred, 114-115

G

George, 80-81
Gilbert, 155-157
Glen, 269-271
Gordon, 137-138
Gregg, 127

H

Harold, 138-140
Harriet, 87-88
Harvey, 56-57, 59
Henry, 35-36
Herman, 122

331

Homer, 113

I

Ike, 142-143
Ira, 71-73
Irving, 37
Irwin, 288-289

J

James L., 151-152, 178, 185
Janey, 182
Jean, 65
Jerry, 241
Jill, 89
Jim, 146-147
John, 35, 107-108, 162
Joseph, 82-84
Joshua, 236
June, 94-95

K

Kathie, 166, 176
Kenneth, 84-85
Kermit, 147-148
Kim, 118-119
Konrad, 251-252, 271

L

L., Dr., 132
Larry, 154-155
Lawrence, 292-293, 295, 298
Leonard, 166
Lester, 119-121
Lincoln, 298
Little Hans, 168-169
Lou, 86-87
Louis, 167-168

M

Madeleine, 98
Malcolm, 169-170
Mark, 122, 175-176
Marshall, 75
Max, 87-88

Melvin, 170-171
Michael, 40-41
Milton, 43
Mimi, 56-57, 59
Myra, 71

N

Nathan, 49, 158-159
Nathaniel, 205-206
Neal, 206-207
Nelson, 279
Noah, 172-173
Norman, 89

O

Olaf, 206
Oliver, 159-160
Orson, 183-185
Oscar, 89-90

P

Patrick, 177
Paul, 92-93
Peggy, 270
Peter, 89, 129, 130-132, 133
Philip, 162-163
Preston, 212-214

R

Ralph, 179
Raul, 167
Richard, 49, 225-231, 238
Robert, 93-95
Roberta, 107
Roger, 62
Ronald, 63-65
Ruth, 71-73

S

Sally, 74, 228
Samuel, 40
Sean, 253-254
Sheldon, 225
Stanley, 76

Stillwell family, 277
Stuart, 133, 154
Susan, 92-93, 181, 241

T

Tad, 254-256
Ted, 185-187, 189
Thelma, 137
Tom, 68-69
Tony, 181-182

U

Ulysses, 187-189, 190

V

Victor, 46
Vincent, 231-323

W

Walter, 76-77, 111-112

Z

Zachary, 233-234

NAME INDEX

A

Abraham, K., 4, 105, 106
Ackerman, N. W., 165
Adam, 1
Adams, P. L., 194, 195
Adler, M., 299
Alexander, F., 44
Allardt, E., 249
Als, H., 165
Anthony, E., 164
Arieti, S., 264
Aristotle, 1-2, 55, 157, 243
Atlas, 14
Augustine, 220

B

Balzac, H., 287
Bartell, G., 79, 81
Barlett, D., 209
Baryshnikov, M., 14
Beck, 163
Bellah, R., 22, 152, 235, 238, 239
Bellak, L., 41
Berengarten, S., 26
Berenson, D., 134
Beres, D., 126
Bergler, E., 287
Berliner, B., 124
Berryman, J., 273-275, 284
Bieber, I., 59, 118

Blackmur, R. P., 273
Bleuler, M., 160
Blumstein, P., 17, 78, 99, 183, 235, 278
Boas, F., 9
Boukydis, C. F. Z., 264
Bourne, E. S., 10
Bowlby, J., 53, 67, 126
Brazelton, T. B., 165
Breuer, J., 223, 263
Brod, M., 300, 301
Brodie, H. U. H., 13
Broun, H., 135
Brown, J., 14
Bruce, L., 301
Burnham, D. L., 124
Burns, R., 222
Burr, A. R., 220

C

Caesar, J., 220
Caine, M. G., 53
Calef, V., 219
Canciano, F. M., 235, 236
Cannon, W., 150
Caplow, T., 183
Cardan, J., 220
Carey, P., 58-59
Carnegie, D., 229
Carpenter, W., 208
Casanova, J., 66-67

335

Cath, S. H., 16
Chafetz, M. E., 134
Chein, I., 129
Cooley, 218
Cornelison, A., 6, 160
Cuber, J., 70, 74, 86, 184, 281
Cunningham, S., 264

D

Dali, S., 298
Daniels, G. F., 136
Dante, 52, 69, 223
Darwin, C., 2, 223
Dean, J., 302
De Mause, L., 53
de Tocqueville, A., 238
Deutsch, F., 92
Deutsch, H., 1, 6, 98
Dickson, W. J., 256
Diener, E., 248
Donne, J., 57-58
Douvan, E., 19, 127, 196, 234-235
Dowling, C., 18
Dublin, L. I., 140
Durkheim, E., 141

E

Edgcumbe, R., 264
Ehrenreich, B., 3, 17, 63, 150
Ehrhardt, A. A., 11
Eidelberg, L., 222
Einstein, A., 301-302
Ekman, P., 150
Eleanor of Aquitaine, 57
Ellis, A., 20, 163
Ellis, G. F. R., 23
Ellis, H., 96
Emmons, R. A., 248
English, D., 3, 150
Erikson, E., 178, 179-180
Evans, D., 121
Evans, N. J., 243
Eve, 1

F

Fenichel, O., 4, 8-9
Fine, B., 293

Fine, B. D., 219
Fine, R., 3, 36, 40, 42, 46, 52, 53,
    57, 88, 97, 117, 128, 145, 165,
    196, 223, 239, 244, 267, 273,
    293, 302
Fink, R., 208
Firestein, S. K., 259
Fischer, D. K., 152
Fiske, D. W., 26
Fitzgerald, F. S., 273, 275
Fleck, S., 6, 160
Fliess, W., 223
Flugel, J. C., 164
Flynn, E., 67
Forrestal, J., 45
Fraiberg, S., 165-166
Framo, J. L., 174
Franks, V., 12
Frayser, S. G., 63
Frederick II, 262
Freedman, D. X., 23, 241
Freud, A., 44, 170, 171-172
Freud, S., 3-6, 7, 8, 18, 19, 25, 27,
    30, 33, 37, 42, 44, 45, 47, 49,
    51, 66, 81, 85, 96-97, 98, 105,
    108, 110, 116, 121, 126, 130,
    139, 142, 146, 157, 159, 164,
    168-169, 172, 175, 198, 203,
    218, 219, 221, 223, 229, 236,
    240, 248, 259, 263, 272, 275,
    283, 286, 288, 289, 290, 299,
    302, 304, 305, 307
Fried, E., 287, 295
Fromm, E., 7
Frosch, J., 6

G

Gabriel, T., 63
Galbraith, J., 244
Galdston, R., 70
Galenson, E., 54, 105
Galois, E., 177
Gardell, B., 248
Gardner, H., 287
Gauguin, P., 284
Gauss, J. K. F., 225
Gebhard, P., 78, 98
Gediman, H., 41
Gedo, M., 287, 290, 291

Geertz, C., 9
Gelles, R. J., 73
Gelman, D., 152
Gibson, W., 124
Gilligan, C., 249
Gitelson, M., 215
Gladstone, A. I., 124
Glass, G. V., 233
Glazer, N., 200
Goldberger, M., 121
Goldensohn, S. S., 207-208
Goldsmith, L., 41
Gomberg, E. S., 12
Gonsiorek, J. C., 118
Good, B., 91
Gordon, M., 164
Gove, W. R., 12
Green, R. J., 174
Greenacre, P., 286, 294
Greenspan, S., 17
Gross, C., 287
Grotjahn, M., 164
Gunderson, J., 208
Gurwitt, A. R., 16

H

Hall, G. S., 149
Halliday, J., 250
Hamilton, A., 243
Hamlet, 51
Hardy, G. H., 286
Harroff, P., 70, 74, 86, 184, 281
Hartmann, H., 4, 44, 126
Hatterer, L. J., 118
Hatton, C. L., 143
Hausfater, G., 12, 53
Hegel, G. W. F., 218
Heidegger, M., 218
Heimann, P., 5, 31, 170-171
Hendin, H., 142
Henry, A. F., 142
Henry, W. H., 27, 28-29, 33
Hepburn, K., 211
Hertzman, M., 134
Herzberg, F., 245, 249-250
Herzog, J. M., 17
Hewlett, S., 247
Hite, S., 282
Hitler, A., 78, 173

Hogarth, R. M., 256
Holt, R. R., 26
Hook, S., 302
Horney K., 7, 130
Hornick, E. J., 207
Horwitz, J., 248
Hosken, F. P., 3
Houpt, K. A., 264
Howard, M., 121
Hoyt, F., 145
Hrdy, S. B., 2, 12, 53
Hughes, H., 128, 209-212
Hunt, M., 2, 22, 58
Hurvich, M., 41
Husserl, E., 218
Huxley, A., 33

I

Ibsen, H., 3

J

Jacklin, C. N., 12
James, W., 179-180, 212, 218, 219
Jarrell, R., 273-274
Jefferson, T., 244
Jellinek, E. M., 134
Jencks, C., 203
Jensen, 272
Joffe, W., 125
Johansson, G., 248
Johnson, S., 55
Johnson, V. E., 3, 99, 100
Jones, E., 4, 223, 240
Jones, E. E., 121
Jones, J., 145
Jung, C., 44, 218

K

Kafka, F., 300-301
Kahn, R., 248
Kant, I., 180
Kaplan, H., 100
Kardiner, A., 7, 151
Karon, B. P., 163, 208-209
Kelly, E. L., 26
Kennedy, J. F., 30, 255
Kennedy, H., 174

Kennedy, R. F., 255
Kerig, P. K., 121
Kernberg, O. F., 32, 219, 265
King, H., 142
Kinsey, A. C., 3, 11, 78, 97, 98, 99,
    100, 101, 105, 116, 118, 278
Klein, M., 5, 31, 170-171
Kleinman, A., 10, 91
Kohut, H., 219, 307
Kolb, L. C., 13
Komarovsky, M., 279-281
Koupernik, C., 164
Kris, E., 126, 284
Krupnik, J. L., 121
Kubie, L., 230, 238
Kulish, N. M., 121, 122
Kulka, R. A., 19, 127, 196, 234-235

L

Lamb, M., 16, 164, 192-193
Lange-Eichbaum, S., 303
Laplanche, J., 23
Lasswell, H. D., 44
Laufer, M., 175
Laufer, M. E., 175
Lawrence, D. H., 278-279
Lazarus, A., 215
Leibnitz, G. W., 219
Leonardo da Vinci, 283
Lester, B. M., 264
Lester, E., 121
Levin, M., 275
Levin, R., 285
Levine, S. V., 178
Levinson, A. J., 15-16
Levy, N. B., 17
Lewis, O., 204
Lidz, T., 6, 160
Lincoln, A., 178
Lindbergh, C. A., 209
Locke, J., 219
Locke, S., 150
Loewenstein, R. M., 126
Lombroso, C., 303
Loomie, L. S., 268
Lowell, R., 273-274
Luborsky, L., 26
Ludwig, A., 265

M

McClelland, D., 223, 244
Maccoby, E. E., 12
McDermott, M., 180
McDougall, J., 110
McGill, V. J., 239
Maetze, G., 26
Marden, O. S., 222
Marsella, A. J., 10
Martin, C. F., 11, 78, 97, 98, 100,
    116, 118
Maslow, A., 248
Masters, W., 3, 99, 100
Maugham, S., 58-59, 89
Mead, G. H., 218
Mead, M., 6-7
Menninger, K., 44
Mensner, B., 245
Mercano, S., 32
Michelangelo, 286, 299
Mill, J. S., 3
Millay, E. S., 286
Miller, A., 215-216
Miller, T. I., 233
Milner, J. R., 194, 195
Money, J., 11
Money-Kyrle, R. E., 5, 31, 170-171
Monroe, M., 211
Moore, B. E., 219
Moss, C., 264
Moynihan, D., 200
Mozart, W. A., 291
Murdock, G., 78, 96

N

Nader, R., 256
Newton, I., 303
Nijinsky, V., 284, 303
Nixon, R. M., 99, 212, 237, 302
Norton, J., 295-297, 298
Nydes, J., 176

O

Offer, D., 175
O'Hara, J., 70
O'Neill, E., 221

O'Neill, G., 81
O'Neill, N., 81
Orlinsky, D., 121
Orwell, G., 264

P

Paffenbarger, R. S., 142
Paige, J. M., 78
Paige, K. E., 78
Palladas, 2
Palmare, E., 247
Pantagruel, 64
Patmore, C., 58
Paul, 1
Peters, J., 209, 211
Pfister, O., 33
Picasso, P., 286-287, 290, 291
Pietropinto, A., 16
Plantagenet, G., 306
Plato, 243
Polgar, S., 294-295
Pollock, G. H., 289
Pomeroy, W. B., 11, 78, 97, 98, 100,
    116, 118
Pontalis, J. B., 23
Portinare, B., 52
Provence, S., 166

R

Rabelais, F., 64
Rado, S., 128, 129
Rangell, L., 219
Rank, O., 284, 301, 304
Ravich, D., 177
Reder, M. W., 256
Redican, W. M., 11-12
Redlich, C., 23, 241
Reich, W., 3, 4, 302-303
Reik, T., 123
Reite, M., 53
Rennie, T., 152
Renouvier, C., 180
Reuben, D., 54
Ribble, M., 5
Rice, E., 210
Richfield, J., 160
Ridley, M., 11

Rink, A., 143
Robards, J., 240
Robertson, J., 239
Rockefeller, J. D., 244
Rodrigue, E., 167
Roe, A., 286
Roethlisberger, F. J., 256
Rogers, C., 20
Roheim, G., 9, 23, 218
Rohner, R. P., 52
Roiphe, H., 54, 105
Roosevelt, F. D., 134
Rosen, J., 6
Ross, J., 198
Ross, J. M., 16
Ross, N., 109, 110
Rubinstein, A., 291
Ruesch, J., 262

S

Sachs, H., 26, 283
Salimbene, 262
Samaras, L., 285
Sandler, J., 125, 174
Sapir, E., 262
Sayre, Z., 273
Schafer, R., 125
Schonberg, H., 291
Schrenck-Notzing, H. A., 118
Schrepf, N. A., 194, 195
Schwartz, D., 273, 274
Schwartz, P., 17, 78, 99, 183, 235,
    278
Selesnick, S., 44
Shakespeare, W., 51, 299
Sharpe, E., 286
Shaw, G. B., 3
Schneidman, E. S., 140-141, 143
Short, J. F., Jr., 142
Shweder, R. A., 10
Simenaur, J., 16
Simmel, G., 129, 130
Simon, H., 256
Simpson, E., 274, 275
Sims, J. H., 27
Slovenko, R., 200
Smith, J. A., 274
Smith, M. L., 233

Snyderman, B. B., 245
Socarides, C., 117
Socrates, 239
Solomon, K., 17
Spence, D., 43
Spiegel, R., 265
Spitz, R., 59, 100, 101
Spray, S. L., 27
Srole, L., 152
Steele, J., 209
Stein, H., 198
Stieper, D. R., 36
Stoller, R. J., 11
Stollworthy, J., 286
Strauss, B., 208
Strean, H., 40, 161
Strindberg, A., 287, 299
Sullivan, H. S., 7, 209, 221-222
Sussman, W. I., 222

T

Tartakoff, H., 214-215
Taub, D. M., 11-12
Tennyson, A., 20
Terman, L. M., 141, 258
Terrace, H. S., 264
Thompson, 7
Thoreau, H. D., 110
Thorpe, W. H., 264
Tissot, R., 208
Tolstoy, L., 224
Tomkins, S. S., 125
Torras de Bea, E., 121
Truman, H., 45
Tuchman, B. W., 203-204
Tyson, R. L., 174

V

Vaillant, G., 14-15
Valente, S. M., 143

Vandenbos, G. R., 163, 208-209
van Gogh, V., 284, 290, 291, 293, 295
Veblen, T., 256
Veith, I., 3
Veroff, J., 19, 127, 196, 234-235
von Frisch, K., 264
von Sacher-Masoch, L., 123

W

Wallace, A. F. C., 8
Wallerstein, R., 30-31, 47, 219
Walter, B., 289
Walter, M.-T., 291
Warner, R., 163, 240-241
Wayne, J., 153
Weber, M., 244
Weinshel, E. M., 219
Weiss, J. M. A., 140
White, G. M., 10
Whiting, B. B., 195
Whiting, J. W. M., 195
Wickler, W., 11
Wiedeman, G. H., 118
Wiener, D. N., 36
Wiener, N., 223-225, 261, 295
Wilson, E. O., 8
Wing, A. L., 142
Winnicott, D., 61
Wolski, T. R., 264
Wordsworth, W., 275

Y

Yankelovich, D., 214, 235, 246
Yanowich, M., 249

Z

Zablocki, B., 52, 179, 216
Zeligs, M. A., 268

SUBJECT INDEX

A

Achievement, need for, 202-212
Acting out: as defense, modifying, 46-47; self-damaging, 145-148
Adjustment disorders: and pain, 127; and price of success, 214; and sexual conflict, 111
Adolescents: family role of, 174-182; groups for, 178-179
Affects, in psychotherapy, 125
Africa, women mutilated in, 3
Aggression: and alcoholism, 136; and suicide, 142
AIDS: and adolescence, 176; and extramarital affairs, 79; and homosexuality, 116; and sexual revolution, 278
Albert Einstein College of Medicine, and residency program, 207
Alcoholics Anonymous (AA), 135, 220
Alcoholism: and acting-out defense, 46-47; and pain, 134-140; and reason, 160-161; as regression in service of spouse, 89-90
American Association for Suicidology, 143
American Psychiatric Association (APA), 22-23, 44, 118

American Psychoanalytic Association, 30, 219, 240, 268
American Psychological Association, 149; Division of Psychoanalysis of, 240
Analytic ideal: components of, 20-22; and emotional problems, 18-24; and psychotherapist activity, 45; and resistance, 38, 39; and transference, 37; uses of, 305-308
Analytic situation: establishing, 34-39; transference in, 36-37
Antabuse (disulfiram), and alcoholism, 135, 137
Anxiety: of castration, 106, 112, 116, 120; concepts of, 5; and drug addiction, 129, 131; of separation, 168
Arapesh, temperament of, 6
Attachments, and reason, 157-158
Australia, self-image in, 9

B

Bachelor, and family role, 183-191
Berlin Psychoanalytic Institute, 26
Brown v. Board of Education, 178

C

California, joint custody in, 198

341

Castration anxiety, and sexual conflicts, 106, 112, 116, 120
Center for Creative Living: and
family role, 167-168, 187-188;
and lying, 266; and retreat from
love, 68
Character structure: and masochism,
124; and pain, 128; in psychotherapy, 34-35, 39, 42; and
symptoms of sexual conflict,
110-115
Child Custody Act of 1970 (Michigan), 200
Children: family role of, 165-183;
and superego formation, 124-
125, 126-127, 132
Communication: and analytic ideal,
21-22; aspects of, 262-282; and
language, 278-279; lie as, 265-
266; manipulative, 264-265;
marital, 279-282; nature of, 262-
264; and private language, 271;
problems of, 264-272; and secrets, 276-278; self-, 271-272;
silence as, 266-271; with writing, 272-275
Creativity: and analytic ideal, 22;
aspects of, 283-304; block to,
287-290; concepts of, 5; gender
differences in, 294-295; and
hero, 302-303; and madness,
303-304; and narcissism, 283-
287; narcissism and depression
linked to, 297-302; nurturing,
290-293; positive aspects of,
304; and psychotherapy, 295-
297; as work, 286-287
Cultural relativism, and masculinity and femininity, 7-8
Cultures: drug addiction in, 128;
father role in, 195; love problems in, 52, 63, 78, 82; masculinity and femininity in, 6-8,
9-10; sexual conflicts in, 96; success in, 216; temperament in, 6;
work in, 249

                    D

Denial, of feelings, 149-150, 153,
155-157

Denmark: and Antabuse, 135; suicide in, 142
Depression: creativity and narcissism linked to, 297-302; and regression in service of spouse, 87;
and therapist activity, 43; and
unattainable love object, 59-61
Diagnosis, or dynamic assessment
by psychotherapists, 43-45
Don Juanism, and unattainable love
object, 62-67
Dreams: and alcoholism, 136-137;
of bachelors, 186-187; and character structure, 112; and communication, 263, 266, 267, 270;
and creativity, 296-297; in depression, 60-61; in Don Juanism,
64-65; and drug addiction, 131;
and feelings, 154, 156; and
homosexuality, 120-121; and
masturbation, 103-104; as patient activity, 41-42; and price of
success, 213; and regression, 87;
and self-image, 228, 229; wet,
101, 104; and work, 253-254,
255, 257-258
Drug addiction: and acting-out defense, 46-47; and pain, 128-133

                    E

Ejaculation, premature, 97-98, 105-
108
Emotional problems: and analytic
ideal, 18-24; aspects of, 1-24;
background on, 1-2; literature
review on, 2-13; and myth of
male superiority, 13-18
Enoch Arden divorce, 188
Epicureans, 33
Ethology, and masculinity and femininity, 11-12
European Economic Community,
249
Extramarital affairs, and marital
conflict, 78-85

                    F

Failure. See Success and failure
Family role: for adolescent boy,
174-182; and analytic ideal, 21;

aspects of, 164-191; for bachelor, 183-191; background on, 164-165; of child, 167-174; as disturbed background, 160; of infant boy, 165-166

Family therapy, effectiveness of, 174

Father: and acting out, 146; and alcoholism, 137; aspects of role of, 192-202; and character structure, 111, 112, 114; and children, 16-17; and communication, 267, 269, 270, 277; and creativity, 291, 292, 293, 294, 300-301; and development of love, 53; and Don Juanism, 64; and drug addiction, 130-131, 133; family role of, 166-169, 173, 179, 182-186, 188-190; and father role for son, 198, 199, 201; and feelings, 154; history of role of, 193-194; and homosexuality, 59, 119-120, 121, 185, 255, 270; and impotence, 109-110; inability for nurturance by, 194-195; as isolated from children, 195, 196, 198; and love and transference, 57; and love problems, 82-83; and marital conflicts, 72, 76; and masculinity and femininity, 5, 6, 11-12; and masturbation, 101-102; and premature ejaculation, 107-108; and self-image, 223-225, 226, 227; and success, 209-210, 213; and suicide, 142; and work, 254-256. See also Men

Fears, and treatment crisis, 49

Feelings: and analytic ideal, 21; aspects of, 149-157; denial of, 149-150, 153, 155-157; elements of, 150; outlets for, 150

Fees: assigning, 47-48; and communication, 265-266; and resistance, 35, 40-41

Femininity, and emotional problems, 2-13

Free association, and patient activity, 41

G

Gallup poll, 245

Gender differences: and assigning fees, 47; in creativity, 294-295; of therapists, and resistance, 38

Gender identity, concept of, 11

Germany: drug addiction treatment in, 129; refugees from, 66, 77-78, 88, 224; and self-image, 10, 218-219; studying in, 180

Group therapy, and self-image, 230-234

Guyana, mass suicide in, 145

H

Harvard University, degree from, 180, 223

Hatred: culture of, 196; in marriage, 70

Hawthorne experiment, 256

Hero, and narcissism, 302-303

Homosexuality: in adolescence, 253; and alcoholism, 136-137, 139; and character structure, 112; concepts of, 117-118; and creative block, 288-289; and drug addiction, 131, 132; and identification with father, 185, 255, 270; overt, 116-121; patient material on, 187; and physiological research, 11; reactions to, 59, 64, 65, 89, 93, 271, 295; and reason, 162-163; repressed wish for, 155; and revenge, 83, 84; secret of, 58, 89, 277; and self-image, 227, 229, 237; and unattainable love object, 59

Husbands: conflict-prone, 73-78; as drifters, 74-75; henpecked, 74; passive, 109-110, 117; violent, 73-74; as workaholics, 75-78. See also Men

Hysteria, concepts of, 3

I

Ideal. See Analytic ideal

Identity diffusion, in adolescence, 179-180

Impotence: and resistance, 35; and
    sexual conflict, 108-110
Infant, family role of, 165-166
Institute for Social Research, 248
Insurance: employee assistance
    plans as, 251; for psychother-
    apy, 33, 208; and social workers,
    259
Internal Revenue Service (IRS),
    142-143, 146-147, 241
International Psychoanalytical As-
    sociation, 30, 240
Introjects: and psychotherapy, 165;
    and superego formation, 124,
    126

                    J

Japan: mass suicide in, 145; and
    self-image, 10
Joint Commission on Mental Illness
    and Health, 234-235

                    L

Laius complex, 198
Language: and communication, 278-
    279; private, 271
Latency period, development of
    love in, 54
Latin America, training of psycho-
    therapists in, 32
Lie, as communication, 265-266
Love: and analytic ideal, 20; as-
    pects of problems with, 51-95;
    background on, 51-52; develop-
    ment of, 52-56; glue, 88, 89, 90-
    91; and marital conflicts, 69-95;
    as primary value, 236, 239, 306-
    307; retreat from unattainable,
    67-69; and suicide, 144; and
    transference, 37, 56-58, 61; un-
    attainable, 58-69

                    M

Madness, and creativity, 303-304
Magna Carta, 178
Marital conflicts: aspects of, 69-95;

and communication, 279-282;
    and conflict-prone husbands, 73-
    78; and extramarital affairs, 78-
    85; and material produced by pa-
    tient, 40; psychosomatic symp-
    toms of, 91-95; and regression
    in service of spouse, 85-91
Marriage: classes of, 70; conflict-
    habituated, 70-71; devitalized,
    70, 74, 184; intrinsic, 70, 86;
    polygyny in, 63; rates of, 183
Masculinity, and emotional prob-
    lems, 2-13
Masochism: concept of, 123-124;
    and drug addiction, 132; and
    love, 57, 71, 73
Masturbation: and character struc-
    ture, 113; fantasy, 175-176, 181;
    and homosexuality, 116; in re-
    gression, 197; as revenge, 86-87;
    and sexual conflict, 100-105;
    and suppression, 269; and ther-
    apist activity, 43, 46
Medications: and psychotherapy,
    33; and schizophrenia, 163
Men: adult development of, 15-16;
    and analytic ideal, 20-22; and
    communication, 262-282; cre-
    ative, 283-304; emotional prob-
    lems of, 1-24; epilogue on, 305-
    308; in family role, 164-191;
    feelings of, 149-157; and feminist
    literature, 17-18; Grant study of,
    14-15; and love, 51-95; and mari-
    tal conflict, 17; and masculinity,
    2-13; pain and pleasure for, 123-
    148; and reason, 157-163; rebel-
    lion by, 17-18; self-image of,
    218-242; sexual conflicts of, 96-
    122; social role of, 192-217; and
    superiority myth, 13-18; ther-
    apeutic principles for, 25-50; in
    transition, 17; and work, 243-
    261. See also Fathers; Husbands
Michigan, child custody in, 200
Michigan, University of, Survey Re-
    search Center at, 235
Michigan State Hospital, schizo-
    phrenia treatment at, 208

Midtown Study, 152
Minnesota, parental leave in, 194
Mother: and alcoholism, 138, 139; and character structure, 112, 113; and communication, 268, 269, 276, 277; and creativity, 289, 293, 301; and depression, 59, 60-61; and development of love, 53-54; and Don Juanism, 65, 67; and drug addiction, 130, 132; and extramarital affairs, 83; family role of, 166-170, 172-173, 176, 181-182, 184-185, 187-188, 191; and father role for son, 196, 199, 201; and feelings, 155-156; and henpecked husband, 74; and homosexuality, 116-117, 119, 120; and impotence, 109-110; in literature review, 5-6; and love and transference, 57; and masturbation, 101; and pain, 126, 127; and premature ejaculation, 107-108; and psychosomatic symptoms, 94, 95; and reason, 159-160, 162; and regression, 87, 90, 91; and retreat from love, 68; and revenge, 61-62; and self-image, 226, 227, 228, 233-234; separation from, 67, 126; and success, 210, 211, 212; and transference, 56; and work, 255; and workaholics, 76. *See also* Women
Mundugumor, temperament of, 6
Mutual parentification, 85

N

Narcissism: and creativity, 283-287; and depression, 297-302; and hero, 302-303
National Center for Drug Addiction, 131
Netherlands, labor policy and work in, 23, 250
Neurosis, concepts of, 22-24, 118
Neutrality, by psychotherapists, 45-46
New York, master's in social work in, 259

New York Center for Psychoanalytic Training, 259-260
New York Health Insurance Plan, 208
Nobel Prize complex, 214-215
Normality: concepts of, 19; and psychotherapist activity, 45
Norway, suicide in, 142

O

Obsession: concepts of, 4; and sexual conflicts, 102-103, 109, 114
Oedipal conflict: and creativity, 301; and extramarital affairs, 83; and family role, 167-168, 169; and father role, 198; and homosexuality, 59; in literature review, 4, 5; rejection in, 53; and secretiveness, 161; and self-image, 233-234
Oral stage, in literature review, 5-6

P

Padua, University of, expulsion from, 66
Pain: and alcoholism, 134-140; aspects of, 123-148; background on, 123-128; and drug addiction, 128-133; and self-damaging acting out, 145-148; and suicide, 140-145
Patients: acting-out defense by, 46-47; activity of, 39-42; instructions to, 41; major role of, 232-233; material produced by, 40-42
Physiology, and masculinity and femininity, 10-11
Pleasure: and analytic ideal, 20-21; and pain, 123-148; pharmacological image of, 128-129
Poland, refugees from, 173
Postgraduate Center for Mental Health, 295
Premature ejaculation: and attitudes, 97-98; and sexual conflict, 105-108

Prohibition Amendment, 134
Psychiatric symptomatology, and analytic ideal, 22
Psychiatry, and masculinity and femininity, 12-13
Psychoanalysis: and self, 218-220; and unconscious, 220-222; visions in, 24
Psychoeconomic disorders, and work, 250-261
Psychology, and masculinity and femininity, 12
Psychosocial moratorium, in adolescence, 178
Psychosomatic symptoms, and marital conflict, 91-95
Psychotherapists: activity by, 42-48; commonalities of, 26; diagnosis or dynamic assessment by, 43-45; dynamic inactivity by, 42; gender of, and sexual conflicts, 121-122; gender differences in, and resistance, 38; and modifying acting-out defense, 46-47; neutrality by, 45-46; personality of, 26-30; psychodynamic language of, 28-29; as secular philosopher, 33, 306; sociocultural origins of, 29-30; specialized world of, 27-28; as trained outside universities, 32; and training analysis, 215; training issues for, 30-32; world view of, 29
Psychotherapy: analytic honeymoon in, 48, 60, 227; analytic situation in, 34-39; aspects of, for men, 25-50; background on, 25; and communication, 263; and creativity, 295-297; and feelings, 153; as fifth profession, 27; frequency of sessions in, 47; patient activity in, 39-42; and personality and training of psychotherapist, 26-34; promise of, 307-308; and psychotherapist activity, 42-48; and reason, 159; relationship established in, 225-227; and rich and famous, 209-

212; and self, 237-242; and social milieu, 33-34; social problems in, 50; and socioeconomic struggle, 203-209; stages in, 48-50; termination of, 50; treatment crisis in, 48-49; working-through process in, 49-50
Puberty, development of love in, 54

R

Reason: and analytic ideal, 21; aspects of, 157-163
Regression: and drug addiction, 129, 130, 132; in service of ego, and creativity, 284; in service of spouse, 85-91; and social problems in psychotherapy, 50
Rejection, to bachelor, 191
Resistance: in analytic situation, 35-36, 37-39; of bachelor, 191; and patient activity, 40; and self-image, 39, 221, 228, 229-230, 233; and training analysis, 215
Revenge: and homosexuality, 83, 84; masturbation as, 86-87; and premature ejaculation, 106; and unattainable love object, 61-62
Rockefeller Institute for Medical Research, 210
Roman Empire, orgies in, 79

S

Schizophrenia: and communication, 262-263, 264, 271; concepts of, 5-6; and family role, 173; and father role, 196; as political phenomenon, 240-241; psychotherapy for, 208; and reason, 158-159, 160, 162, 163; and regression in service of spouse, 90; and retreat from love, 68; and success and failure, 205, 208
Secrets: and communication, 276-278; and reason, 161-162
Self: concepts of, 218-219; and psychoanalysis, 218-220; and psychotherapy, 237-242

Self-image: and analytic ideal, 21; aspects of, 218-242; changing, 225-234; development of, 223-225; and group therapy, 230-234; and hidden fears and memories, 227-228; and masculinity and femininity, 9-10; and resistance, 39, 221, 228, 229-230, 233; and social revolution, 234-237; traditional, 221; and unconscious, 220-222; and working-through process, 222, 228-229

Separation anxiety, and Oedipal conflict, 168

Sex, and analytic ideal, 20. See also Love

Sex therapy, relative merits of, 100

Sexual conflicts: of adolescents, 175-177; aspects of, 96-122; and attitudes, 96-100; in children, 167-171; and gender of therapist, 121-122; and impotence, 108-110; literature review on, 3-4; and masturbation, 100-105; and overt homosexuality, 116-121; and premature ejaculation, 105-108; preventing adequate performance, 100-110; and resistance, 38; symptoms of, and character structure, 110-115; and transference, 37; and treatment crisis, 49

Silence, as communication, 266-271

Social revolution, and self-image, 234-237

Social role: and analytic ideal, 21; aspects of, 192-217; as father in family, 192-202; and price of success, 212-217; success and failure in, 202-212

Society for Self Psychology, 219

Sociobiology, and masculinity and femininity, 8-9

Socioeconomic struggle, and psychotherapy, 203-209

South America, coca use in, 128

Stoics, 33

Substance abuse. See Alcoholism; Drug addiction

Success and failure: aspects of, 202-212; price of, 212-217; for rich and famous, 209-212; and socioeconomic struggle, 203-209; and work, 248-250

Suicide: characteristics of, 141; and pain, 140-145

Suicide Prevention Center, 143-144

Superego: childhood formation of, 124-125, 126-127, 132; and family role, 174, 178; and overachievement, 261; and secrets, 276; and self-image, 222

Sweden: paternity leave in, 194; suicide in, 142; work and health in, 248

Swinging, and marital conflict, 78-85

T

Taiwan, and healing process, 10

Tchambuli, temperament of, 6

Tegel Sanitarium, drug addiction treatment at, 129

Termination, of psychotherapy, 50

Thematic Apperception Test, 162, 272

Therapeutic revolution: and analytic ideal, 307-308; and feelings, 152-153; and price of success, 214-215

Transference: and alcoholism, 138, 139; in analytic situation, 36-37; for children, 170; and communication, 269, 271-272; and family role, 184, 185, 186-187, 189; and feelings, 156, 157; and fees, 48; and love, 37, 56-58, 61; and self-image, 227, 228, 229, 232; and sexual conflicts, 102, 103-104, 108, 121; and work, 255-256

Tufts College, degree from, 223

Tuscarora Indians, and modal personality, 8

U

Unconscious, and self-image, 220-222

Union of Soviet Socialist Republics: attack by, feared, 45; social milieu in, 34; work in, 249, 250

United Kingdom, work and health in, 250

U.S. Bureau of the Census, 63

U.S. Department of Labor, 247

U.S. Naval Academy, 100

U.S. Secretary of Health, Education, and Welfare, 245-246, 247

V

Veterans Administration, 93, 139, 205, 206, 207

Violence, in husbands, 73-74

Virgin-whore split, 54-55, 186-187

W

Womanizing, and unattainable love object, 62-67

Women: and analytic ideal, 20-22; considered repressed, 277-278; denigration of, 1-2; and femininity, 2-13; sadistic medical treatment of, 2-3; at work, 247. *See also* Mother

Women's Christian Temperance Union, 134

Work: and analytic ideal, 21; aspects of, 243-261; creativity as, 286-287; dissatisfaction with, 256-257; evolution of ethic of, 244-245; historical view of, 243-244; inability in, 251-252; incapacity for, 252-254; instability in, 254-256; and overachievement, 260-261; and psychoeconomic disorders, 250-261; source of dissatisfaction with, 245-250; and success, 248-250; and underachievement, 257-260

Workaholics, husbands as, 75-78

Working-through process: and drug addiction, 132; and feelings, 153; in psychotherapy, 49-50; and revenge, 62; and self-image, 222, 228-229

Writing, communication through, 272-275

Y

Yale University, schizophrenia studies at, 160

Young Men's Temperance Union, 137